Brilliant
Laptops for the Over 50s

Joli Ballew

PEARSON
Prentice
Hall

Harlow, England • London • New York • Boston • San Francisco • Toronto • Sydney • Singapore • Hong Kong
Tokyo • Seoul • Taipei • New Delhi • Cape Town • Madrid • Mexico City • Amsterdam • Munich • Paris • Milan

Pearson Education Limited
Edinburgh Gate
Harlow CM20 2JE
United Kingdom
Tel: +44 (0)1279 623623
Fax: +44 (0)1279 431059
Website: www.pearsoned.co.uk

First published in Great Britain in 2009

© Joli Ballew 2009

The right of Joli Ballew to be identified as author
of this work has been asserted by her in accordance
with the Copyright, Designs and Patents Act 1988.

ISBN: 978-0-273-72055-3

British Library Cataloguing-in-Publication Data
A catalogue record for this book is available from the British Library

Library of Congress Cataloging-in-Publication Data
Ballew, Joli.
  Brilliant laptops for the over 50s / Joli Ballew. -- 1st ed.
    p. cm.
  ISBN 978-0-273-72055-3 (pbk.)
  1. Laptop computers. I. Title.
  QA76.5.B262 2008
  004.16--dc22
                        2008043544

10 9 8 7 6 5 4 3 2 1
13 12 11 10 09

Set in 11pt Arial Condensed by 30
Printed and bound in Great Britain by Ashford Colour Press Ltd, Gosport, Hants

The publisher's policy is to use paper manufactured from sustainable forests.

Brilliant guides

What you need to know and how to do it

When you're working on your computer and come up against a problem that you're unsure how to solve, or want to accomplish something that you aren't sure how to do, where do you look? Manuals and traditional training guides are usually too big and unwieldy and are intended to be used as end-to-end training resources, making it hard to get to the info you need right away without having to wade through pages of background information that you just don't need at that moment – and helplines are rarely that helpful!

Brilliant guides have been developed to allow you to find the info you need easily and without fuss and guide you through the task using a highly visual, step-by-step approach – providing exactly what you need to know when you need it!

Brilliant guides provide the quick easy-to-access information that you need, using a table of contents and troubleshooting guide to help you find exactly what you need to know, and then presenting each task in a visual manner. Numbered steps guide you through each task or problem, using numerous screenshots to illustrate each step. Added features include 'See also...' boxes that point you to related tasks and information in the book, while 'Did you know?...' sections alert you to relevant expert tips, tricks and advice to further expand your skills and knowledge.

In addition to covering all major office PC applications, and related computing subjects, the *Brilliant* series also contains titles that will help you in every aspect of your working life, such as writing the perfect CV, answering the toughest interview questions and moving on in your career.

Brilliant guides are the light at the end of the tunnel when you are faced with any minor or major task.

Publisher's acknowledgements

The author and publisher would like to thank the following for permission to reproduce the material in this book:

Microsoft product screen shots reprinted with permission from Microsoft Corporation.

Every effort has been made to obtain necessary permission with reference to copyright material. In some instances we have been unable to trace the owners of copyright material, and we would appreciate any information that would enable us to do so.

About the author

Joli Ballew is a technical author, a technology trainer and website manager in the Dallas area. She holds several certifications including MCSE, A+ and MCDST. In addition to writing, she occasionally teaches computer classes at the local junior college, and works as a network administrator and web designer for *North Texas Graphics*. She's written almost two dozen books, including *Brilliant Microsoft Windows Vista for the Over 50s*, *Degunking Windows*, *CNet's Do It Yourself 24 Mac Projects*, *PC Magazine's Office 2007 Solutions*, and *Breakthrough Windows Vista with Microsoft Press*.

Joli can be contacted at www.joliballew.com

Contents

Introduction	ix

1. Introduction to laptops — **1**

Laptop advantages	2
Access media and games	4
Use the web to find your way	6
Entertain your grandchildren	7
Tablet PC support	8
Use your laptop ergonomically	9
Get started	10

2. Choosing and using a laptop — **11**

Things to consider when shopping for a laptop	12
Shopping checklist	15
Choosing a rugged laptop	17
Extended warranties	18

3. Exploring the outside of the laptop — **19**

Locate and use various features	20
Explore additional ports	28

4. Exploring the inside — **29**

Basic functionality	30
Keys common to most keyboards	33

5. Windows Vista — **39**

Starting and activating Windows Vista	41
Explore the Welcome Center	42
About Vista editions	47
Explore the desktop	49
Explore Vista	54
Explore the taskbar	67
Explore Sidebar	70
Instant search	76
Shut down Windows	79

6. Tweaking the look of Windows Vista   **83**

Personalise the desktop with Aero   84
Windows backgrounds   88
Screen savers   91
Changing desktop icons   95
Screen resolution   105
Mouse/screen pointers   108
Font size   113

7. Configuring accessibility options   **115**

Configure the Narrator   116
Working with the Magnifier   119
Using the on-screen keyboard   122
Make the keyboard easier to use   125
Explore keyboard shortcuts   128
Explore additional ease of access options   130
Using speech recognition   133

8. Safety and security   **141**

User accounts and passwords   144
Protecting your laptop   154
Protecting your family and your data   165
Staying safe online   171
Help and support   174

9. Connecting to the Internet   **183**

Choose among dial-up, broadband, mobile, wireless and satellite   184
Configuring your home Internet connection   186
Creating a wireless satellite connection   190
Viewing and managing network connections   192
Using a free WiFi hotspot   194

10. Working with media and media applications   **199**

Rip a CD in Media Player   200
Playing music in Media Player   202
Burn a CD in Media Player   204
Import pictures   207
Edit photos   210
Share photos   217
Watch DVDs   220
Burn a data DVD   226
Movie Maker basics   229
Watching live television   246
Record television   249

11. Instant and video messaging   255

Get Live Messenger   257
Configure Live Messenger   261
Messaging   266
Voice and video communications   272

12. The Mobility Center   279

Explore Mobility Center   281
Extend battery life   283
Wireless connectivity   286
Exploring presentation settings   287
Sync Center   289
Using an external display   295

13. Tablet PC features for tablet PCs and laptops   297

Tablet PC tools   298
Using the tablet PC's input panel   304
Configure tablet PC features   307
Snipping Tool   316
Sticky Notes   321
Handwriting recognition   325
Gestures   335
Flicks   337
Windows Journal   341

14. Holidays with a laptop   347

Back up your laptop before you leave   348
Be sure you need your laptop   358
Packing your laptop   359
Taking your laptop on an airplane   361
Getting online access   368
Physically secure your laptop   375

15. Maintaining and upgrading your laptop   377

Maintain your laptop   370
Upgrading your laptop   393

Appendix: Avoiding laptop disasters   401
    Commonsense precautions   401
    Health precautions   402
    Laptops and physical precautions   402

Jargon buster   **403**
Troubleshooting guide   **415**

Introduction

Welcome to *Brilliant Laptops for the Over 50s*, a visual quick-reference book that shows you how to make the most of your laptop computer, particularly if it is your first one, or if you are new to the world of computers! It will give you a solid grounding on how to choose the right laptop for you, how it works and how to get the best out of your laptop – a complete reference for the beginner and intermediate user who hasn't grown up with a laptop.

Find what you need to know – when you need it

You don't have to read this book in any particular order. We've designed the book so that you can jump in, get the information you need, and jump out. To find the information that you need, just look up the task in the table of contents or Troubleshooting guide, and turn to the page listed. Read the task introduction, follow the step-by-step instructions along with the illustration, and you're done.

How this book works

Each task is presented with step-by-step instructions in one column and screen illustrations in the other. This arrangement lets you focus on a single task without having to turn the pages too often.

How you'll learn

Find what you need to know – when you need it

How this book works

Step-by-step instructions

Troubleshooting guide

Spelling

Step-by-step instructions

This book provides concise step-by-step instructions that show you how to accomplish a task. Each set of instructions includes illustrations that directly correspond to the easy-to-read steps. Eye-catching text features provide additional helpful information in bite-sized chunks to help you work more efficiently or to teach you more in-depth information. The 'For your information' feature provides tips and techniques to help you work smarter, while the 'See also' cross-references lead you to other parts of the book containing related information about the task. Essential information is highlighted in 'Important' boxes that will ensure you don't miss any vital suggestions and advice.

Troubleshooting guide

This book offers quick and easy ways to diagnose and solve common problems that you might encounter, using the Troubleshooting guide. The problems are grouped into categories.

Spelling

We have used UK spelling conventions throughout this book. You may therefore notice some inconsistencies between the text and the software on your computer which is likely to have been developed in the USA. We have however adopted US spelling for the words 'disk' and 'program' as these are commonly accepted throughout the world.

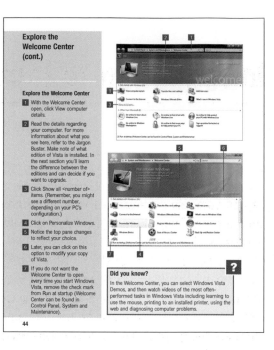

Troubleshooting guide

Choosing and buying a laptop

What should I consider when buying a laptop?	12
What is ergonomics?	13
What types of connections should I insist on?	14
What questions should I ask the salesperson?	15
What is a 'processor' and 'RAM' and how much should my new laptop have?	15
What is a hard drive, and how big a hard drive should my laptop have?	15
What type of laptop should I buy if I just want to use email?	16
What type of laptop should I buy if I want to create my own home films on DVDs?	16
What should I look for on the manufacture's website?	17
I plan to take my laptop on a safari and on a mountain climbing trip. Should I get a 'rugged laptop'?	17
Should I invest in an extended warranty?	18

The outside of the laptop

How can I find out what all of this stuff is on the outside of my laptop?	20
What is a USB port and how do I use it?	22
What is FireWire and how do I use it?	22
What is Ethernet and how do I use it?	23
What is Bluetooth and how do I use it?	24
How do I add another monitor?	25
How do I add external speakers?	26
What port do I use to configure a dial-up connection to the Internet?	26
How do I insert or remove the battery?	27
What additional ports do I have (S-Video, DVI, SD, ExpressCard, etc.)?	28

The inside of the laptop

Where's the power button?	30
Where's the volume?	30
Where's the microphone?	31
Where's the webcam?	32
What do all of these weird keyboard keys do?	33/36
What is a touchpad and how do I use it?	38

Troubleshooting guide 415

Introduction to laptops

Introduction

Laptop computers are smaller versions of their desktop counterparts. They often do everything a desktop will, and offer portability. If you travel a lot now or are planning to, a laptop is certainly something to consider. With a laptop, you'll always have access to your favourite games, music and media (pictures and video), as well as e-mail, the web and travel directions (provided you have an Internet subscription). If these are things you want to have handy when you travel, a laptop is the way to go.

You may want to purchase a laptop even if you don't travel though. You can take a laptop with you anywhere, including hospitals, friends' and relatives' homes, the local pub, or even just your back garden.

What you'll do

Watch a DVD

Play games

Get directions online

Laptop advantages

In addition to being portable and offering access to personal data and the web, there are other advantages to having a laptop. These include:

- Disconnecting from mains power and using the laptop's built-in batteries in airplanes, cars and trains.
- Storing and travelling with pictures, videos and documents.
- Having access to a music player and DVD player.
- Being able to play games when there's nothing else to do.
- Installing a GPS so you always know where you are and how to get where you're going.
- Always on the web and e-mail.
- Having something to keep your grandchildren busy on long car journeys.

Yes, you can take it with you! With a laptop you can bring along your favourite photos, documents, address books, journals, videos and any other digital data you keep. Having this information at your fingertips makes travelling easier, and also allows you to show off pictures of your family to people you meet along the way. You can also bring data with you to share. You may not be able to bring your boat, but you can show off a video you took on your boat to friends and relatives. With Windows Vista you can even offer people (or yourself) a slide show of your pictures. Windows Photo Gallery, shown here, lets you play a slideshow of images by hitting the F11 key on the keyboard or by clicking the Play Slide Show button at the bottom of the screen. You'll never have to spend a moment away from your digital photo album!

Access media and games

With a Windows laptop, you'll also have access to a media player (Modia Player 9), a digital journal (Windows Journal), an image-editing application (Windows Photo Gallery) and games. Here's Windows Media Player 9, where you can listen to music and watch DVDs.

It's simple to watch a DVD too; no experience necessary.

In addition to watching DVDs, you can play games. You don't need to bring your own games though, Vista comes with plenty! To find the games on your laptop, click the Start button and then Games.

Watching a DVD

1 Press the button on the side of your laptop that opens the DVD drive.

2 Carefully place a DVD in the tray and let it slide back in.

3 When prompted, choose Play DVD Movie using Windows Media Player.

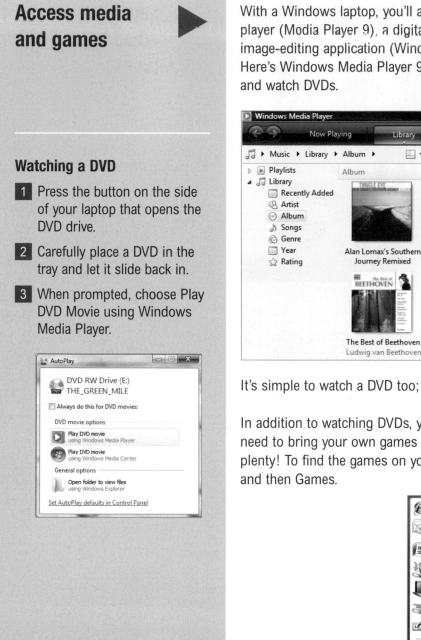

Playing games

1 Click Start.

2 Click Games.

3 Double-click any game to start it.

For your information

There are some games here you may not have. That's because my computer came with lots of games installed by the manufacturer.

Use the web to find your way

You can also use your laptop to stay safe while travelling. You can get directions from websites such as **www.multimap.com** and access phone numbers from sites like **www.yellowpages.com**. You can follow the weather. You can check petrol prices, read reviews of local restaurants, and find out which places are safe to visit and which are not. You can make air and hotel reservations, check flight arrivals and departures, and read reviews of hotels and camping grounds. If you opt for a GPS add-on, you can even have your laptop read directions aloud while you drive. You can also download maps.

Getting maps and directions online

1 Log on to your ISP so that you have web access.

2 Go to **www.multimap.com**.

3 Under the find a map tab, type an address, town or postcode.

4 Click find.

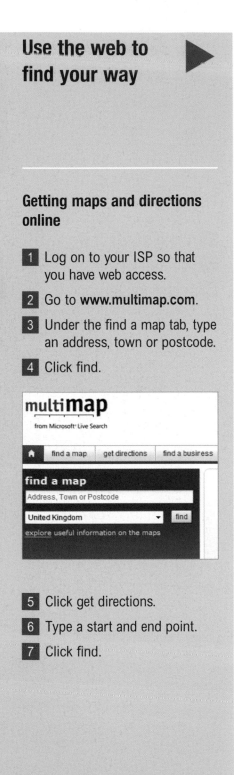

5 Click get directions.

6 Type a start and end point.

7 Click find.

You can use a laptop to entertain your grandchildren too. They can play games, of course, but they can also use Paint to 'draw', Windows Mail to send e-mail, Windows Media Center to work with any type of media, Windows Movie Maker to edit uploaded raw video footage from a DV camera, and to use programs you allow them to install, such as their own games or applications. Here's Windows Media Center, an all-in-one media application (that's included with Windows Home Premium and Windows Ultimate editions).

Tablet PC support

If you have a tablet PC, that's a PC you can write on using a stylus, you can use Vista's Tablet PC options for inputting and manipulating data. Here's the Tablet PC input panel. You can write right on the screen and have Vista covert your scrawl to text! That text can be input into any application that accepts text.

Because laptops are small, in general, they are harder to use than desktops. Keyboards aren't ergonomic and it's hard sometimes to find a comfortable position for long-term use. For best results, try the following:

◀ Use your laptop ergonomically

1

- Sit in a chair that is comfortable and that you can lean back in.

- If possible, buy a laptop 'desk'. You place the desk on your lap, and the laptop on top of it. Men, note that the heat from a laptop can decrease sperm count, which is another plus for a laptop desk.

- Angle the laptop's screen so that you don't have to strain your neck or eyes to see it.

- When working at a desk at home or in the office, consider a computer monitor pedestal and use a 'real' keyboard and mouse. You can connect these via a USB connection.

Get started ▶

A laptop is a great piece of equipment. It's awesome for travel, and lets you keep in touch with friends and family no matter where you are or where you're going. And Vista is a great operating system. In this book we'll cover both of these topics.

Here, you'll learn about laptops, including what each port on the outside of the laptop does. You'll also learn about things specific to a laptop keyboard. With that done, you'll explore Vista, including the applications you'll need to use your laptop effectively. You'll also learn about tools specific to laptops, such as the Tablet PC tools available in Vista. If you're ready, let's get started!

Choosing and using a laptop

Introduction

If you've yet to buy a laptop or are considering replacing one you have, read through the tips in this chapter. There are lots of things to consider, including the weight and size of the laptop, its cost and related features, Internet connection options, and things like the amount of memory, hard drive space and processor speed. You'll also want to consider things like laptop bags, additional batteries, extended warranties and set-up services. Some of these aren't necessary, and are a waste of money.

What you'll do

Visit a computer shop and ask questions.

Check out the manufacturer's website.

Make the purchase.

Things to consider when shopping for a laptop

▶

If you're shopping for a laptop or if you're considering replacing an older laptop or desktop PC, there are several things to consider before you buy. If you're planning to travel on airplanes, for instance, you'll want to know the laptop's weight and size. The smaller and lighter the laptop is, the easier it will be to travel with. If you travel mostly by car, weight and size may not be an issue. In both cases though, the laptop needs to be large enough so that you can use it easily, making these factors even more complex. You'll also want to consider cost, features, speed and how the keyboard feels when you type on it.

Weight and size

A typical laptop weighs 2kg–4kg (4–8lb). You can get 'ultralight' models that weigh about 1.5kg, but they can be much more expensive and often lack features other laptops have, like DVD drives. When purchasing a laptop, make sure it's not too heavy if you plan to travel with it, like on an airplane. However, if your main mode of travel is a cruise ship or car, a heavier laptop may actually be an asset, because it will be less likely to fall when you're in motion.

When a laptop is small, it may be hard to use the keyboard and pointing device. You should consider carrying a small mouse with you on your travels.

Ergonomics

You'll want to test the keyboard before you buy a laptop. The finest laptop will become a burden if you can't type effectively. This happens more often than you think; I have a laptop whose keyboard is so hard to use that I actually bring along an external keyboard and mouse, and connect them using the laptop's USB ports. This defeats the main purpose of the laptop, of course, portability and convenience.

A laptop's small size can make it less comfortable to use too. Often, your laptop's display is not set at eye level, and the keyboard is not positioned for best posture. If possible, try to improve your position by putting the laptop on a hotel room's desk, raising or lowering your chair, or building a table or tray for your car.

Cost and features

PC desktops are less expensive than laptops, and are more easily upgraded if you need or want additional features. Because it's nearly impossible to add features internally to a laptop, like a DVD drive, FireWire port or larger hard drive, it's important to find a laptop you really like and offers the features you want from the beginning. I'll spell out later what you should look for, but make sure you save enough money to get the laptop you need, and not the laptop you can afford.

One thing you'll need to decide is if you like the touchpad offered on many laptops, or if you'd like to shop for something else. Many people have a touchpad but connect a mouse. It's up to you.

Things to consider when shopping for a laptop (cont.)

Reliability

Laptops are more prone to accidents than desktops because you take them with you, and can be damaged if they are exposed to too much heat, humidity or vibration. Of course, a laptop can be stolen, lost or damaged more easily. When considering a laptop, know that you'll have to be extremely careful with it, and keep it safe from harm. Make sure, when you purchase a laptop, that you can secure it with a lock, preferably a Kensington lock.

Connectivity

When purchasing a laptop, make sure it includes Ethernet and wireless networking. You don't know where your travels will take you, and it's best to be prepared for any type of connection. Here's an Ethernet cable.

I can't tell you exactly what you'll need in a laptop, but I can help you choose one by providing a list of things you'll probably want. Here are some things to consider:

- A capable processor. Almost all laptops have a processor that is fast enough to handle e-mail, web surfing, uploading and viewing photos, and keeping a journal. That said, you may not need to buy a laptop with the fastest processor to get a laptop you'll love. If you plan to render movies in Movie Maker though, or if you need to use Photoshop or other high-end graphics software, you'll need a faster processor than what you'll find in a basic laptop.

- Additional processors. If you play games that require lots of fast graphics, create your own movies, or perform other resource-intensive tasks (you'll know if you do), consider additional processors. Some laptops come with dual processors or graphics cards with processors built in.

- More RAM. Random access memory is where your laptop will temporarily store information while it processes it. You should get a laptop that has at least 1 gigabyte (GB) of memory. Get more if you can afford it.

- Hard drive space. A hard drive is where your data is stored. Digital music, photos and video take up a surprisingly large amount of hard drive space. Make sure you get at least 160 GB of hard drive space, and get more if you can afford it.

- Size and weight. Carefully consider a laptop's weight. Although 3kg may not feel like a heavy piece of equipment now, after carrying it, along with a power cable, adapters, computer case and other peripherals from your car to the airport terminal, you'll be wishing you'd opted for the lighter model. Trust me on this.

- Battery life. Always look at battery life, and if you can't afford a model that offers long battery life, get an extra battery.

For your information

The best way to compare battery life, weight, processor speed, RAM and other components is to go to an electronics shop where laptops are offered side-by-side, and where you can compare price and features.

Shopping checklist

Visit a computer shop and ask questions

2

1. If you're close to a computer shop, visit it in person.

2. Ask the following questions:
   a. What is your least expensive laptop?
   b. What is your most expensive laptop?
   c. What are the differences?
   d. What features are absolutely necessary?
   e. What features are not necessary?

3. Tell the salesperson how you plan to use the laptop.

4. Ask the salesperson the following:
   a. What laptop would you suggest?
   b. Will a less expensive model work?
   c. Is this laptop rugged enough for what I want to do?
   d. Can you show me any independent reviews of this laptop?

5. Leave the shop without buying anything.

Shopping checklist (cont.)

- Wireless. The laptop should have Ethernet and wireless capabilities

- Dimensions. The size of the screen is a big part of selecting a laptop. It may seem like a 17-inch or 19-inch screen is best, until you try to use it on an airplane. And, a 12.5-inch or 15-inch screen may seem perfect too, until you want to do some image-editing. Of course, it's likely the larger screen will be heavier. You'll have to consider carefully where and how you'll use your laptop before deciding on a screen size.

- DVD drive: opt for a laptop that can, at the very least, play DVDs. If possible, spend the extra money to get a drive that can write to blank DVDs.

To sum up:

- If you only want to check e-mail, surf the web, keep a journal and upload a picture or two, compare the prices of brand-name computers. Any laptop these days can handle these tasks, no matter how slow the processor or how little RAM (provided it's new, that is). Make sure, if you buy a lower-end laptop that it comes with Ethernet and wireless capabilities.

- If you travel a lot, focus on weight, battery life and how well the keyboard responds to your typing style. Make sure you get at least 1 GB of RAM, 160 GB hard drive and wireless capabilities.

- If you play a lot of games, make sure you get a high-end graphics chip, graphics card and a powerful processor. You'll also want a 17-inch or larger, high-resolution monitor.

- If you love all things media and/or want to create home movies, focus on getting a large hard drive (500 GB), dual core processor and 2GB+ of RAM. You may even want to buy an external hard drive, shown here.

Yes, there is such a thing as a rugged laptop. You'll want to consider one if you plan to take your laptop with you on a safari or mountain climbing, for instance. Rugged laptops have sealed keyboards and casings and are thus better protected from water, humidity, sand and dust. Even the external ports are protected with plastic covers.

Rugged laptops also have a stronger outer shell, offering internal protection for the CPU, hard disk drive and optical drives. This means, if you drop it, it's less likely to be damaged and it's less susceptible to shock and vibration than other laptops. Many rugged laptops can also repel rain, snow, sleet, hail, wind, fog, dust, sand, extreme cold and heat, salt spray and/or humidity.

If your travels will take you places where a normal laptop would fail, consider a rugged laptop. (A rugged laptop may be just what your clumsy partner needs too!)

◀ Choosing a rugged laptop

Checking out the manufacturer's website

2

1 After you've selected the laptop you want to buy, or have narrowed it down to a few makes and models, visit the manufacturers' websites.

2 Browse through the site. Look for support and/or help pages.

3 See if there is an online or chat option for getting support.

4 Call the manufacturer's help line to see how long it takes to talk to a support person.

5 See how expensive additional components are, such as RAM and external speakers.

6 See how much it would cost to buy the laptop though this website, versus a shop.

Extended warranties ▶

Making the purchase

1. Make sure the laptop meets your needs.

2. Do not buy an additional warranty or sign up for any 'services'. You can load anti-virus software, configure a screen saver and input your user name.

3. Buy an additional battery if you think you will be away from power sources often.

4. Purchase an Ethernet cable and keep it with you.

5. Consider a second power supply to keep in the car so you don't have to pack it when you leave.

6. Consider buying a laptop desk.

7. Look over Internet subscription plans if you don't have one. Don't purchase a plan at the shop though; just look at the options.

8. Look at computer bags. Before purchasing one, read the information in the appendix of this book.

9. If you don't already have one, buy a surge protector.

There's no doubt you'll be asked to buy an extended warranty with your laptop. This warranty is supposed to cover everything from drops to spills to hard drive crashes to mechanical failures. Don't fall for this. It's highly unlikely you'll need the cover, and unlikely you'll be covered if something does happen.

An extended warranty is supposed to act as an insurance package. The long document you sign when you purchase it will explain what the extended warranty covers. If you really are sold on the idea of an extended warranty, ask to see the agreement. Read it carefully, ask questions and beware of vague references to what 'damage' is covered. If you really want to insure your laptop, consider your own home or car insurance company, or opt for a company that is in the business of covering electronics.

Exploring the outside of the laptop

Introduction

A laptop is much smaller than a desktop PC, but the ports you'll have are basically the same. Like a desktop PC, there will be USB ports, an Ethernet port and an external monitor port. You'll probably also see a place to connect speakers or headphones. There may also be a place to plug in a phone cord to access the Internet via dial-up, a FireWire port, or even a slot for inserting a SD card from a digital camera. Depending on the make and model, there may be other options, like a serial port or additional USB ports. Practically all laptops come with a disk drive for viewing and/or burning CDs/DVDs too. You may even have a Bluetooth connection. It's a lot to explore.

What you'll do

Locate and use the power cable

Locate and use USB ports

Locate and use FireWire ports

Locate and use Ethernet ports

Locate and use Bluetooth technology

Locate and use an external monitor port

Locate and use sound ports

Locate and use a modem port

Locate and insert or remove the battery

Explore additional ports

Locate and use various features

The best way to find out what's on your laptop is to read the documentation. If you can't find the physical guide, there may be one on the laptop. To find out, click Start, and in the Start Search window, type user guide (or user's guide). If you find one, click on it to open it.

```
Programs
  AcerSystem User's Guide
Files
  Guide
  cookies
  Chapter 27
  Chapter 25
  Chapter 13
  Chapter 9
  Chapter 5
Communications
  Information you should have already b...
  RE: MVP News- Post Global Summit Ed...


  Search Everywhere
  Search the Internet

User Guide                              ✕
```

Such a guide will help you discover more about the laptop, as you can see opposite. I've expanded, from the left window, 'Your Acer notebook tour' and under that 'Left view'. The user guide shows the left side of the laptop, with a Kensington slot (to connect to a Kensington type security lock), an Ethernet port, two USB ports and a five-in-one card reader that accepts camera memory cards.

You can also find out what's installed using Device Manager or System Information, both included with Windows Vista and both equally cryptic when it comes to discovering what's inside your computer. However you find out what is available on your laptop, even if it's simply looking at what's on the outside, you need to know what each of these ports looks like, what they do and how to use them.

For your information

If a user guide is not available, you can probably download one from the manufacturer's website.

Screenshot of Adobe Reader:

Guide.pdf - Adobe Reader

File Edit View Document Tools Window Help

38 / 119   74.8%   Find

Bookmarks   Options

- Acer eDataSecurity Management
- Acer eLock Management
- Acer eRecovery Management
- Acer eSettings Management
- Windows Mobility Center
- Your Acer notebook tour
  - Top view
  - Closed front view
  - Left view
  - Right view
  - Rear view
  - Base view
- Specifications
- Indicators
- Easy-launch buttons

Left view

1 2 3 4 5 6 7 8 9 10

#	Icon	Item	Description
1		Kensington lock slot	Connects to a Kensington-compatible computer security lock.
2		External display (VGA) port	Connects to a display device (e.g., external monitor, LCD projector).
3	DVI-D	DVI-D port	Connects to a display device with DVI-D input. (for selected models)
4		Ethernet (RJ-45) port	Connects to an Ethernet 10/100/1000-based network.
5		2 USB 2.0 ports	Connect to USB 2.0 devices (e.g., USB mouse, USB camera).
6		S-video/TV-out (NTSC/PAL) port	Connects to a television or display device with S-video input.
7	1394	4-pin IEEE 1394 port	Connects to IEEE 1394 devices.
8		Unlimited volume control wheel	Adjust the volume of the audio-out.
9		5-in-1 card reader	Accepts Secure Digital (SD), MultiMediaCard (MMC), Memory Stick (MS), Memory Stick PRO (MS PRO), xD-Picture Card (xD).
10	ExpressCard / 54	ExpressCard/54 slot	Accepts one ExpressCard/54 module.

A power cable will connect the laptop to the mains socket. You can connect and disconnect the power cable even when the computer is running. When you connect the power cable both to the laptop and the power outlet, the laptop will use the power from the outlet and charge the battery at the same time. When you unplug the laptop from the mains, the laptop will run on stored battery power. Leave the laptop plugged in when you can, that way the battery will always be charged.

Locating and using the power cable

1 Locate the power cord. It may consist of two pieces that need to be connected. One end will be small and plug into the power port on your PC; the other end will plug into a wall outlet.

2 Connect the power cord to the back or side of the laptop as noted in the documentation. In almost all cases, there is only one port that a power cord can fit in to. It if doesn't fit, it's not the right port. You may see a symbol similar to the one shown here.

2 Plug the power cord into the mains socket.

3

Locate and use various features (cont.)

Locating and using USB ports

1. Locate a USB cable. It can be rectangular on one end and almost square on the other, or it may be rectangular on both ends.
2. Plug the cable into the PC and the device.
3. Often, you'll need to turn on the USB device to have Vista recognise it, but not always. You do not generally have to 'turn on' USB storage units, like flash drives.

Locating and using FireWire ports

1. Locate your FireWire cable.
2. Plug the appropriate end of the cable into the FireWire device.
3. Plug the other end of the cable into the FireWire port on the laptop. (Not all laptops have this port.)
4. Often, you'll have to turn on the FireWire device for Vista to recognise it.

USB ports, or Universal Serial Bus ports, offer a place to connect USB devices. USB devices include mice, external keyboards, mobile phones, digital cameras, printers and flash drives. You may have a USB printer or scanner for instance, or a flash drive for backing up data. USB cables don't always come with USB devices you purchase, so although you may have a USB device, unless you've bought a USB cable separately, you may not have one.

The symbol for USB is shown here. Two USB ports are shown as well. The picture of the USB port was taken from my laptop's user guide, and you may be able to find a similar user guide with pictures on your laptop. USB ports are rectangular, and small. Your laptop probably includes at least two of these ports, but may have four or more.

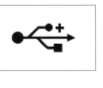 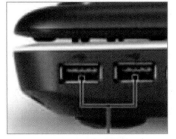

FireWire, also called IEEE 1394, is often used to connect digital video cameras, professional audio hardware and external hard drives to a PC. FireWire connections are much faster than USB, and are better than anything else when you need to transfer large amounts of data, such as digital video.

Unlike USB peripherals, devices that require a FireWire cable often come with one. When searching for a FireWire port on your newer laptop, look for an extremely small, rectangular port, with the numbers 1394 beside it, or a symbol similar to the one shown here. On an older laptop, the FireWire port may be larger,  but often these larger FireWire ports are used only on older desktop PCs.

Ethernet, also called RJ-45, is used to connect a laptop to a local network. If you have a cable modem, router or other high-speed Internet device at home, you'll probably use Ethernet to connect to it. If you want to connect to a hotel network, you may use Ethernet to do that too. An Ethernet cable looks like a telephone cable, except both ends are slightly larger. Both ends of an Ethernet cable are the same though, which is unlike the other cables discussed so far. The symbol for Ethernet is shown here.

When looking for an Ethernet port on your laptop, look for this symbol and/or an almost square port. The Ethernet cable will snap in.

If you've seen people talking on their mobile phones using a headset (while leaving the phone in their pocket or handbag), you've seen Bluetooth in action. Bluetooth is used to create 'personal' networks, to connect devices that are in close range. A laptop may come with built-in Bluetooth capabilities (although this is not common), or you can add it by installing a USB Bluetooth 'dongle'. A Bluetooth dongle is about the size of a flash drive and connects directly to a USB port on the laptop.

Once the dongle is installed, Bluetooth connections can be made between your laptop and Bluetooth-enabled devices such as mobile phones, other laptops, PCs, printers, GPS receivers, digital cameras and game consoles. The universal symbol for Bluetooth is shown here.

Locating and using Ethernet ports

1 Locate an Ethernet cable. You should have one if you've installed a local network at home. You may have to borrow one from reception if you're using a hotel network.

2 Connect the cable to both the PC and the Ethernet outlet on a router or cable modem (or a wall in a hotel).

3

For your information ⓘ

Bluetooth is best used when the two devices are close together and very little data needs to be transferred (as is the case with a mobile phone and headset).

Locate and use various features (cont.)

Locating and using Bluetooth technology

1 If necessary, insert the Bluetooth dongle and install any drivers required.

2 On the laptop, click My Bluetooth Places, or whatever icon represents the Bluetooth device you installed.

3 Turn on the external Bluetooth device.

4 Click Bluetooth Setup Wizard.

5 Work through the setup process as prompted.

6 Click View Devices in Range to see the connected devices.

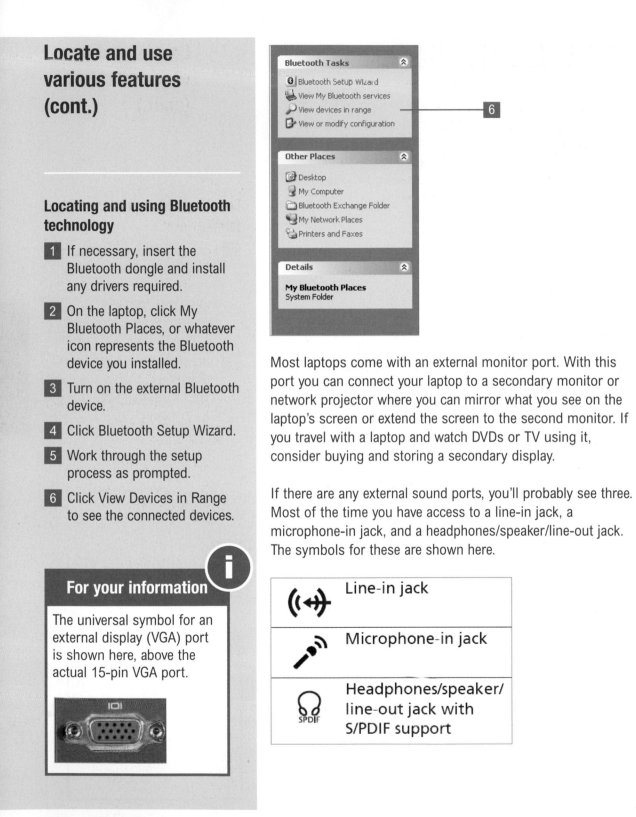

Bluetooth Tasks
- Bluetooth Setup Wizard
- View My Bluetooth services
- View devices in range — 6
- View or modify configuration

Other Places
- Desktop
- My Computer
- Bluetooth Exchange Folder
- My Network Places
- Printers and Faxes

Details
My Bluetooth Places
System Folder

Most laptops come with an external monitor port. With this port you can connect your laptop to a secondary monitor or network projector where you can mirror what you see on the laptop's screen or extend the screen to the second monitor. If you travel with a laptop and watch DVDs or TV using it, consider buying and storing a secondary display.

If there are any external sound ports, you'll probably see three. Most of the time you have access to a line-in jack, a microphone-in jack, and a headphones/speaker/line-out jack. The symbols for these are shown here.

((↔))	Line-in jack
🎤	Microphone-in jack
⌒ SPDIF	Headphones/speaker/line-out jack with S/PDIF support

For your information

The universal symbol for an external display (VGA) port is shown here, above the actual 15-pin VGA port.

24

New Display Detected

Choose the appearance of your display

[two display thumbnail illustrations]

○ Duplicate my desktop on all displays (mirrored)

4 ○ Show different parts of my desktop on each display (extended)

○ Show my desktop on the external display only

To select different settings, go to Display Settings in Control Panel.

| Apply | OK | Cancel |

A line-in jack accepts audio from devices such as CD players. A microphone-in jack accepts input from external microphones. A headphone or speaker jack lets you connect your laptop to an external source for output, such as speakers and headphones.

A modem port lets you connect your laptop to a phone jack using a standard telephone cord. Once connected, you can connect to the web using a dial-up connection, provided you've signed up for a dial-up Internet subscription. The telephone cable must be connected to both the wall and the laptop to connect. Here's the symbol for a dial-up modem.

Locate and use various features (cont.)

Locating and using an external monitor port

1 Locate a port on your laptop that is in the shape of a trapezoid and contains 15 pin holes. Look for this icon.

3

2 Connect a VGA display to this port using the cable attached to the display.

3 Turn on the display.

4 When prompted, select how to use the display.

Locate and use various features (cont.)

Locating and using sound ports

1. If necessary, plug the device into an electrical outlet (speakers) or insert batteries (portable music players).

2. If necessary, turn on the device.

3. Insert the cables that connect the device to the laptop in the proper port. Remember, line-in jacks bring data into the laptop; line-out jacks port data out to external devices like speakers or headphones.

4. If prompted, work through any set-up processes.

Locating and using a modem port

1. Connect the laptop to a phone jack using a telephone cord.

2. Connect using your dial-up Internet connection.

There are several items that have to do with the battery, and they're usually on the underside of your laptop. Before you turn the laptop upside-down to look at them, make sure to turn it off and unplug it.

You'll probably find the following items regarding the battery:

- Battery bay. This holds the computer's battery. Sometimes you have to use a screwdriver to get inside the battery bay, other times you simply need to slide out a door.

- Release latch. This holds the battery in place, even after the bay's door has been opened. You'll need to release this latch to get to the battery.

- Battery lock to fix the battery in position.

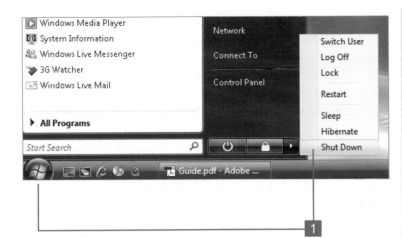

Locating and inserting or removing the battery

1 Turn off the laptop properly, using Start, and Shut Down.

2 Unplug the laptop from the mains and remove the power cable. Set the power cable aside.

3 Carefully turn the laptop upside down and place it on a desk or table.

4 Locate the battery bay and open it.

5 Unlatch the battery latch.

6 Remove or install the battery.

7 Lock the battery into place.

8 Secure the latch.

9 Close the battery bay door.

3

Explore additional ports ▶

The ports detailed in this chapter are common on laptops. However, high-end laptops have other ports. You may have one or more of the following:

- Kensington lock slot to connect the laptop to a lock to prevent it from being stolen from a hotel or vehicle.
- DVI port to connect the laptop to a television set or other DVI device.
- S-Video to connect to a television or other display.
- SD card slots or card readers that accept digital memory cards found in digital cameras.
- ExpressCard to expand a laptop's capabilities. ExpressCards are often used to offer wireless capabilities.
- AV-in accepts input from audio/video devices.
- RF-in accepts input signal from digital TV tuners.

Exploring the inside

Introduction

When you open your laptop for the first time, you should be able to find the power button, keyboard keys, touchpad or trackball, and the display screen, but you can be sure there are plenty of hidden features. There may be a microphone, webcam, speakers, and 'easy-launch' buttons, for a starter. To get the most out of your laptop you should be aware of all of the features, and if configurable, personalise them.

Your laptop is probably not the same model as mine, nor will it be the same as other readers', so this chapter may seem a bit generic. All laptops do have display screens, keyboards, arrow keys, specialised keys and function keys. Most have buttons that you configure too, buttons that will open, with a single click, your email application, web browser, music software or favourite application. We'll look at all of this here, starting with basic functionality.

What you'll do

Locate basic features

Use the touchpad

Use common keys

Use the arrow keys

Use the function keys

Important !

The best way to find out what's available on your laptop is to read the documentation that came with it, as noted in Chapter 3. If you can't find a physical guide, there may be one installed on the laptop. To find out, click Start, and in the Start Search window, type user guide (or user's guide). If you find one, click on it in the Start menu results to open it. If a user's guide is not available, you can probably visit the manufacturer's website and download one.

Basic functionality

Some features are included in all laptops. There's a latch for opening the laptop, a power button for turning it on, some sort of pointing device (often a touchpad, see page 38), and of course, the display. There may also be a microphone or webcam. Let's find them.

Locating basic features

1. Locate the latch on the outside of the laptop to open the lid.

2. Locate the power button. It may have the universal power button symbol on it. Press it to boot the computer.

3. Watch the computer's progress on the display screen.

4. When the computer has finished its start-up tasks, look at the bottom of the display screen. Locate the speaker icon in the 'notification area' at the bottom right.

5. Click the volume icon once.

6. Use the slider to increase or decrease the volume.

7. Follow the sound to locate the speakers.

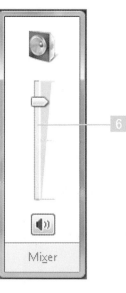

Basic functionality (cont.)

8 Click Start.

9 In the Start Search window, type sound.

10 Click sound under programs.

11 Click the recording tab.

12 Locate a working microphone. There are two shown here, and the headset microphone is active.

13 Speak into the microphone. Watch while the bars next to the microphone move upward.

14 Click OK.

15 Look for a small camera eye, which should be located at the top of the display. This is the webcam. You may or may not see a webcam lens and/or a webcam may not be included with your laptop. To find out, complete steps 16-20.

4

Basic functionality (cont.)

16 Click Start.

17 In the Start Search window, type webcam. If you do not see a webcam listed under programs in the results, as shown here, try typing web cam, or simply web.

18 If, under the Programs results, you see something related to an installed webcam, click on it.

19 You should see yourself as others would see you if you were having a webcam conversation.

20 Look for tools included in the program. Click them to apply webcam settings.

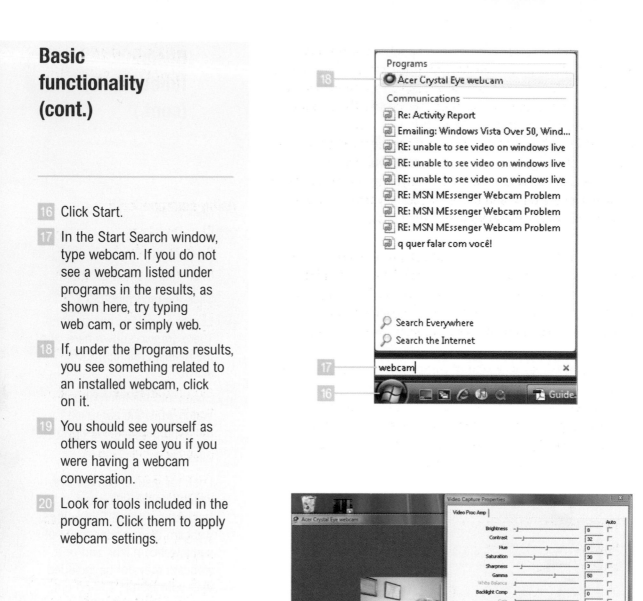

Most laptop keyboards have more than a few universal keys, and much of the time these keys offer the same things across makes and models. For instance, pressing F1 almost always opens a Help window for the open application. The Windows key opens the Start menu, and the Windows key in combination with other keys will do other things, such as minimise all windows (Start + M) or lock your computer (Start + L). The Caps Lock key makes sure anything you type appears in capital letters only, and the Num Lock key makes sure your number pad offers numbers and nothing else.

There are arrow keys too, which you can use to move around in a web page, document or other window. Page Up and Page Down keys let you move around as well. And there are always function keys, which offer shortcuts to specific computer-related functions, most of which are make and model specific.

There are hundreds of keyboard shortcuts, and my goal in this chapter does not include listing them or suggesting you learn them. However, the Windows Start key, also called the Windows logo key, can be a real time saver if you can get in the habit of using it regularly. That said, here are a few shortcuts you can commit to memory:

- Windows Start key: open the Start Menu.
- Windows Start key + E: open My Computer.
- Windows Start key + D: show Desktop (and minimise all open windows).
- Windows Start key + M: minimise all windows.
- Windows Start key + L: switch between users or lock the laptop.
- Windows Start key + F: open Search.
- Windows Start key + F1: open Help and Support.

Using common keys

1. Click the Windows Logo Key to the Start Menu.
2. Click the Windows Logo Key (which I'll call the Start key from here on) to close the Start Menu.
3. Click the Start key + E to open Computer.
4. Click the Start key + F to open a search window.
5. Click the Start key + F1 to open Help and Support.
6. Click the Start key + D to show the Desktop.
7. Click the Start key + Shift + M to maximise all minimised windows.
8. Click the X symbol at the top of each of the open windows to close it.

9. Click Start.
10. In the Start Search window, type WordPad.

Keys common to most keyboards (cont.)

11 From the Programs results, click WordPad to open it.

Programs
⬚ WordPad

Communications
⬚ Emailing: Windows Vista O‹

🔍 Search Everywhere
🔍 Search the Internet

Wordpad|

12 Click Ctrl + O to see the Open dialogue box, shown here.

13 Click Cancel to close.

14 Click Ctrl + P to open the Print dialogue box.

15 Click Cancel to close.

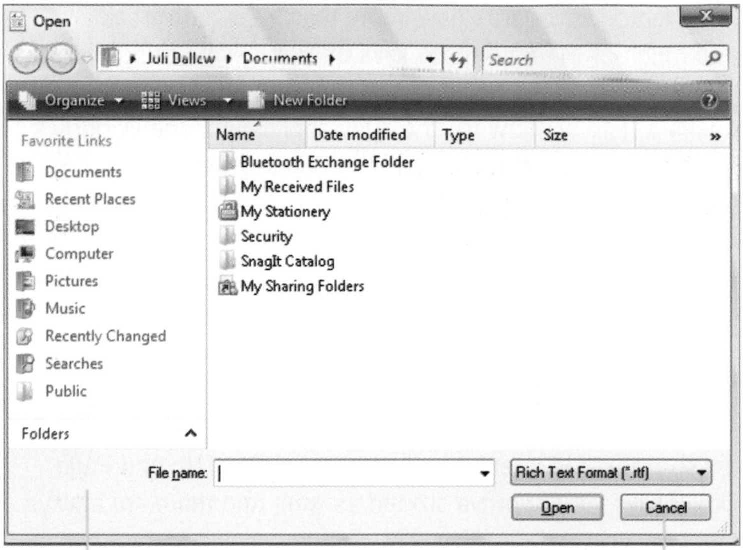

Open

◉ ◉ | 📁 ▸ Juli Dallew ▸ Documents ▸   ▾ ⁺⁺ | Search   🔍

🔹 Organize ▾ 🔲 Views ▾ 📁 New Folder   ?

Favorite Links | Name ▴ | Date modified | Type | Size | »
📄 Documents | 📁 Bluetooth Exchange Folder
📄 Recent Places | 📁 My Received Files
🖥 Desktop | 📁 My Stationery
🖥 Computer | 📁 Security
📁 Pictures | 📁 SnagIt Catalog
🎵 Music | 📁 My Sharing Folders
📁 Recently Changed
📁 Searches
📁 Public

Folders   ︿

File name: | ▾   Rich Text Format (*.rtf) ▾

Open   Cancel

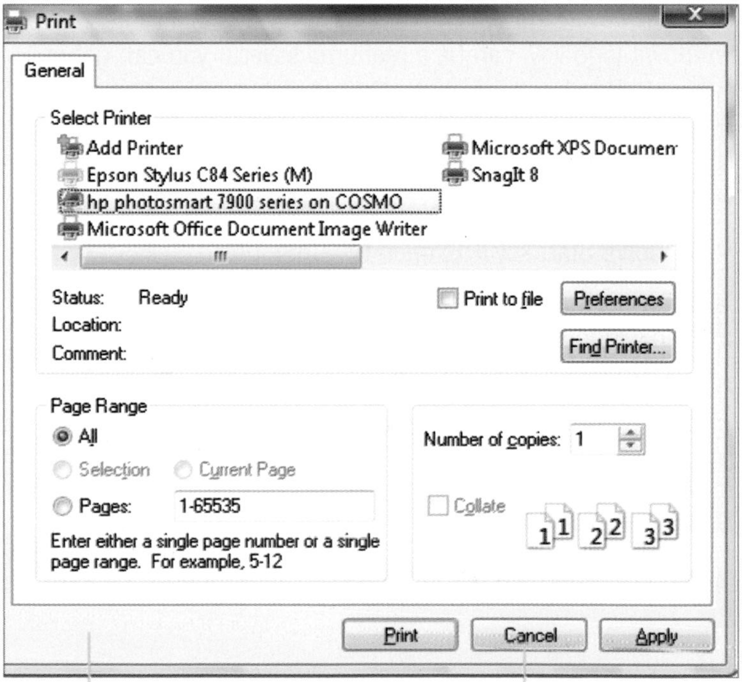

Print

General

Select Printer
🖨 Add Printer   🖨 Microsoft XPS Documen‹
🖨 Epson Stylus C84 Series (M)   🖨 SnagIt 8
🖨 hp photosmart 7900 series on COSMO
🖨 Microsoft Office Document Image Writer

◂ | ⸺ | ▸

Status: Ready   ☐ Print to file   Preferences
Location:
Comment: Find Printer...

Page Range
◉ All   Number of copies: 1 ⬍
○ Selection   ○ Current Page
○ Pages: 1-65535   ☐ Collate
Enter either a single page number or a single   1¹ 2² 3³
page range. For example, 5-12

Print   Cancel   Apply

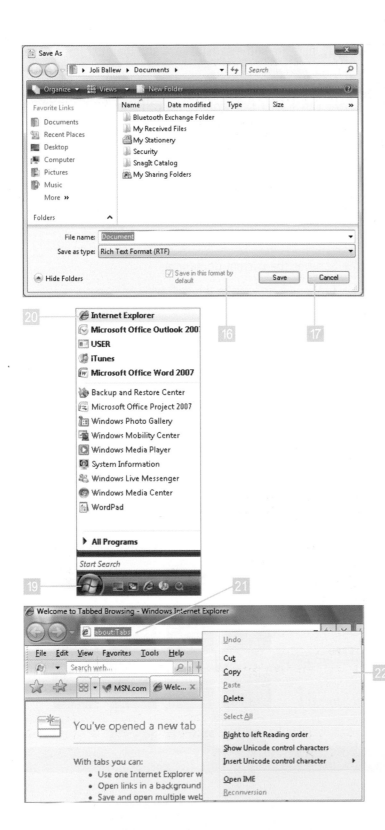

16 Click Ctrl + S to open the Save As dialogue box.

17 Click Cancel to close.

18 Click the X in the top of WordPad to close it.

19 Click Start.

20 Click Internet Explorer.

21 Click Ctrl + T to open a new tab (where you can type a website address).

22 Click Shift + F10 to open a context menu you'd normally get by right-clicking inside web browser.

23 Close Internet Explorer.

Keys common to most keyboards (cont.)

Using the arrow keys

1 Click Start.

2 Click All Programs.

Windows Defender
Windows DVD Maker
Windows Live Mail
Windows Live Photo Gallery
Windows Mail
Windows Media Center
Windows Media Player
Windows Meeting Space
Windows Movie Maker
Windows Photo Gallery
Windows Update
Accessories
Acer Crystal Eye webcam
Acer Empowering Technology
Acer GameZone
AcerSystem
AT&T
Crystal Eye webcam

3 Click Windows Photo Gallery to open it.

4 Select any picture.

5 Use the arrow keys on the keyboard to move from picture to picture.

6 Click the Page Up key to go to the first picture.

Additionally, here are some general keys and their common uses.

The **Ctrl** key rarely does anything by itself, but is used with other keys. Ctrl + Alt + Del (hold down Ctrl and Alt, press Del) opens a new screen where you can lock the computer, switch users, log off, change a password or start Task Manager, for instance. Here are a few options you may want to explore:

- Ctrl + O: opens the Open window where you can search for and open a file, folder or program.
- Ctrl + P: opens the printing dialogue box.
- Ctrl + S: saves the current document.
- Ctrl + T: opens a new tab in the web browser.

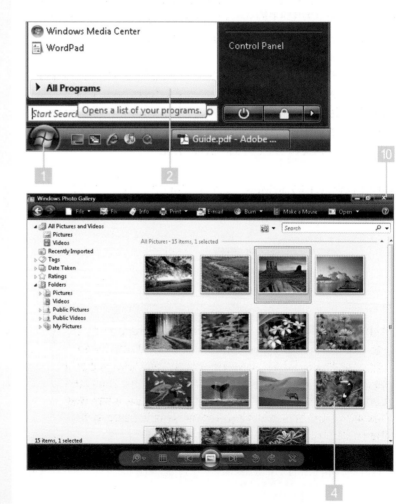

Esc stops the current activity, usually.

Tab advances the cursor to the next Tab stop.

Shift, like the Ctrl key, generally does nothing by itself, but when used with other keys, performs tasks. Here are a few options:

- Shift + F10: opens a context menu you'd normally get by right-clicking.
- Shift + Delete: deletes the selected item permanently.
- Shift + any letter: in a word processor, capitalises the letter you type.

Home moves the cursor to the beginning of a paragraph, line or document, depending on where the cursor is. **End** moves to the end of the paragraph, line or document.

Fn, like Shift and Ctrl, doesn't do anything by itself, but instead is used to access items listed on the function keys (F1, F2, F3, etc). The items listed are laptop-specific and may offer options to change the volume, lock the laptop, put the laptop to sleep, set number lock or scroll lock, and more.

Scroll Lock varies in its use depending on the application open, and is rarely used on today's laptops.

For your information

Although most laptops offer an Fn key, some do not. If you don't see an Fn key, take a look at the items listed underneath F1, F2, F3, F4, and so on. They will probably be a different colour to the default keys on the keyboard. Locate a key that is the same colour as these, a key that has an F on it or something similar. This is likely to be the Fn key we're talking about here.

Keys common to most keyboards (cont.)

7 Click the Page Down key to go to the last picture.

8 Click the Home key to go to the first picture.

9 Click the End key to go to the last picture.

10 Click the X in the top right corner of Photo Gallery to close it.

Using the function keys

1 Locate the Fn key on your keyboard. If you do not see an Fn key, read the For your information box below. The Fn key is used with other keys to perform a task, such as changing the volume or opening Help.

2 Notice the colour of the text or images under F1, F2, F3, and other function keys. It will be different from the keyboard letters. Under F1 you may see a blue question mark, for instance. This alternative-coloured information tells you what will happen when you press the Fn key and this key at the same time.

3 Press Fn + F1. This will probably open Help.

4

Keys common to most keyboards (cont.)

4 Press Fn + F2. Make a note of what happens as well as what is listed under F2 on the key itself.

5 Continue in this manner until you've explored all the function keys, up to F12. (Some keys may not do anything.)

6 Look for other keys on the keyboard that have additional information on them other than letters or punctuation. For instance, you may see additional functions on the arrow keys (which is where you might access the volume or brightness), or on the Page Up and Page Down keys (where you may find options to scroll left or right). Explore these keys.

Using the touchpad

- The touchpad or other pointing device is usually located in the centre of the keyboard or at the bottom of it. Place your finger on the touchpad or trackball and move it around. Notice the screen pointer moves.

- If there are buttons, for the most part the left button functions in the same way as the left button on a mouse. Double click to execute a command, click once to select something. (Often you can click one time with the left button and use your finger to drag the mouse pointer across text to select it.)

- The right button functions the same way as the right button of a mouse. Right click one time to open context menus to access copy, select all, and similar commands.

- If there is a centre button, this is often used to scroll through pages. Try clicking and holding it to move up, down, left, or right on a page.

Windows Vista

Introduction

Windows Vista is the most important software on your computer. Although you may have other programs (such as Microsoft Office or Photoshop Elements), Vista is your computer's *operating system*, it's what allows you to operate your computer's *system*. You will use Vista to find things you have stored on your computer, go online, send and receive email, and surf the web.

You don't need to be a computer guru or have years of experience to use Vista. The Start button offers a place to access just about everything you'll need, from photos to music to email; the Recycle Bin holds files you've deleted; and the Sidebar is full of gadgets such as a clock, the weather and news headlines. In this chapter you will learn how to get started with Windows Vista.

What you'll do

Start and activate Windows Vista

Explore the Welcome Center

Explore the Desktop

Discover Windows Vista applications

Discover Windows Vista accessories

Explore the Taskbar

Enable the Sidebar

Personalise gadgets

Configure the Sidebar

Adding and remove gadgets

Search with Instant Search

Shut down Windows

> **! Important**
>
> Windows Vista comes in several versions and computer manufacturers often add their own touches. As a result, your screen may not look exactly like the screenshots in this book (but it'll be close).

One of Vista's main jobs is to act as a liaison between you and your laptop. When you move the mouse or place your finger on the touchpad, Vista helps the laptop move the cursor on the desktop. When you save a file, Vista interacts with the hard drive to offer a place to save the information and remembers where it is stored. If you want to print a web page, Vista communicates with the printer and sends the required information to it. And, when you want to burn a CD or DVD, Vista communicates with those drives too, making sure what you want to do is completed successfully. Vista's work is behind-the-scenes, making sure that you never have to worry about how anything works.

Vista also offers applications to help you be more productive. For instance, there's a calendar, and software to help you create DVDs, fax and scan, send and receive email, and Windows Photo Gallery, Media Center and Movie Maker help you handle media files. You also get Internet Explorer for surfing the web and the Sync Center for adding portable players for music, photos, videos and ebooks.

You probably have other programs installed. You may have Microsoft Office, Photoshop or an art program. You may even have applications that were installed by the computer manufacturer, like a PDF reader, firewall, PC update software, music players or anti-virus software.

If this is your first time you've booted your laptop, you'll be prompted to enter some information. Specifically, you'll type your name as you'd like it to appear on your Start menu (capital letters count), activate Vista, and if desired, register your copy of Vista. It's important to know that while activation is mandatory, registration is not. You'll learn more about both of these things shortly.

Starting and activating Windows Vista

Starting and activating Windows Vista

1 If applicable, open the laptop's lid.

2 Press the power button. It's generally located towards the top of the keyboard (to keep you from accidentally turning on the laptop when the lid is closed or when typing).

3 Work through the activation and registration process, if applicable. Just follow the directions, clicking Next to move from one page of the activation wizard to the next.

4 Click your user name and input a password, or just wait for Windows to start. What happens here depends on your current set-up.

5 Wait a few seconds for Vista to initialise.

6 Click the Start button on the Desktop. It's in the bottom left hand corner.

7 Locate your user name in the Start Menu.

Explore the Welcome Center

When you first start Vista, the Welcome Center opens. There are at least two sections: Get started with Windows and Offers from Microsoft, and perhaps others. Often, computer makers add their own listings and links to help you learn about your computer and the applications installed, as well as links to their own Help files or website.

Using the Get started with Windows section you can choose:

- View computer details: see what edition of Vista is installed (probably Basic, Home Premium or Ultimate), the processor type and speed, the amount of memory (RAM) and other details.

- Transfer files and settings: learn how to use Windows Easy Transfer, an application that helps you transfer accounts, files and folders, program settings, Internet settings and bookmarks, and email settings, contacts and messages from an older computer to your new one. (You can use this at any time.)

- Add new users: learn how to secure your computer with user accounts for each person who will access it. If two people share a single laptop, each can have his or her own user account, where documents, email, photos and other data is secure. You can also customise settings and set up parental controls here.

- Connect to the Internet: use Vista wizards to help you set up an online connection. You can use an existing account or choose from a list of service providers (ISPs).

- Ultimate extras: available only on Vista Ultimate edition, this section allows you to access programs, services and publications for Vista Ultimate.

- What's new in Vista: information regarding what's been added since Windows XP, such as keeping devices synchronised, backing up and encrypting files, faxing and scanning documents, and creating, saving and using Search folders.

- Personalise Windows: change the picture that appears on your Desktop, change your screen saver, sounds and fonts.

- Register: go online to register your copy of Windows. This lets you get tips and ideas for Vista.

- Windows Media Center: available in the Home Premium and Ultimate editions, this option allows you to watch, pause and record live television, locate, download, and/or listen to music and radio, view, edit and share photos and videos, and play DVDs (among other things).

- Windows basics: learn how to use the mouse and keyboard, work with files and programs, use email, connect to the Internet, surf the web, secure your PC and work with digital pictures.

- Ease of Access Center: make your computer easier to see, hear and use by adjusting the display and other settings.

- Back Up and Restore Center: copy important files once or on a schedule. If you have Vista Ultimate you can create a copy of your entire PC.

- Demonstrations: watch videos to learn to work with programs, files and folders, use email and the Internet, print documents, secure your PC, set up user accounts and solve problems.

- Control Panel: use this to change settings such as the clock or time zone, the colour scheme, and if you want to share files with other users, add or remove programs, search and configure network settings.

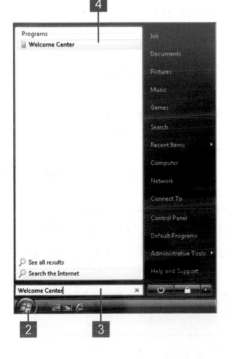

Explore the Welcome Center (cont.)

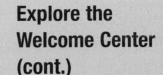

Important

What you see in your Welcome Center may differ from what you see here. For instance, this screen shows some things that only come with Vista Ultimate.

Show the Welcome Center

1 To show the Welcome Center, turn on the PC.

2 If the Welcome Center does not open automatically, click on the Start button.

3 In the Start Search window, type Welcome Center.

4 Under Programs, in the Start Menu, click on Welcome Center.

5

Explore the Welcome Center (cont.)

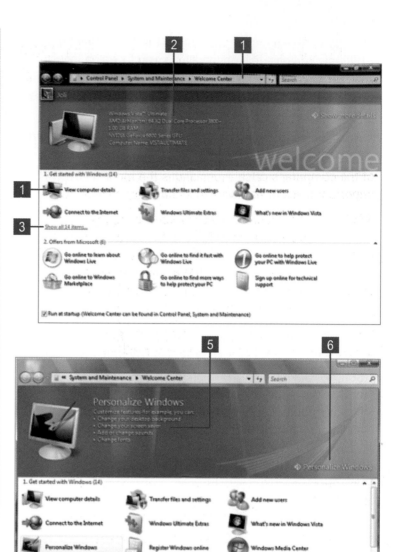

Explore the Welcome Center

1 With the Welcome Center open, click View computer details.

2 Read the details regarding your computer. For more information about what you see here, refer to the Jargon buster. Make note of what edition of Vista is installed. In the next section you'll learn the difference between the editions and can decide if you want to upgrade.

3 Click Show all <number of> items. (Remember, you might see a different number, depending on your PC's configuration.)

4 Click on Personalize Windows.

5 Notice the top pane changes to reflect your choice.

6 Later, you can click on this option to modify your copy of Vista.

7 If you do not want the Welcome Center to open every time you start Windows Vista, remove the check mark from Run at startup (Welcome Center can be found in Control Panel, System and Maintenance).

Did you know?

In the Welcome Center, you can select Windows Vista Demos, and then watch videos of the most often-performed tasks in Windows Vista including learning to use the mouse, printing to an installed printer, using the web and diagnosing computer problems.

Jargon buster

Processor – short for microprocessor, it's the silicon chip that contains the central processing unit (CPU) inside a computer. Generally, the terms CPU and processor are used interchangeably. The CPU does most of the computer's calculations and is the most important piece of hardware in a computer system.

RAM – short for random access memory, it's the hardware inside your computer that temporarily stores data that is being used by the operating system or programs. Although there are many types of RAM, generally, the more RAM you have, the faster your computer will (theoretically) run and perform.

GPU – short for graphics processing unit, it's a processor used specifically for handling graphics. It frees up the main CPU, allowing it to work faster on other tasks.

GHz – short for gigahertz, this term describes how fast a processor can work. One GHz equals one billion cycles a second, so a 2.4 GHz computer chip will execute calculations at 240 billion cycles per second. Again, it's only important to know that the faster the chip, the faster the PC.

Using the Welcome Center's Offers from Microsoft section allows you to go online to learn about Windows Live, visit the Windows Marketplace, find ways to protect your PC, and sign up for online technical support. These are all extras and include things you may want to explore later.

Explore the Welcome Center (cont.)

As an example, as you acquire and/or begin to use applications such as Hotmail, Messenger, Mail and Photo Gallery, you may begin to want to integrate these technologies. With Windows Live, you can. For instance, Windows Live offers a Windows Live Toolbar for searching from any web page and gaining immediate access to Hotmail, Windows Live Mail and other Live services like Windows Live Spaces. With Windows Live Spaces you can create your own free website, and then use Live Writer to create your own blog, complete with photos, videos and any other content. But we're getting ahead of ourselves. For now, let's focus on getting to know Vista!

You saw in the Welcome Center what edition of Vista was on your PC. This information is available from the View computer details section. Here, the computer is running Windows Home Premium edition.

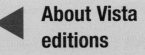

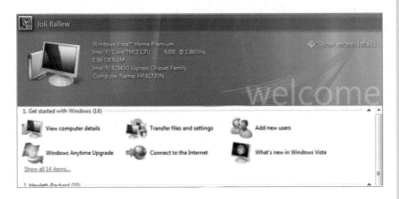

There are four Windows Vista editions:

■ Basic: this edition includes necessary security features, network connectivity tools, Internet Explorer and Search features. If you have this edition, don't think that you're not appropriately covered, PC-wise; you have all you need to perform basic computing tasks such as email, creating documents, storing pictures and videos and surfing the web.

■ Home Premium: an upgrade to Basic that adds features such as a different display feature (Aero): Tablet PC support for laptops and portable PCs; Media Center for watching and recoding television, among other things; creating scheduled back-ups; DVD maker; more games; Meeting Space (a way to hold virtual meetings from anywhere); and the ability to create your own videos in high definition.

■ Business: another upgrade to Basic that adds Aero; mobility and Tablet PC support; a back-up program for your entire PC; fax and scan facilities; the ability to access your PC remotely; and business tools such as Meeting Space. It does not include Media Center, the games in Home Premium or the ability to create videos in high-definition.

■ Ultimate: with this edition you get everything in all of the other editions; the ability to encrypt data to make it more secure; tablet and touch technology (meaning you can touch the screen of compatible hardware to perform computer-related tasks); Ultimate Extras; language packs; a multiple-user language interface; and secure online back-up.

5

About Vista editions (cont.)

Did you know?

Starter is an affordable way for emerging markets to gain access to Windows Vista. Starter is not available in high income markets such as the European Union, the United States and Australia. This version is designed for users with little or no computer experience and in countries where PCs have previously been unavailable or unwarranted due to price and/or lack of user experience.

Not every feature of Vista has been mentioned, but the information here can give you an idea whether or not you'd like to upgrade. For instance, if you have Basic or Business, and you want to watch, record and pause live TV, you're going to need to upgrade to Home Premium or Ultimate. However, if your laptop does not include a TV tuner card and you don't want to buy one, there's no reason to upgrade. (Don't worry, if you choose to upgrade, you'll get a nice, organised report regarding your PC's compatibility, and what you'll need to buy and add on to use the additional features in the upgraded edition.)

If you're interested in upgrading, click Start, and type Windows Anytime Upgrade. Follow the prompts to see if an upgrade is possible and to perform the upgrade if desired.

What you see on the Desktop will vary depending on how long you've been using your laptop. If it's new, you may only see the Recycle Bin and the Sidebar. If you've been using Vista for a while, you may see other things, including Computer, Network, Control Panel or a folder with your name on it (for storing your personal files). You may even see icons with names of applications or internet service providers written on them. Here you can see a sample Desktop.

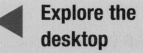
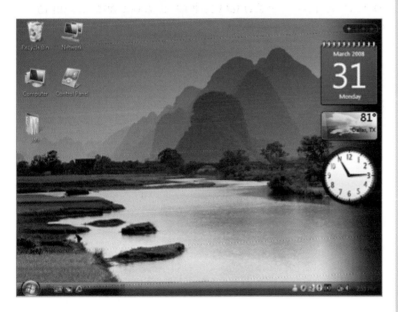

When you double-click on any icon, the associated folder, file or application opens. Vista icons are shown here. You can add or remove icons from the Desktop if you desire. You'll learn how to do that in Chapter 6. Here are a few of the things you may find on the Desktop:

■ Recycle Bin: holds deleted files until you decide to empty it. This serves as a safeguard, allowing you recover items accidentally deleted, or items you thought you no longer wanted but later decide you need. Note that once you empty the Recycle Bin, the items in it are gone forever. (You can empty the bin by right-clicking it and choosing Empty Recycle Bin.)

Explore the desktop (cont.)

■ Sidebar: this lies *on top of* the Desktop. It's transparent and offers by default, a calendar, the weather and a clock. You can delete and add items, called gadgets, to show the information you want to see. You can also hide the Sidebar. You'll explore this later.

■ Network: double-clicking on this icon opens a window where you can see the computers on your network. If you are not connected to a network, you'll see the following.

■ Computer: double-clicking on this icon opens the window shown here. You can see your hard drive(s) where the operating system, installed applications and personal data are stored, along with CD or DVD drives and sharing folders. You'll learn more about sharing folders in Chapter 8.

■ Control Panel: double-clicking on this icon opens the Control Panel window. Here, you can change settings related to system maintenance, user accounts, security, appearance, networks and the Internet, the time, language, region, hardware and sounds, visual displays and accessibility options, programs and additional options.

Explore the desktop (cont.)

■ Your personal folder: the name of this folder is the user name you created when you set up Vista. Every user account has a personal folder. Double-clicking the folder icon opens it, and inside are subfolders named documents, music, saved games, pictures, downloads, searches, videos and more. You'll use these folders to store your personal data.

Explore the desktop

1. If the Welcome Screen is open, close it by clicking the X in the top right corner.

2. Locate the Recycle Bin.

3. You may see other icons, like the ones shown here, including Network, Computer, and Control Panel. The folder named Joli is my personal file folder, inside it are my saved documents, pictures, e-books and videos. Your folder will have your name (not mine).

4. Locate the Start button. It's in the bottom left corner.

5. Locate the Quick Launch area.

6. Locate the clock and volume. (You may see additional icons.)

In addition to the icons on the Desktop, you'll also notice the Start button, Quick Launch area and the Notification area.

- Start Button: you'll use this to locate programs and data stored on your computer. Click it once to open the Start menu, right-click it to see additional options as shown here.

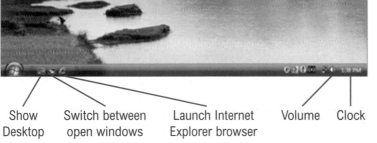

Show Desktop   Switch between open windows   Launch Internet Explorer browser   Volume   Clock

- Quick launch area: you'll use this to see the Desktop (if there are open windows on it, switch between open windows, access Internet Explorer and so on).

- Notification area: the icons here differ, depending on your PC's set-up and installed programs. However, you will see some Windows icons there, including the Clock and Volume icons.

7 Locate the Sidebar.

Explore Vista

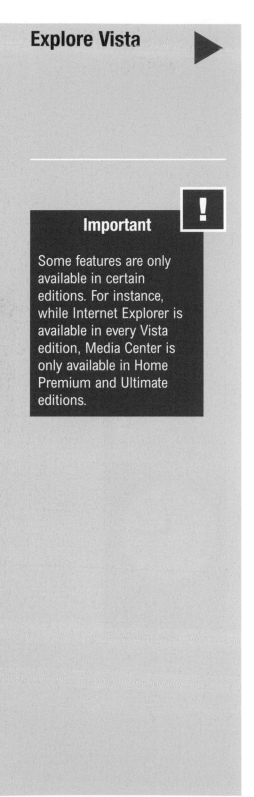

Just about anything you want to access on your computer can be accessed through the Start menu. You can open office applications, graphics applications, games and personal folders. You can access computer, network and control panel too, as well as help and support. In this section though, we'll only look at one part of the Start Menu, the All Programs menu.

Vista comes with just about everything you need when it comes to applications and software. There's Internet Explorer for surfing the web, a calendar for keeping track of tasks and appointments, a DVD maker for burning your own DVDs, and a media player for listening to music. But there are far more features than that. In this section you'll learn a little about many of the Vista features, and you can decide if there's something you want to explore and use or not. With that out of the way, you can then skip around the book for the information you need on using and applying the feature, and ignore those you don't need or want to use.

Here are some of the more commonly-used features, all available by clicking the Start button and then clicking All Programs:

- Internet Explorer: one option for accessing and surfing the web. Internet Explorer offers tabbed browsing, meaning you can have several web pages open at the same time; a place to store links to your favourite pages; a pop-up blocker; and the

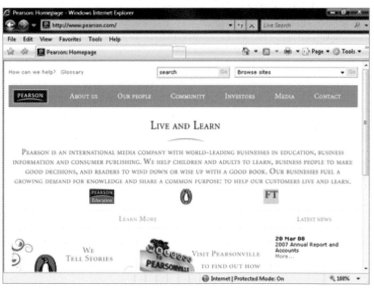

ability to zoom, change the text size, print, and subscribe to RSS feeds among other things.

- Calendar: a way to create, edit, save and publish a calendar for you, your children or your business. With it, you can add tasks and appointments, make notes, and even import and export calendar data.

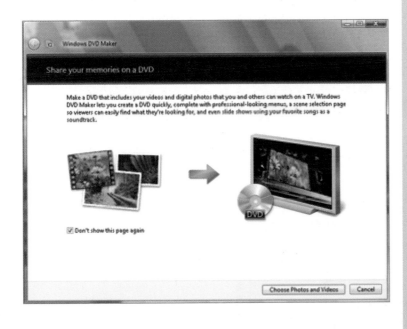

- DVD Maker: an application that lets you create DVDs by working through the steps offered by a 'wizard'.

Explore Vista (cont.)

■ Fax and Scan: this helps you scan and then fax documents, or fax documents created on your PC. It looks like Outlook Express, so if you're familiar with that program, this one will be easy. Although you won't find information in this book about using Fax and Scan, if you learn how to use Mail you can use that knowledge for Fax and Scan. (Note that you'll need a modem and a phone line to use the program to fax data.)

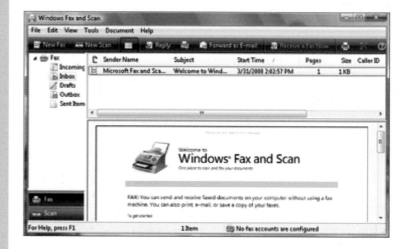

■ Live Messenger: to exchange instant messages.

■ Mail: for sending, receiving, storing and organising email and contacts.

■ Media Center: allows you to watch, record, fast-forward and (after recording or pausing a TV show) rewind live TV. You can also listen to music on your PC; locate and watch sports programmes; view, download and/or purchase online media; burn CDs and DVDs; connect portable music devices; and view and organise pictures and videos. To use all of these features though, you'll need a TV tuner, CD and DVD burner, Internet connection, large hard drive and lots of RAM.

5

Explore Vista (cont.)

■ Media Player: helps you to store, access, play and organise music on your PC. You can also 'rip' music (that means copying music CDs you own to your PC's hard drive), burn CDs and connect portable devices.

■ Movie Maker: helps you import videos from a camera and edit them. You can add effects, music, transitions and audio.

- Photo Gallery: to import, access, view, send, store and organise pictures and videos. You can create picture galleries that contain only the images you want, and organise photos easily by year, subject or ratings.

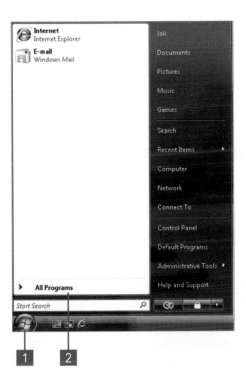

Discover Vista applications

1 Click the Start button.

2 Click All Programs.

Explore Vista (cont.)

3 If necessary, use the scroll bar to move to the top of the All Programs list.

4 Locate Internet Explorer. Do not click it or it will open.

5 Locate the calendar. Do not click it or it will open.

6 Continue down the list, noting what programs and applications are available in your edition of Vista.

For your information

The Accessories folder is located underneath Windows Update in this list. We'll talk about the items in that folder next.

Accessories

Vista also comes with a lot of accessories. These applications are simpler than the applications so far. Two examples are the calculator and notepad. Accessories are located in the Accessories folder, which you can access from the Start button and the All Programs list.

The accessories include:

- A calculator for basic mathematical tasks. Click the View menu and choose Scientific to see the calculator shown here.

- Command Prompt is a way to communicate with Vista's underlying operating system. A task you are unlikely to need to do.

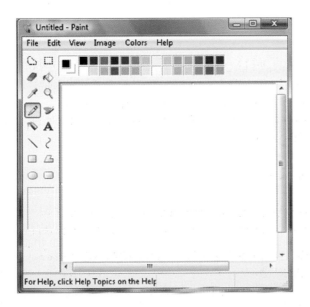

- Connect to a network projector for presentations.

- Notepad: a basic word processor that enables you to type notes and save them. Using this application, you can also print, cut, copy and paste, find and replace words, and select a font, font size and script.

- Paint can be used to create drawings either on a blank canvas or on top of a picture. You can use the toolbar to draw shapes, lines, curves and input text. You can use additional tools including paint brushes, pencils, airbrushes and the like, as well as choose colours.

Explore Vista (cont.)

■ Remote Desktop Connection: a program you can use to access your computer from somewhere else, such as an office or hotel room.

■ Run: a dialogue box where you can type a command. There are many commands, one example is sfc/scannow, which will prompt Vista to find and fix any problems with the operating system, and msconfig, which opens a dialogue box where you can control what programs load when you start Windows, among other things.

■ Snipping Tool: use this to copy any part of any screen, including information from a web page, part of your desktop, or even part of a picture.

■ Sound Recorder: use this to record your own voice. You can use the voice clips as reminders for tasks and you can add them to video files or a web page.

■ Sync Center: this lets you set up partnerships between Vista and devices such as portable media players, ebook readers, and portable PCs or phones. After a partnership is set up, each time you connect the device to your PC, the information that has changed is updated, as per your instructions during set-up.

- Welcome Center: as discussed earlier in the chapter, a place for Vista to 'welcome' you by offering quick links to tasks such as setting up the Internet, viewing computer details and securing your PC.

- Explorer: opens an 'explorer' window where you can browse for files, programs, pictures, music and videos. However, it's generally easier to locate these items in their respective folders or from the Start menu. Here Public folders are selected. (You'll store items in these folders when you want to share them with others who use your PC or are on your local network.) In the Explorer window you can also change how you share files and burn CDs.

- Sidebar: opens the Sidebar, detailed later in this chapter.

- WordPad: a wordprocessor where you can create, edit, save and print files. Like Notepad, you can cut, copy and paste, find and replace words, and select a font, font size and script.

Explore Vista (cont.)

However, you also have access to a formatting toolbar, a ruler and other options. You can insert the date and time into a document, and an object, like a graph or chart, or a compatible picture. WordPad's toolbars and interface are shown here.

■ Ease of Access folder: holds tools that make using the computer easier for people with disabilities. Items include a magnifier and narrator.

■ System Tools: to maintain your computer's health. These include but are not limited to disk clean-up, defragmenter and system restore. You'll learn more about these in Chapter 15.

■ Tablet PC: you'll only see this option if you have a laptop with Vista Home Premium or Ultimate, or if your PC runs Ultimate. Accessories include tools related to mobile PCs such as the Tablet PC input panel and Windows Journal. You'll learn more about Tablet PC options in Chapter 13.

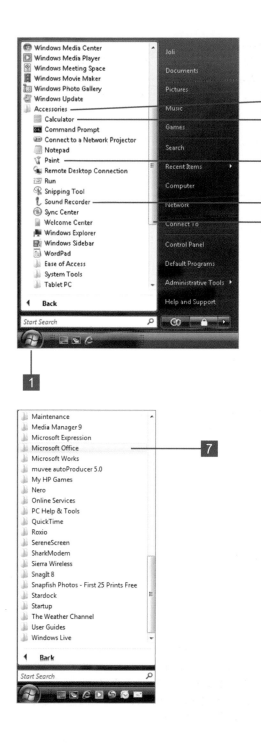

Explore Vista (cont.)

Discover Windows Vista accessories

1 Click on the Start button. Click on All Programs.

2 Use the scroll bar to move down the list until you see Accessories.

3 Click Accessories.

4 Click Calculator. Close the program using the red X in the top right corner.

5 Repeat steps 1–4, and open Paint. Close the program by clicking the red X in the top right corner.

6 Repeat steps 1–4, and open Sound Recorder. Close the program by clicking the red X in the top right corner.

7 Continue exploring the features. You'll also want to explore applications you've purchased and installed. To find these, click on folder names such as Microsoft Office, QuickTime, Roxio and Windows Live.

5

Explore Vista (cont.)

8 When you open other folders, you can access the software. Here, My HP Games is expanded. Notice all of my third-party games; these came with my laptop.

The taskbar is the bar that runs across the bottom of your screen. It contains three areas:

Explore the taskbar

- Quick Launch toolbar. This opens programs with a single click. The toolbar stores shortcuts to programs so you can easily access and open them. By default, three items are stored there, but you can easily add your own. Programs and features with links include the Show desktop icon, which lets you access the desktop immediately no matter how many windows are open; the Switch between Windows icon, which lets you move easily between open windows; and Internet Explorer, for surfing the web.

- The middle section displays icons for open programs and documents. When nothing is open, it's blank. When programs and documents are open, you'll see their names here. You can easily open any window by clicking on its icon in the taskbar. By default, similar taskbar buttons are grouped.

Grouped documents   Notification area

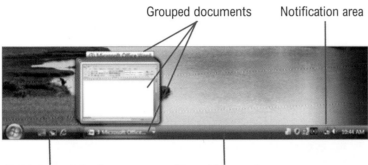

Quick Launch toolbar   The middle section

- The notification area includes the clock and the volume icons. It also holds icons for applications that are running in the background. You may see icons for your anti-virus software, music players, updates or Windows security alerts.

You can configure the taskbar just as you can configure the other aspects of Vista. To access the configuration settings, right-click on the taskbar and click on Properties. There are features specific to the taskbar that you may want to tweak.

5

Explore the taskbar (cont.)

■ Lock the taskbar. Enabling this will keep the taskbar in its default position, across the bottom of the screen. When unlocked, it is possible to drag the taskbar to other areas of the screen and/or to change how thick the taskbar is, as shown here. (To move or resize the taskbar, just click an empty area of the taskbar and drag it to another area of the desktop.)

■ Auto-hide the taskbar: enabling this will cause the taskbar to disappear when not in use. It will reappear when you move your mouse over the area of the screen where the taskbar lies.

■ Keep the taskbar on top of other windows: enabling this will keep the taskbar on top of any windows that are open. By default this is not selected because it is generally better to keep the taskbar behind open windows so that you have more screen 'real estate'.

- Group similar taskbar buttons: enabling this will allow open files from programs and folders to be grouped together to save taskbar real estate. When not grouped, the taskbar can become cluttered.

- Show Quick Launch: enable this to show the Quick Launch area.

- Show windows previews (thumbnails): this shows thumbnails (small pictures) of items shown on the toolbar. Here you can see that Windows Photo Gallery is open and a thumbnail for it is showing. A thumbnail is a smaller version of the actual open window. Note that the thumbnail only shows when you hover the mouse over the item in the taskbar.

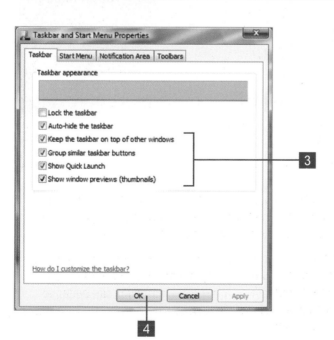

Explore the taskbar (cont.)

Did you know?

You don't have to configure the taskbar. If you're happy with it the way it is, just skip this section.

Configuring the taskbar

5

1 Right-click an empty area of the Taskbar in the middle section.

2 Click Properties.

3 In the Taskbar and Start Menu Properties dialogue box, select or deselect any feature by clicking in its checkbox.

4 Click OK.

?

Did you know?

If you can't find an empty area of the taskbar to right-click, you can right-click the Start menu. When the Properties dialogue box opens, choose the Taskbar tab.

Explore Sidebar

Sidebar sits on your desktop and offers information on the weather, time and date, as well as access to your contacts, productivity tools and CPU usage. You can even have a slideshow of pictures. You can customise the sidebar by hiding it, keeping it on top of or underneath open windows, adding or removing 'gadgets', and even detaching gadgets from the sidebar for use anywhere on the desktop. Here you can see the parts of the sidebar.

Detached gadget   Windows Sidebar   Add gadget icon

Sidebar gadgets   Windows Sidebar icon

It's easy to add gadgets. Just click the Add Gadget icon. There are several default options, such as calendar, clock, notes and weather. It's important to understand that much of this data comes from the Internet. Your computer doesn't know what the weather is like outside, but when you're online, that information is automatically retrieved and updated on the sidebar. The same is true of news headlines and share prices. If you're not online, you won't have up-to-date information.

You can add gadgets by clicking Get more gadgets online. If you're connected to the Internet when you click on the link, you'll be taken to a web page where you can review, choose and download and install just about any gadget imaginable. Gadgets are categorised by their function, and you can search for gadgets that involve games, mail, instant messaging, music, film, TV, news feeds, safety, security, search tools and utilities.

Important

Make sure you read the gadget reviews before downloading and installing them. Although the gadgets you'll find here are almost always harmless, you might run across one or two that don't work or cause computer problems. Don't be afraid to get gadgets online, just be careful before installing them.

Enabling the sidebar

1. If the sidebar is not on the desktop, click Start.

2. In the Start Search window, type Sidebar.

3. Under Programs, click Windows Sidebar.

Explore Sidebar (cont.)

Personalising sidebar gadgets

1 Position the screen pointer over the clock in the sidebar. Look for the X and the wrench to appear.

2 Click the arrow in the Time zone window and select your area from the list.

3 Click the right arrow underneath the clock to change the clock type. You might choose the one shown here.

4 Click OK.

5 Drag the weather sidebar to the desktop. Notice the gadget gets bigger.

For your information

Clicking the X will remove the gadget from the sidebar. Clicking the wrench will open the gadget's properties, if properties are available.

Important

To get the most out of the Sidebar, connect to the Internet.

Important

If the weather gadget is not on the sidebar, skip these steps. You will learn how to add a gadget shortly.

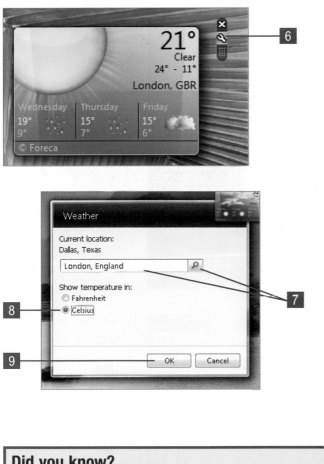

6 Hover the pointer over the weather gadget and click the wrench icon.

7 In the weather dialogue box, type your location. Click the search button (it looks like a magnifying glass).

8 Choose fahrenheit or celsius.

9 Click OK.

10 If desired, drag the weather gadget back to the sidebar.

11 Repeat these steps to personalise more gadgets as desired.

5

?

Did you know?

You don't have to configure the sidebar. If you're happy with it the way it is, just skip this section.

Explore Sidebar (cont.)

Configuring the sidebar

1 Right-click on an empty area of the sidebar. (Try the area to the left of the Add Gadgets icon.)

2 Click Properties.

3 In the Sidebar Properties dialogue box, make changes as desired. For instance, if you do not want the sidebar to start each time you start your PC, deselect 'Start Sidebar when Windows starts'.

4 To keep the sidebar on top of other windows, select 'Sidebar is always on top of other windows'.

5 To reposition the sidebar to the left or right side of the screen, make the appropriate selection as shown here.

6 If you have more than one monitor screen, choose which one to display the sidebar on.

7 To view a list of running gadgets, click on 'View list of running gadgets'.

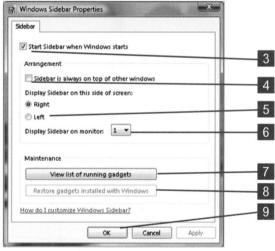

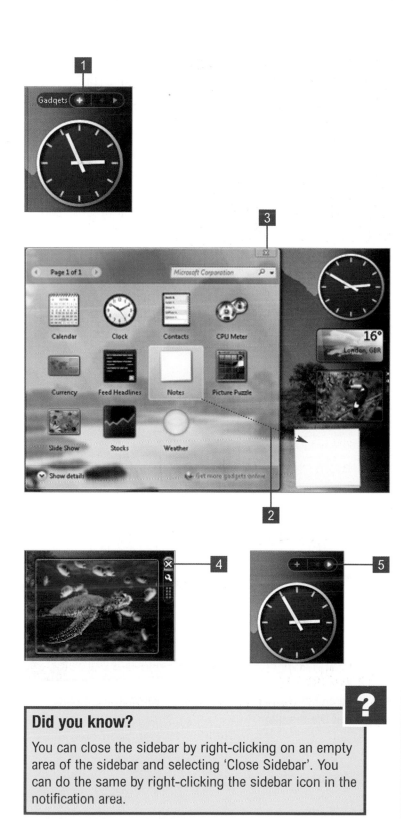

8 To restore gadgets installed with Windows, if you've deleted gadgets in the past, select 'Restore gadgets installed with Windows'. (This will be in grey out if it is not applicable.)

9 Click OK.

Adding and removing gadgets

1 To add a gadget, click the Add Gadget icon on the sidebar.

2 In the gadget gallery, drag the gadget you want to add to the sidebar and drop it there. (Repeat as desired.)

3 Click the X in the gallery to close it.

4 Click the X in any gadget to remove it from the sidebar. This does not remove it from the computer. Remember the X will not appear until you hover the mouse over it.

5 If you add more gadgets than you have space for on the desktop, click the forward arrow (or the back arrow) to move to the next batch of added gadgets.

Did you know?

You can close the sidebar by right-clicking on an empty area of the sidebar and selecting 'Close Sidebar'. You can do the same by right-clicking the sidebar icon in the notification area.

Instant search

In previous exercises you learned to click the Start button and in the Start Search dialogue box, type the name of the program you were looking for. You can use this technique to locate files, folders, pictures, music, documents, programs and even a lost email – most things stored on your PC. Here's an example: say you received an email from a friend that included information about the bowls-like game bocce. You can't remember when you received it and you can't find it in Windows Mail. It's OK. You can search for bocce from the Start Search window, and Vista will find it for you.

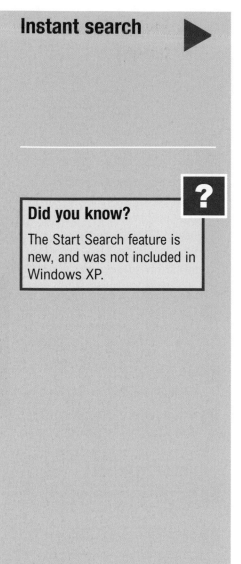

Of course, not all search results only offer the exact item you're looking for, so you should try to search for lost items using words that are not common. Searching for bocce was a better choice than searching for games, for instance. If you search with a word that appears often on your PC, like your name, you'll see all kinds of results. Here I've searched for music. Note all of the results.

There are lots of results including a program called Music Café, a folder for iTunes Music, the Music folder, Recent Music, Sample Music and more, and even a few emails that contain the word 'music' in them.

Now watch what happens when I search for something more specific: Bob Marley. The results now offer much tighter results – two folders and two songs, all having to do with Bob Marley. Clicking on any item in the list will open it, and if it's a song, play it!

You may have noticed that when you type something into the Start Search dialogue box you have the option to search just the computer or to search the Internet. By default, Vista will search everywhere. This means that you might see a link to a web page from your list of favourites, a picture, a song, a file, or an email, just to name a few. These are items on your laptop. You can click on 'Search the Internet' though, and doing so will result in a search of the web.

Instant search (cont.)

For instance, typing bocce in the Start Search window and clicking 'Search the Internet' offers the results shown here. One thing I like to do is to type my own name in the Start Search dialogue box and clicking for an Internet search. Try it with your own name!

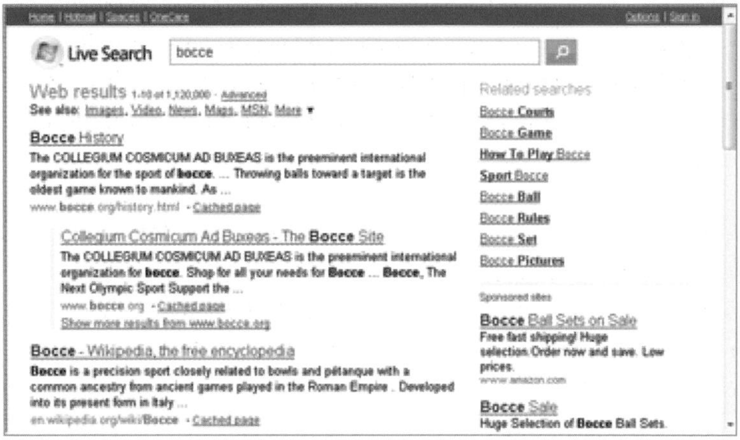

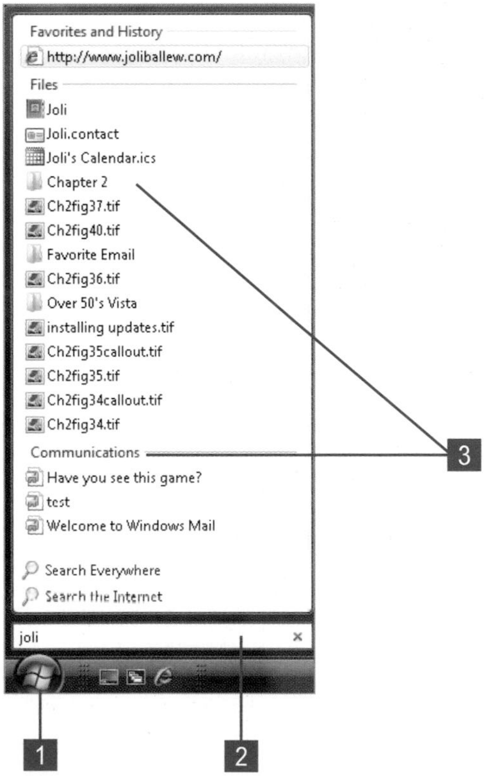

Searching with instant search

1 Click Start.

2 In the Start Search dialogue box, type your first name.

3 Note the results.

4 In the dialogue box, type the name of your home town.

5 Click for an Internet search.

6 Note the results.

By default, Vista will turn off the display and put the computer to sleep after a certain amount of idle time. The length of time that must elapse before this happens depends on the power settings that you've configured for your laptop, the settings configured by the manufacturer, or the operating system's default. There are different settings for when the laptop is plugged in and when it's running on batteries. It's important to note that when the computer goes to sleep, it uses very little power. Because of this, there's often no need to turn off your laptop, unless you plan to move it, not use it for a few days, or if you're energy-conscious.

That being said, if you do want to turn off your laptop, don't just press the power button. You need to let Vista handle the shutting-down process. Remember, Vista is an operating system, and is here to help you operate your computer system safely and properly.

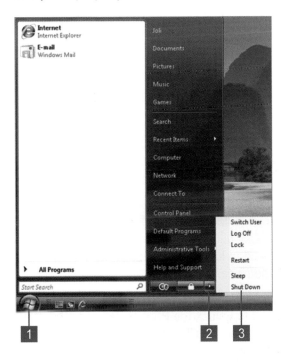

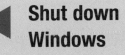

Shut down Windows

Did you know?

Many computers now come with a Sleep button on the outside of the PC tower or on the inside of a laptop. Clicking the Sleep button puts the computer to sleep immediately. If you're taking a break, you may want to try that now.

5

Shut down Windows

1 Click on the Start button.

2 Click on the arrow in the bottom-right corner of the Start menu.

3 Click on 'Shut Down'. Note that you can also choose to put the computer to sleep, restart the computer, switch users, log off, or lock the computer.

Shut down
Windows (cont.)

The options

The options in the list shown here include:

- Switch User: if more than one user account is available on the PC, select this to switch to another user. Switching users is different from logging off. When you choose to switch users, the current user's program, files, folders and open windows remain intact. When you switch back you do not need to reopen these items. Switching users has nothing to do with putting the computer to sleep or turning it off.

- Log Off: choose this option when you want to finish your computer session. This does not shut down or put the computer to sleep, but will bring up the log-in screen. Once logged off, you'll need to log back on, usually by typing in your user name and/or password.

- Lock: use this option to lock the computer. You'll have to input your password to unlock the PC if one is assigned. If a password is not assigned, you'll simply click your user name.

- Restart: use this option to restart the laptop. You should restart your PC when you're prompted to (usually after a Vista update or installing a program), when you know an application has stopped working, or the computer seems slow or unresponsive.

- Sleep: use this option to put the laptop to sleep. Vista's sleep state uses very little energy and is a better option than turning the computer off, unless, of course, you do not plan to use the PC for a couple of days or longer.

- Shut Down: choose this option when you want to shut down the laptop completely. Shutting down a computer is harder on the components than simply letting the computer sleep. However, if you do not plan to use the computer for two days or longer, turning it off is the best option.

Shut down Windows (cont.)

Jargon buster

Operating system: the software and code responsible for basic computer system operations and to control and manage computer hardware.

5

Tweaking the look of Windows Vista

Introduction

Now that you've explored the outside of your laptop, opened it up, turned it on and taken a look inside, it's time to personalise it to suit your preferences and needs. In this chapter you'll learn how to tweak the look of Vista including changing the picture on the desktop, selecting a screensaver, and creating shortcuts to programs or folders so they can be found quickly. You may also want to enable Aero, Vista's new interface option, or change the screen resolution, colour or appearance. This isn't a must-read chapter, though; either you want to change how Vista looks or you like it the way it is. You can always come back here if you decide you want to apply a theme or change the desktop background. However, if you're ready to explore the options, read on!

What you'll do

Enable Windows Aero

Change the background

Change the screen saver

Change the Vista icons on the desktop

Create desktop shortcuts for programs, files and folders

Remove icons and shortcuts from the desktop

Change the screen resolution

Choose a new mouse pointer

Use the Windows Classic theme

Adjust the font size

Personalise the desktop with Aero

Aero is an interface option in Vista. However, you can only use Aero if your hardware supports it, meaning that the components on your laptop meets Aero's minimum requirements and that you are running something other than Vista Basic (i.e. Home Premium, Ultimate or Business). Aero builds on the Vista interface and offers (among other things) the translucent effect of Aero Glass with reflections and 'soft' animations.

Did you know?

You don't have to use Aero. If you prefer the usual Vista, you can turn Aero off.

You can see Aero in action here. Note that you can see 'underneath' the Start menu, and see the outline of the Control Panel and Media Player.

Another Aero feature we'll discuss is Windows Flip 3D, which offers a new way to switch among the windows on your laptop's screen. Here you can see Flip 3D.

Enabling Windows Aero

1 Right-click on an empty area of the desktop.

2 Click on Personalize.

Instead of spelling out what is actually required to run Windows Aero, let's just see if you can enable it. If you can, your hardware supports it; if you can't, it doesn't. Once enabled, you'll learn how to use Flip and Flip 3D.

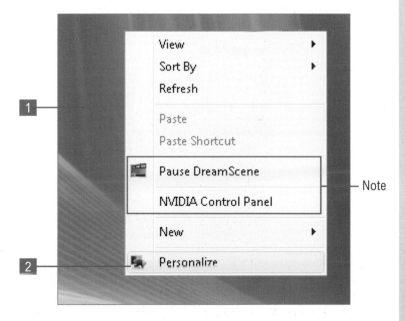

Note that you may see items in this list that are not shown here or vice-versa.

Personalise the desktop with Aero (cont.)

3 Click on 'Windows Color and Appearance'.

4 If you're using Vista Basic, you'll see the 'Appearance Settings' dialogue box.

5 If you're currently using Windows Aero, you'll see the Aero options, where you can select a different colour scheme, enable transparency, make changes to the colour intensity, or show the colour mixer.

6 To change from Vista Basic to Windows Aero, select Windows Aero in the 'Color Scheme' options, and then click on OK.

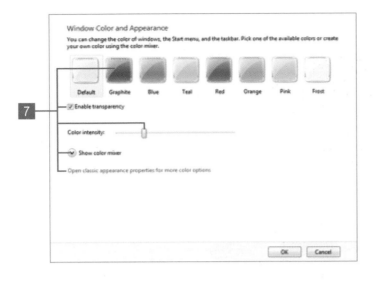

Window Color and Appearance

You can change the color of windows, the Start menu, and the taskbar. Pick one of the available colors or create your own color using the color mixer.

| Default | Graphite | Blue | Teal | Red | Orange | Pink | Frost |

7 ☑ Enable transparency

Color intensity:

Show color mixer

Open classic appearance properties for more color options

OK   Cancel

7 To change the Aero defaults:

- Select a different colour by clicking once on the one you want.

- Disable transparency (that's disabling the Aero Glass feature) by deselecting the box.

- Change the colour intensity by moving the slider to the right or left (moving the slider to the right alters a colour by darkening it).

- Show the 'Colour Mixer' to access sliders for changing hue, saturation or brightness.

- Open classic appearance properties for more options (this opens the window shown in step 6)

8 To use Windows Flip, hold down the Alt key and click Tab; to use Windows Flip 3D, hold down the Windows key and click Tab.

?

Did you know?

You can't use Flip 3D unless Aero is enabled.

Windows backgrounds

The background is the picture you see on the desktop when no windows are open. Vista comes with lots of backgrounds to choose from, and you can access them from the personalisation window that you accessed earlier by right-clicking on the desktop.

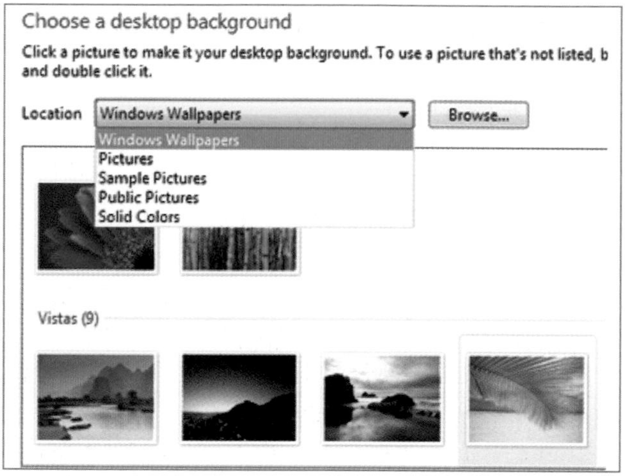

Choose a desktop background

Click a picture to make it your desktop background. To use a picture that's not listed, b and double click it.

Location: Windows Wallpapers ▾ Browse...

- Windows Wallpapers
- Pictures
- Sample Pictures
- Public Pictures
- Solid Colors

Vistas (9)

There are many kinds of backgrounds including:

- Wallpapers: images included with Vista are categorised into black and white, light auras, paintings, textures, vistas and widescreen.

- Pictures: this folder is empty, but you can click the browse button to locate a picture you've saved on your laptop.

- Sample pictures: images included with Vista such as autumn leaves, desert landscape and forest.

- Public pictures: this folder is empty, but as pictures are added to the public pictures folder, they also appear here.

- Solid colours: backgrounds of a single colour.

If you use Vista Ultimate, and have downloaded the extra features, you'll see many more options. As shown here, there are Windows DreamScene Content, Videos, Sample Videos and Public Videos. More options may come.

Note that you can also position the pictures (or videos) you add to fill the entire screen, to tile across the screen, to appear in the centre of the screen, to maintain aspect ratio, and to crop to fit the screen. Generally you'll want to leave the default – to fill the entire desktop screen, but there are times when other choices may suit better. (For instance, if the image is too large to fit on the desktop, you could crop it to fit.)

Changing the background

1 Right-click on an empty area of the desktop.

2 Click on Personalize.

Windows backgrounds (cont.)

3 Click 'Desktop Background'.

4 For Location, select Windows Wallpapers. You can repeat these step and the remaining ones using other options, if desired.

5 Use the scroll bars to locate the wallpaper to use as your desktop background.

6 Select a background to use.

7 Select a positioning option (the default is the most common).

8 Click on OK.

For your information

If you don't find what you want in the desktop background options, you can click Browse in any option to locate and find a file stored on your computer.

A screen saver is a picture or animation that covers your screen and appears after your computer has been idle for a specific amount of time that you set. It used to be that screen savers 'saved' your computer screen from image burn-in, but that is no longer the case. Now, screen savers are used for either visual enhancement or as a security feature. As an extra measure of security, you can configure your screen saver to require a password on waking up, which happens when you move the mouse or press a key on the keyboard. Requiring a password means that once the screen saver is running, no one can log on to your computer but you, by typing in your password when prompted.

Screen savers come in many forms, and Vista comes with several; the Bubbles screensaver is one I like. As with enabling Aero or changing the desktop background, you access the settings by right-clicking an empty area of the desktop and selecting Personalize, and then Screen Saver.

Screen savers (cont.)

Changing the screen saver

1 Right-click an empty area of the desktop.

2 Click on Personalize.

You can also find screen savers online and buy them. However, screen savers from such places are notorious for containing, at the very least, annoying pop-up ads and, at worst, viruses. Before you download and install a screen saver from a third-party, make sure you've read the reviews and are positive it's from a worthy and reliable source. One screen saver I particularly like is called MarineAquarium2 from www.serenescreen.com. Pay for the full version or you'll be prompted to buy it each time it runs.

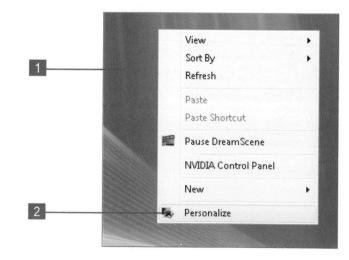

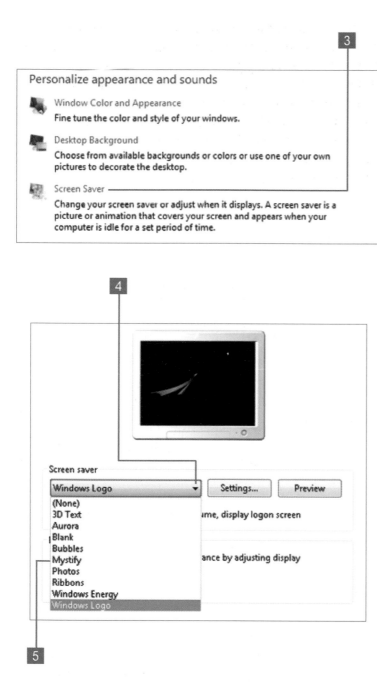

Personalize appearance and sounds

Window Color and Appearance
Fine tune the color and style of your windows.

Desktop Background
Choose from available backgrounds or colors or use one of your own pictures to decorate the desktop.

Screen Saver
Change your screen saver or adjust when it displays. A screen saver is a picture or animation that covers your screen and appears when your computer is idle for a set period of time.

4

Screen saver

| Windows Logo ▾ | Settings... | Preview |

(None)
3D Text   ıme, display logon screen
Aurora
Blank
Bubbles
Mystify   ance by adjusting display
Photos
Ribbons
Windows Energy
Windows Logo

5

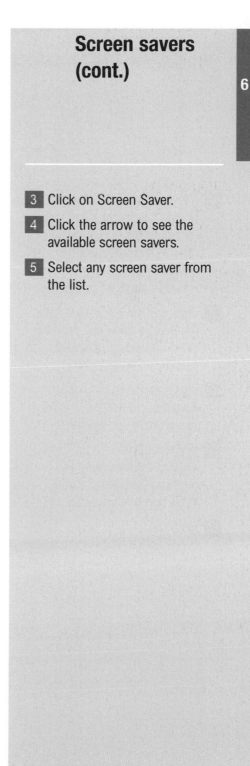

Screen savers (cont.)

6

3 Click on Screen Saver.

4 Click the arrow to see the available screen savers.

5 Select any screen saver from the list.

Screen savers
(cont.)

?

Did you know?

Select Photos and your screen saver will be a slideshow of photos stored in your Pictures folder.

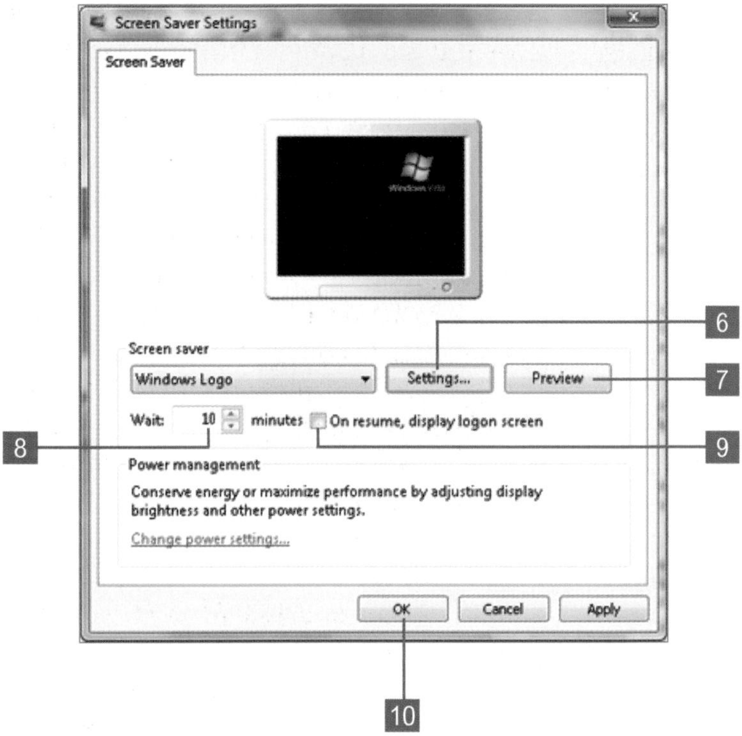

6 Click on Settings. A few screen savers have settings, including 3D Text, but most do not. If settings are available, accept the defaults or make changes as desired.

7 Click on Preview to see what the screen saver will look like. Press any key on the keyboard to disable the preview.

8 Use the arrows to change how long to wait before the screen saver is enabled.

9 If desired, click 'On resume, display logon screen' to require a password to log back into the computer.

10 Click OK.

When Vista started the first time, it may have had only one item on the desktop, the Recycle Bin. Alternatively, it may have had 20 or more. What appears on your desktop the first time Windows boots up depends on a number of factors.

If you installed Vista yourself, and you chose not to upgrade from another version of Windows but instead to perform a 'clean' installation, you are likely to see only one icon, the Recycle Bin. If you installed Vista as an upgrade from another operating system version, such as Windows XP, then you'll see the Vista-related icons you had on your computer before the upgrade. These may include Documents, Pictures or even shortcuts to programs. If you purchased a laptop with Vista installed, you could have icons on your desktop for an Internet service provider (ISP) such as AOL, or any number of others. You may also see icons for anti-virus software such as McAfee or Semantic. There may also be links to what's called OEM software, that is software installed on your laptop by the maker that you may or may not want, including image editing applications, music players and wordprocessors or databases. Whatever the case, the desktop is unlikely to match your needs exactly, and so needs to be tweaked. With time, your needs change, so adding and deleting desktop icons is a common task and will be discussed in depth.

Besides the icons on the desktop by default (depending on the installation configuration), there are Vista icons you can add or remove. You can choose to view or hide Computer, Recycle Bin, Control Panel, Network and your personal user folder.

You can also choose to add shortcuts to programs you use often. You may want to add shortcuts to the desktop for folders you create, programs you use often, or network places, such as folders stored on other computers. You can even add a shortcut to a public folder, or a single file or picture!

Changing desktop icons

6

Changing desktop icons (cont.)

Changing Vista icons on the desktop

1 Right-click on an empty area of the desktop.

2 Click on Personalize.

3 Click on Change desktop icons.

4 Select the desktop icons you want to appear on your desktop.

5 Click on OK.

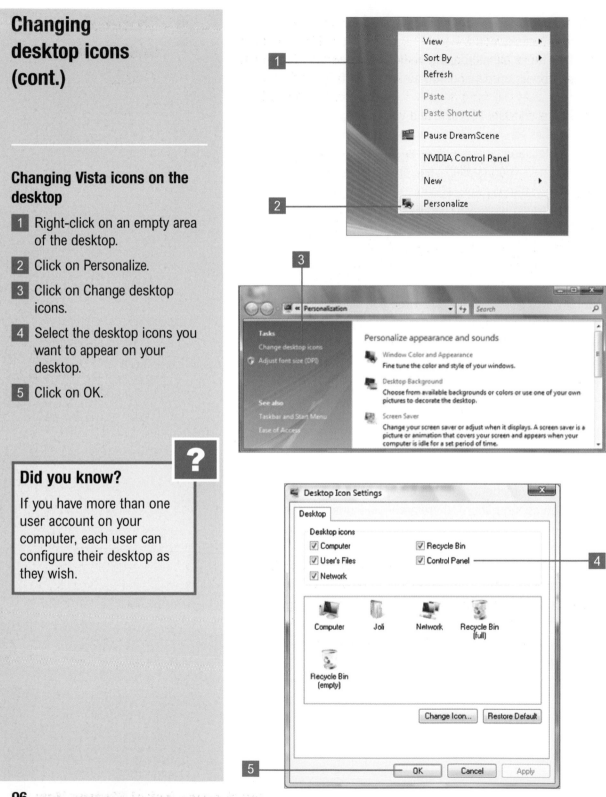

A shortcut always appears with an arrow beside it (or on it, actually). Shortcuts enable you to access folders, files, programs and other items on your laptop without the hassle of drilling into the Start Menu or using the search box. In this figure there are three shortcuts and five Windows icons. Sometimes, a shortcut will even have the word shortcut in its name.

These are
Windows
icons and
are not
shortcuts.

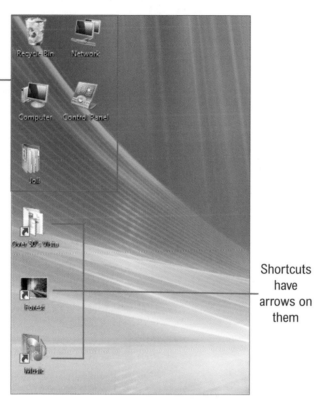

Shortcuts
have
arrows on
them

There are several ways to create a shortcut. One is to right-click an empty area of the desktop, click New, and then Shortcut. Performing these steps will bring up a dialogue box where you can 'browse' to the location of the file, folder or program for which you want to create the shortcut.

Changing desktop icons (cont.)

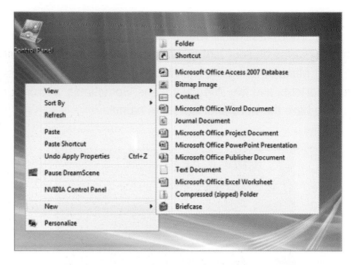

However, this method requires you understand a bit more about how files and folders are managed in Vista, as well as where programs files are located and what file actually starts the program. Anyway, this is really the long way around the issue of creating a shortcut. There's a better way, and that involves finding the item to create a shortcut for in the Start Menu, and dragging it to the desktop, or locating the item and right-clicking on it.

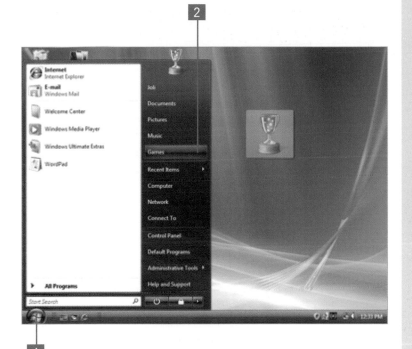

Creating shortcuts for programs, files and folders

1 Click on Start.

2 If you see the item for which you want to create a shortcut, click it and drag it to the desktop. Here, we create a shortcut for the Games folder. Note that as you drag a shortcut arrow appears.

3 To add a shortcut for a program, in the Start menu, click on All Programs.

4 In the All Programs list, locate the program for which to create a shortcut.

5 Right-click on the program name.

6 Click on Send To.

7 Click on Desktop (create shortcut).

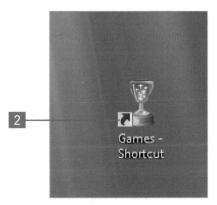

Important

This is the only time you should use the drag and drop method for creating a shortcut on the desktop. Most of the time, you'll right-click the item, as noted next.

Changing desktop icons (cont.)

Important !

For some reason known only to Microsoft, if you drag and drop a program from the All Programs menu, the actual program files will be moved. You don't want to do that. You want the program files to stay where they are. Additionally, when you drag and drop a file from inside a folder, such as a file, picture, video or song, those files are moved out of the folder and on to the desktop too. If you see Move to Desktop when you drag and drop as shown here, drag the mouse right back to where you started, and use the right-click method instead. You don't want to move the file; you only want to create a shortcut for it.

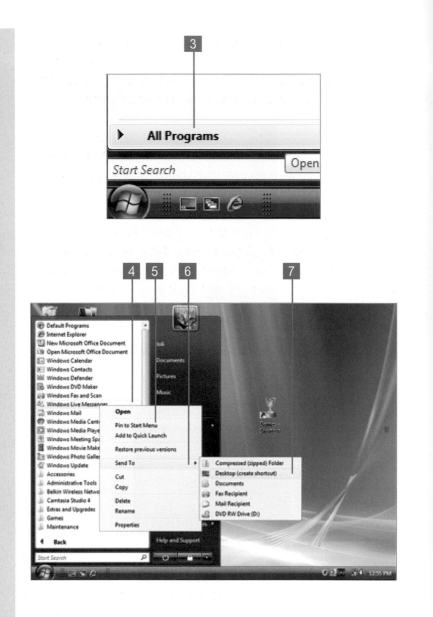

So, to repeat, and listen carefully – when you are in the All Programs menu, and in all other instances (with the exception of the Start menu items), to create a shortcut, always right-click the file, folder or program (verses dragging and dropping).

When you're ready to remove items from the desktop, you'll use the right-click method again. The options you'll have when you right-click an item on the desktop will differ depending on what type of icon you select.

When you right-click the Vista icon for Control Panel, you are given four choices: Open, Explore, Create Shortcut and Delete. When you click Delete, you are prompted about how to add the icon again, if desired. Note that nothing is actually deleted when you do this; all of the Vista files, icons and data are still on your laptop and can be easily added to the desktop again at any time.

When you right-click on the Games shortcut you created, you'll see more choices. One is to create a shortcut, interestingly. A shortcut of a shortcut! When you click Delete here, you are prompted to move the file to the Recycle Bin. Since it's a shortcut, that's just fine. You're not going to delete the Games folder or the games in it; you are simply deleting the shortcut. No worries here.

Changing desktop icons (cont.)

Right-clicking on a shortcut to a picture (or video, song or file) offers even more choices. Again, Delete simply removes the shortcut. You don't actually delete the picture itself. (Now, if this was an actual picture and not a shortcut to one, you'd delete the picture, but as long as you're deleting a shortcut, that's fine.)

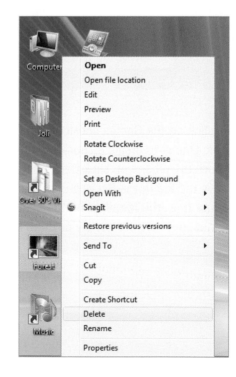

Important

If the item you want to remove from the desktop is actually stored there, don't delete it. If you want it off the desktop, drag and drop it into one of your personal folders.

Here's an actual picture file. Note that there is no shortcut arrow beside it. Right-clicking this picture and choosing Delete offers up this warning 'Are you sure you want to move this file to the Recycle Bin?' If you click Yes, the file is deleted. Well, unless you 'restore' it from the Recycle Bin.

Changing desktop icons (cont.)

Removing icons and shortcuts from the desktop

1. Right-click on the icon to remove.

2. Click on Delete.

3. Carefully read the information in the resulting dialogue box. Click Yes to delete or No to cancel.

For your information

If you are deleting a shortcut, you may still see a warning that you are moving a file to the Recycle Bin, when in reality you are not. Remember, you can always delete a shortcut, even if prompted as if it's a file.

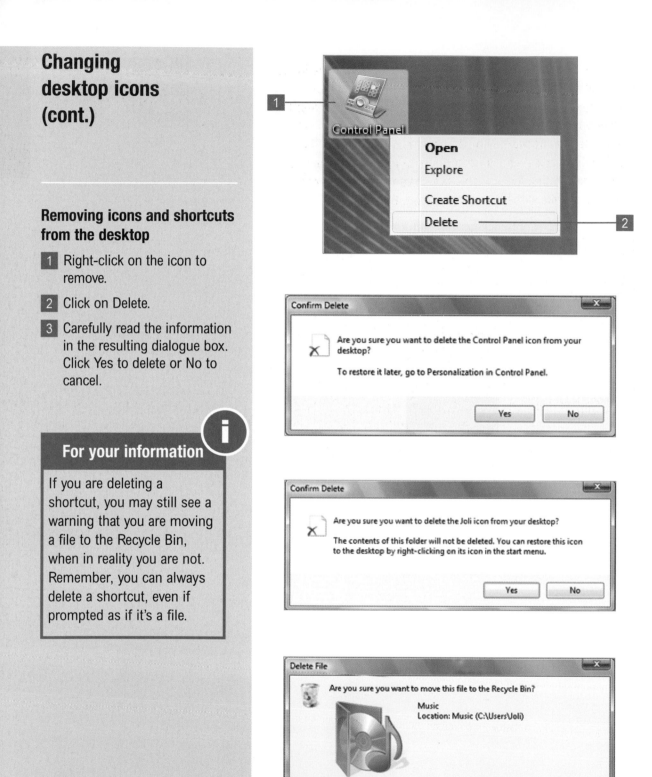

104

There are even more ways to change how Windows Vista looks. One is to change the screen resolution. While the science behind resolution is complex, suffice it to say that the lower the resolution, the larger your stuff appears on the monitor; the higher the resolution, the smaller your stuff appears on the monitor. With a higher resolution, you can have more items on your screen; with a lower resolution, fewer. Here's what my screen looks like at the lowest resolution, 800 by 600 pixels.

Screen resolution (cont.)

And here's what my screen looks like at its highest available resolution, 1280 by 1026 pixels.

As you can see, the higher resolution settings make it harder to see what's on the screen, and that includes what you see in dialogue boxes, windows and menus. Note how small the desktop icons are. With the lower resolution, everything is bigger, including the icons, and what you'll see in dialogue boxes, windows and menus. For your over 50 eyes, you may be more comfortable with one of the lower resolution settings.

If you're interested, technically, choosing 800 by 600 pixels means that the desktop is shown to you with 800 pixels across and 600 pixels down. A pixel is the smallest unit that can be displayed on a computer. So, when you increase the resolution, you increase the number of pixels on the screen. This makes items on the screen appear smaller and allow you to have more items on the screen.

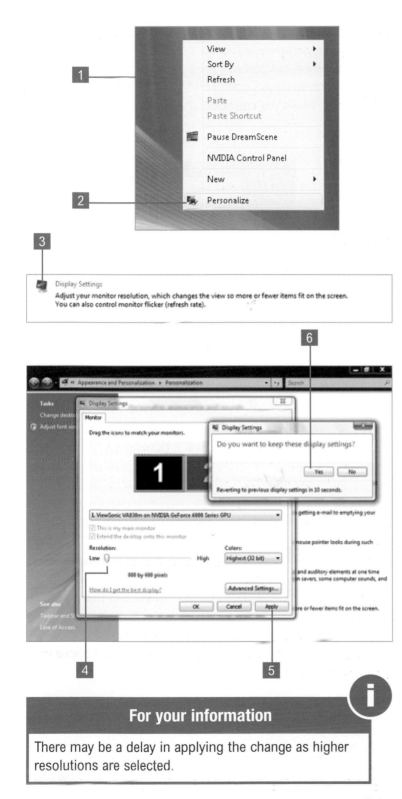

Changing the screen resolution

1 Right-click on an empty area of the desktop.

2 Click on Personalize.

3 Click on Display Settings.

4 Move the resolution slider to the far left position (unless it's already there).

5 Click on Apply.

6 If prompted to keep these settings, click on Yes. Note how the appearance of the screen changes.

7 Move the resolution slider one position to the right, and click on Apply.

8 If prompted to keep these settings, click on Yes. Note how the appearance of the screen changes.

9 Repeat these steps as desired, and select the resolution that is best for you.

For your information

There may be a delay in applying the change as higher resolutions are selected.

Mouse/screen pointers

You have the option of choosing a different version of the pointer you see on the screen, which is controlled by your mouse or touch pad. As you can probably guess, the settings are in the personalisation window. Clicking on Mouse Pointers opens a dialogue box, where you can select the pointers you prefer.

Choosing a screen pointer

1 Right-click on an empty area of the desktop.

2 Click on Personalise.

3 Click on Mouse Pointers.

4 Click on the down arrow to list additional schemes.

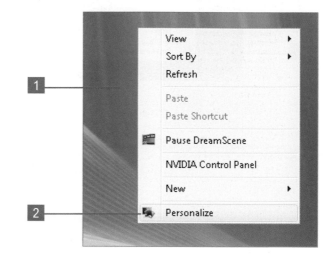

1	View	▶
	Sort By	▶
	Refresh	
	Paste	
	Paste Shortcut	
	Pause DreamScene	
	NVIDIA Control Panel	
	New	▶
2	Personalize	

Screen Saver
Change your screen saver or adjust when it displays. A screen saver is a picture or animation that covers your screen and appears when your computer is idle for a set period of time.

Sounds
Change which sounds are heard when you do everything from getting e-mail to emptying your Recycle Bin.

Mouse Pointers
Pick a different mouse pointer. You can also change how the mouse pointer looks during such activities as clicking and selecting.

3

5 Select 'Windows Black (extra
large) (system scheme)'.

6 Click on Apply to select the
new mouse pointer.

7 Select other pointers by
repeating steps 4 to 6. Try
Magnified, Conductor and
Variations.

If you prefer the look of an older operating system and the
Vista interface and all of its fancy graphics don't do anything
for you, you can use the Windows Classic theme. This look
dates back to 2000 or so, when the interface was blue and
white, and menu bars were grey.

Mouse/screen pointers (cont.)

This screen shot shows the classic theme in conjunction with the Classic Start menu.

Selecting the Windows Classic theme

1 Right-click on an empty area of the desktop.

2 Click on Personalize.

3 Click on Theme.

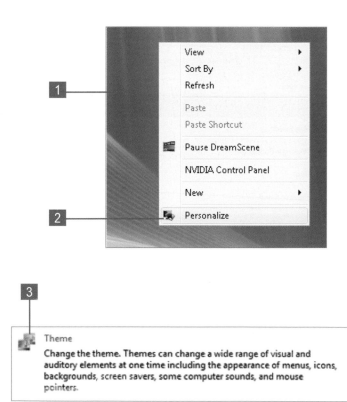

Theme
Change the theme. Themes can change a wide range of visual and auditory elements at one time including the appearance of menus, icons, backgrounds, screen savers, some computer sounds, and mouse pointers.

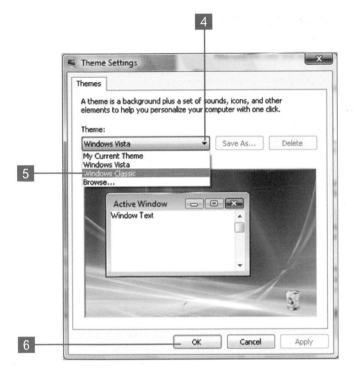

4 Click on the down arrow to show the available themes.

5 Click on Windows Classic.

6 Click on OK.

7 Right-click on the Start button.

8 Select Properties.

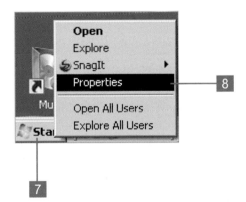

Mouse/screen pointers (cont.)

9 Select Classic Start Menu.

10 Click on OK.

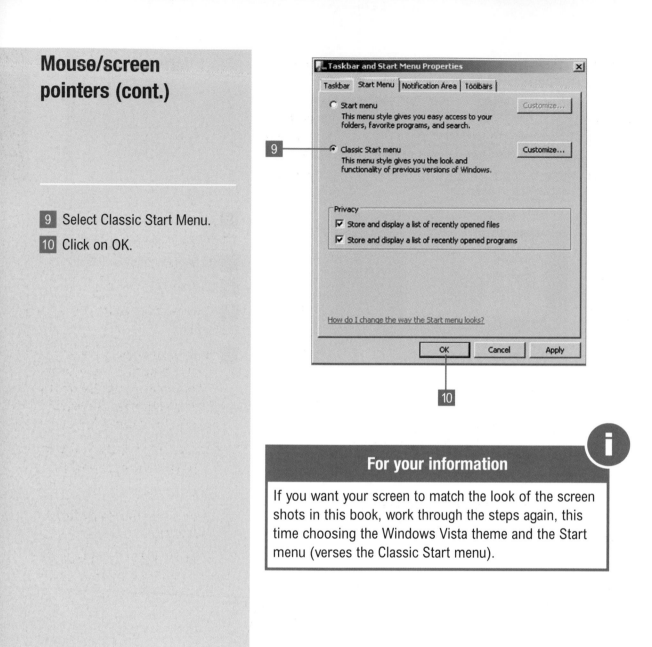

Although Vista includes features to make the computer more easily accessible for people with disabilities, including applications such as Magnifier, Narrator and On-Screen Keyboard, there is a way to increase the system font size if need be. If you've changed the screen resolution to 800 by 600 and still have to wear reading glasses to make out what's on the monitor, including desktop icons, increasing the font size may fit the bill.

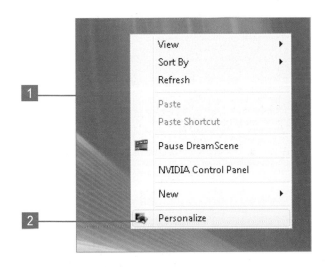

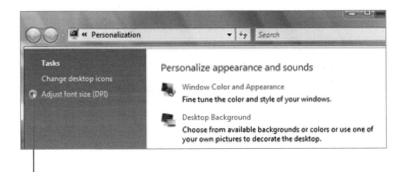

Adjusting font size

1. Right-click on an empty area of the desktop.

2. Click on Personalize.

3. Click on 'Adjust font size (DPI)'.

4. You'll be prompted to enter administrator's credentials or click Continue if you're signed in as an administrator. Input the proper credentials.

5. Select 'Larger scale (120 DPI) – make text more readable'.

6. Click on OK.

7. Click on Restart Now when prompted.

8. After restarting, everything appears much larger with 120 DPI selected.

Font size (cont.)

Jargon buster

Boot up: when a computer is switched on, it goes through a sequence of tasks before you see the desktop. This process is called the 'boot up' process. Computers can be rated by many factors, and one of those factors is how long the process takes.

Browse: browsing for a file, folder or program is the process of drilling down into Vista's folder structure to locate the desired item.

DPI: dots per inch refers to how many dots (or pixels) per inch on a computer screen.

Configuring accessibility options

Introduction

Vista offers the Ease of Access Center to help you turn on and configure settings that will make using the laptop easier if you have a disability. You can optimise the display for blindness, or just make the items on the screen easier to see. You can use the computer without a mouse or keyboard by using an on-screen keyboard or the built-in speech recognition software. You can make the keyboard easier to use by configuring sticky keys, toggle keys, filter keys and more. Also, you can use the built-in Narrator application to read what's on the screen out loud, so you don't have to squint to read it yourself. If you're having trouble accessing your laptop, this chapter is for you.

Did you know?

After turning 50, two-thirds of us experience vision, hearing or dexterity problems that affect how well we use our computers. Getting older doesn't mean the end of using a computer though; PCs can be customised to meet the needs of those that are blind, deaf and quadriplegic, as well as people with the usual over-50 vision and hearing problems, or manual deftness.

What you'll do

Use the Narrator

Use the Magnifier

Use the on-screen keyboard

Make the keyboard easier to use

Explore keyboard shortcuts

Explore additional ease of access options

Set up the speech recognition system

Train the speech recognition system

Use speech recognition

Configure the Narrator

The Narrator is a screen reader. That means it will read text that appears on the screen, while you navigate using the keyboard and mouse. You can choose what text Narrator reads, change the Narrator's voice, and even configure it to describe events, such error messages (or not). There isn't much to configuring Narrator; the art lies in learning to use it properly. Here you see the Narrator dialogue box, where you can have Narrator put voice to your keystrokes, announce system messages, announce when you scroll, and whether or not you want to start Narrator minimised (that means Narrator will appear on the taskbar, and not on the screen when you boot up Windows).

Narrator is not a cure-all for those who want to have everything read to them. It's not designed to read content in every program you have; it's really just a *screen reader*. Additionally, Narrator may not pronounce all words correctly, cannot read text that appears below collapsed headings in Help topics, and has other limitations. However, in the absence of a third-party accessibility program, Narrator will do at a pinch.

Narrator is one of the Ease of Access applications and you can open it by searching from the Start Menu. As soon as you click the Narrator link, it starts reading. In fact, it talks, and talks, and talks. It first announces that Microsoft Narrator is running, and then continues on by reading the entire dialogue box shown earlier. Once it stops reading that, it announces each thing you do with the touch pad or keyboard. For instance, if you hover over the Internet Explorer icon, it says: 'Launch Internet

Explorer Browser. Finds and displays information and websites on the internet. Tooltip.' It may also say things like 'Window opened' or 'Window closed.' Now all of this is great, except that you might not need every little thing read to you. That's what keyboard shortcuts are for. Clicking Ctrl will cause the reading to stop, at least for the current event.

Narrator reads the following items displayed on your screen:

- Contents of the open window.
- Menus and menu options.
- Text you have typed.
- Tool tips.
- Events such as minimising and maximising windows.

Narrator doesn't read email, although it can read the subject line. It doesn't read web pages, although it will read what appears on the web browser tab. When you hover over a folder on the desktop, it will read the tool tip describing what it is. It won't read a document, but it will read the title of the document, as it appears on the screen.

To use Narrator effectively then, you need to understand the keyboard shortcuts associated with it. Table 7.1 shows these shortcuts.

Table 7.1 Keyboard shortcuts for Narrator	
Ctrl+Shift+Enter (Hold down Ctrl and Shift and press Enter)	Get information about the current item
Ctrl+Shift+Spacebar	Read the entire selected window
Ctrl+Alt+Spacebar	Read the selected window layout
All+Home	Get information about the current item
Alt+End	Get a sumamry of the current item
Ctrl	Stop Narrator from reading text

If you learn these shortcuts you'll be much happier with Narrator.

Configure the Narrator (cont.)

Important !

According to Microsoft, the Narrator will read documents, PDFs, web pages and more. But I can't get it to work that way. Sure, it will read anything I click on, what I'm doing to the windows, and if I'm scrolling or not, but getting it to read documents is another story. Lots of people have difficulties with it, too, not just you and me. If you find you're having problems making Narrator work, consider Dspeech. It's free to download: (**http://www.tucows.com/preview/500654**).

Did you know? ?

Microsoft offers help for those with disabilities at **www.microsoft.com/enable**.

Configure the Narrator (cont.)

Using Narrator

1 Click on Start.

2 In the search dialogue box, type Narrator and click Narrator in the results.

3 Select or deselect options to configure Narrator to your needs. The default, shown here, is a good place to start.

4 Click the Start button. If you can't hear the Narrator say 'Start. Tool tip,' turn up or plug in your speakers.

5 Click inside the Start Search dialogue box while Narrator reads what's on the Start menu.

6 Type Internet Explorer.

7 Press the Ctrl key to stop Narrator from continuing to read.

8 Click on Exit to turn Narrator off and exit the program.

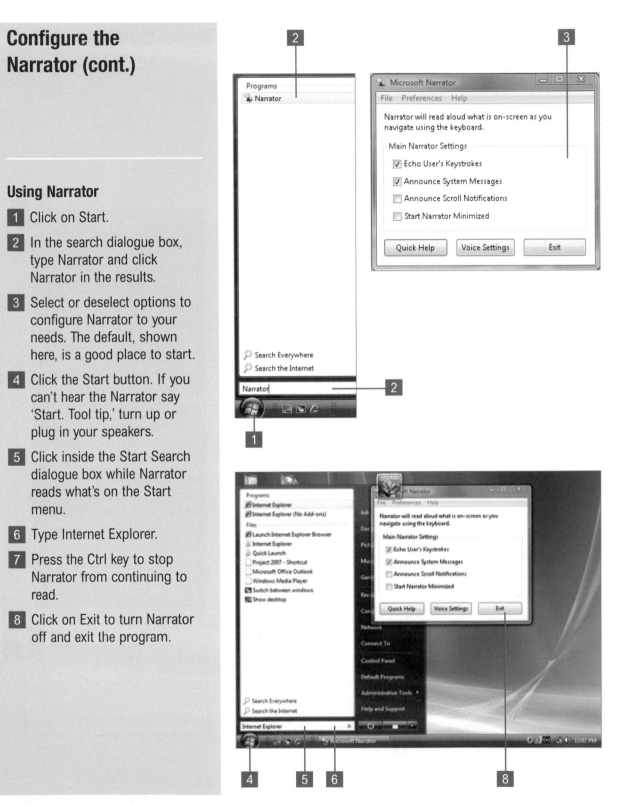

The Magnifier is another tool in the access suite. As with Narrator, you can find Magnifier from the search box, by typing Magnifier. However, you can also open Magnifier from the Ease of Access Center in Control Panel. For the sake of exploring these features and controls, here we've opened our accessibility program from the Ease of Access Center. Note that Narrator is here too.

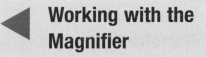

There isn't anything to configure in Magnifier. As with Narrator, the art lies in your ability to use it. When you click on Start Magnifier, you'll see a large rectangular box at the top of the page. What you see in this box is a magnification of the area of the screen where your screen pointer is positioned. As you move the pointer around, other parts of the screen are magnified.

You can move this rectangular box around the screen using the four-headed arrow that appears when you position the pointer inside the rectangle.

Working with the Magnifier (cont.)

My mouse is positioned here.

The area where my mouse is positioned is magnified here.

This application works much better than Narrator. You are in complete control of the touchpad or mouse, and thus, what is magnified in the magnification window. Although you can't enlarge the window, you can at least move it around. Here you can see an open window and Magnifier in action.

Notice in the previous image how the Network window is positioned, above the magnifier. If you maximise the open window, the Magnifier sits 'underneath it', and you can't see the Magnifier! A small glitch in the system, but at least there's a way around this. Just position the open window above or below the Magnifier window.

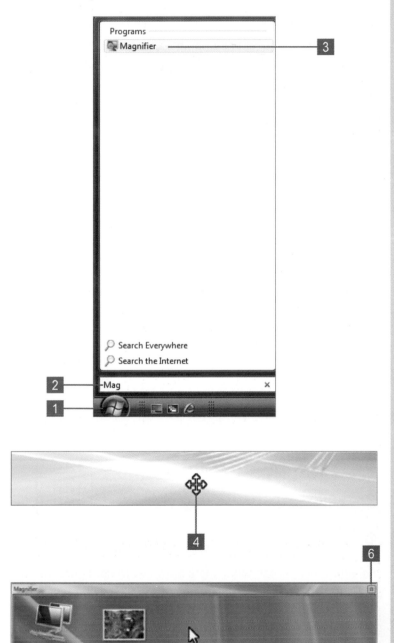

Using the Magnifier

1 Click on Start.

2 In the search box, type Mag. Note that you do not have to type the entire name.

3 Click on Magnifier.

4 Position the mouse inside the Magnifier window. When you see a four-headed arrow, drag the window to the bottom of the screen.

5 Move the mouse around the desktop to explore Magnifier.

6 To close Magnifier, click the X in the Magnifier window.

Using the on-screen keyboard ▶

If you can't use a mouse, don't like the touch pad or you can't use a keyboard, you can still input data to your computer. You can use a joystick, tracker ball, modified switch, touch screen or electronic pointing device to input data using the screen keyboard feature. If your hands shake, if your fingers are too big for the tiny keyboard keys, or if you can't use your hands at all because of arthritis or a similar condition, there are options. A large joystick is one of them. If you're a quadriplegic there are options too. One is the sip/puff switch. This switch controls the screen pointer with a sip or a puff on a device that is kept at the mouth. Every week there seem to be advancements in input devices. Whatever hardware you choose, the screen keyboard should work, though some devices may come with their own software.

To use the screen keyboard, you use whatever pointing device that works for you to click the keys desired on the screen.

As with other access tools, there are ways to configure the keyboard. You'll want to define how you will select a key. Will you click it (using a pointing device), hover over it (with a pointing device), or will you use a joystick or other method? You define that in the Typing Mode settings.

Typing Mode

- ○ Click to select
- ○ Hover to select
  Minimum time to hover: [▼]
- ○ Joystick or key to select
  Scan interval: [▼] [Advanced...]

[OK] [Cancel]

Once that is configured and you begin using the keyboard, you can choose the following:

- Enhanced or standard keyboard: select the option from the keyboard menu.

- Regular or block layout: select the desired option from the keyboard menu.

- 101, 102 or 106 keys: select from the keyboard menu.

- To hear a click sound (or not) when a key is 'pressed' on the screen: select the option from the settings menu.

- To select a font, style and size: select the font option from the keyboard menu.

- Get help with the keyboard: select Contents from the Help menu.

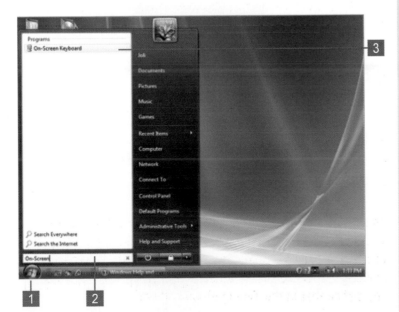

Using the on-screen keyboard

1 Click on Start.

2 In the search box, type On-Screen.

3 Under Programs, click on On-Screen Keyboard.

7

Using the on-screen keyboard (cont.)

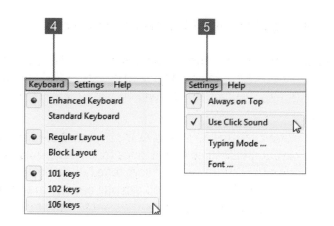

4 Click on Keyboard to select enhanced or standard; regular or block; and 101, 102 or 106 keys. You could also accept the defaults, and not change anything. To make a choice, click on it to highlight the button.

5 Click Settings to select Use Click Sound. Each time you click a key, a clicking sound will play.

6 Click on Start.

7 In the Start Search dialogue box, use your mouse to type the word Internet. Note the results.

8 To close the keyboard, click the X in the top-right corner.

There are ways to make the keyboard easier to use:

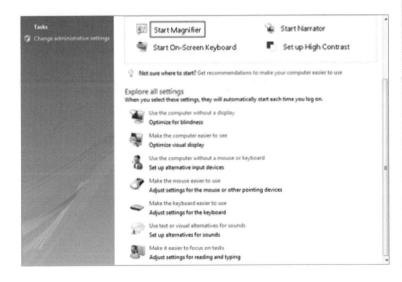

- Mouse Keys let you forgo using the mouse; instead, you can use the arrow keys on your keyboard or the numeric key pad to move the screen pointer around the desktop or inside programs and documents.

- Sticky Keys allow you to configure the keyboard so that you never have to press three keys at once (such as when you must press the Ctrl, Alt and Del keys together to log on to Windows). With Sticky Keys, you can use one key to perform these tasks. You configure the key you want to use for this.

- Toggle can be configured to sound an alert when you press the Caps Lock, Num Lock or Scroll Lock keys. These alerts can help prevent the aggravation of unintentionally pressing a key and not realising it.

- Filter Keys let you configure Windows to ignore keystrokes that occur in rapid succession, such as when you accidentally leave your finger on a key for too long.

- Underline keyboard shortcuts and access keys. This option makes dialogue boxes easier to work with by highlighting the access keys used to control them.

- You enable these features in the Ease of Access Center, under 'Make the keyboard easier to use'.

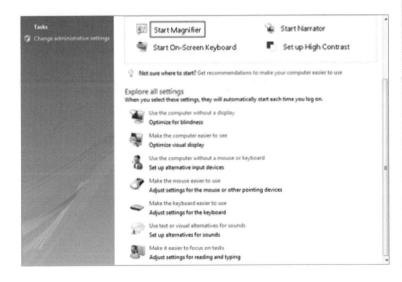

Make the keyboard easier to use (cont.)

Make the keyboard easier to use

1. Click on Start.

2. Type ease of access.

3. Select 'Ease of Access Center' from the results.

4. In the access center, use the scroll bar to locate 'Make the keyboard easier to use'. Click on it.

5. Place a tick mark in the accessibility options to enable.

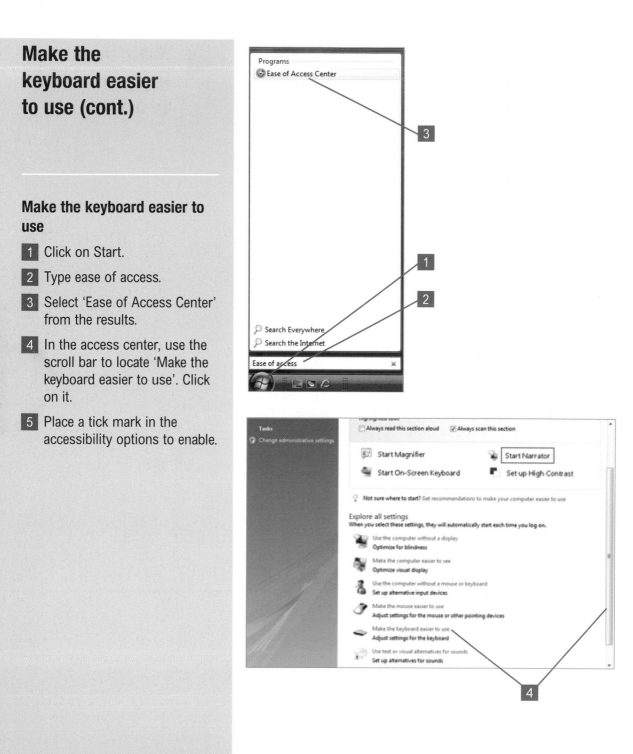

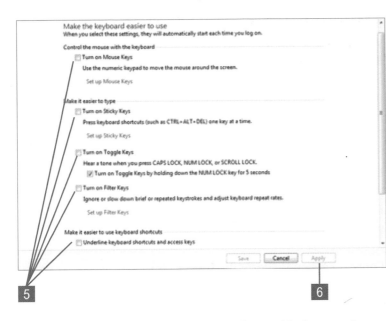

Make the keyboard easier to use
When you select these settings, they will automatically start each time you log on.

Control the mouse with the keyboard
☐ Turn on Mouse Keys
Use the numeric keypad to move the mouse around the screen.
Set up Mouse Keys

Make it easier to type
☐ Turn on Sticky Keys
Press keyboard shortcuts (such as CTRL+ALT+DEL) one key at a time.
Set up Sticky Keys

☐ Turn on Toggle Keys
Hear a tone when you press CAPS LOCK, NUM LOCK, or SCROLL LOCK.
☑ Turn on Toggle Keys by holding down the NUM LOCK key for 5 seconds

☐ Turn on Filter Keys
Ignore or slow down brief or repeated keystrokes and adjust keyboard repeat rates.
Set up Filter Keys

Make it easier to use keyboard shortcuts
☐ Underline keyboard shortcuts and access keys

Save   Cancel   Apply

5

6

There are keyboard shortcuts that go along with these options. They include:

- Hold Num Lock for 5 seconds: turn toggle keys on or off.

- Hold down right arrow for 8 seconds: turn filter keys on and off.

- Press Shift five times: turn sticky keys on or off.

Make the keyboard easier to use (cont.)

6 Click on Apply.

7 Each item you select can be configured. For now, the defaults are fine. However, note that you can return to the access centre to refine how these features perform. There's more on this later in the chapter.

7

Configuring accessibility options 127

Explore keyboard shortcuts

▶

It doesn't matter if you're over 50, disabled, have arthritis in your hands, or are just lazy, learning and using keyboard shortcuts can be one of the best ways to spend your time. Such shortcuts let you do things more quickly. For instance, to open Help and Support you could click Start, and then Help and Support, or you can do it with one finger by pressing the F1 key on the keyboard. Instead of highlighting text in a document and searching for the menu or button that makes that text bold, just hold down Ctrl and press B (Ctrl+B). And there's more where this came from. In the following sections I'll list the best shortcuts, but if you want more, just search the web for 'Windows keyboard shortcuts'.

General keyboard shortcuts

- Alt+Esc: cycle through items in the order in which they were opened.
- Alt+F4: close the active item, or quit the active program.
- Alt+Print Screen: copies an image of the selected window to the clipboard.
- Alt+Tab: switch between open items.
- Ctrl+A: select all items in a document or window.
- Ctrl+Alt+Del: displays options for: lock this computer; switch user; log off; change a password; and start Task Manager.
- Ctrl+Alt+Tab: use the arrow keys to switch between open items.
- Ctrl+C: copy the selected item.
- Ctrl+Esc: open the Start menu (the Windows logo key works too).
- Ctrl+V: paste the selected item.
- Ctrl+X: cut the selected item.
- Ctrl+Y: redo an action.
- Ctrl+Z: undo an action.
- Delete: delete the selected item and move it to the recycle bin.
- Esc: cancel the current task.
- F1: display help.

- F5: refresh the active window.
- Print Screen: copies an image of the entire screen to the clipboard (key may be marked PrtScn).
- Shift+F10: display the shortcut menu for the selected item.

Dialogue box shortcuts

- Alt+underlined letter: perform the command (or select the option) that goes with that letter.
- Arrow keys: select a button if a group of option buttons is active.
- Backspace: open a folder one level up if a folder is selected in the Save As or Open dialogue box.
- Ctrl+Shift+Tab: move back through tabs.
- Ctrl+Tab: move forward through tabs.
- Enter: replaces clicking the mouse for many selected commands.
- Shift+Tab: move back through options.
- Spacebar: select or clear the check box if the active option is a check box.
- Tab: move forward through options.

Explore keyboard shortcuts

1 Click the Windows key on the keyboard. If you don't see a Windows key, click the Start key. The Start Menu opens.

2 Click the Tab key on the keyboard. Notice what is selected in the Start Menu.

3 Use the arrow keys on the keyboard to move through the Start Menu items.

4 Press the Enter key to open the selected item.

7

Explore additional ease of access options

There are too many accessibility options in Vista to cover each and every one. But now that you're familiar with some of them, configuring and using the features we haven't covered will be a little more intuitive.

One of the options in the Ease of Access Center is: 'Make the mouse easier to use'. If you click on that, you see the settings shown here. You can see that it is easy to select a different colour or size for your screen pointer. Note that you can also turn on mouse keys and set up mouse keys.

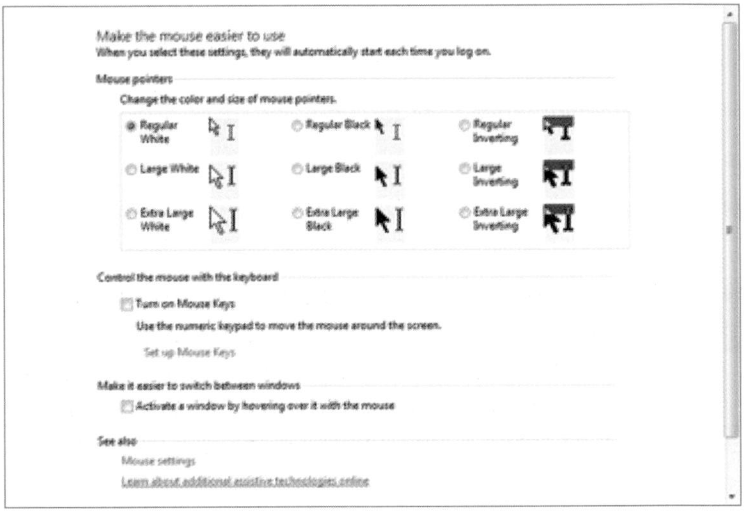

Another option is 'Use text or visual alternatives for sounds'. Here, you can turn on visual notifications of sounds that play on your computer as well as text captions for spoken dialogue.

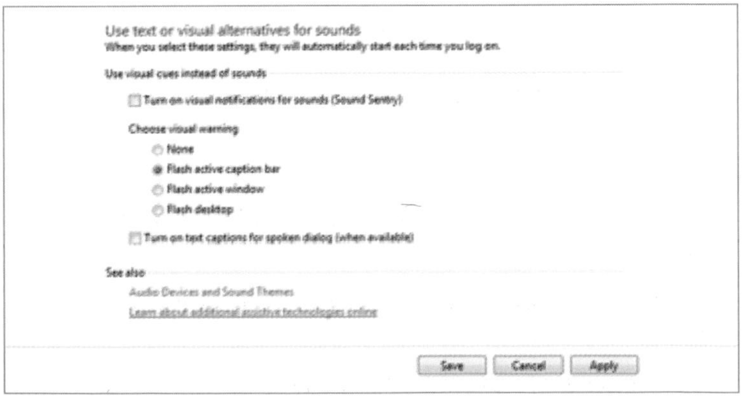

You can also select 'Use the computer without a display'. Here, you can turn on Narrator and Audio Description. The latter lets you hear descriptions of what's happening in the videos you watch, if it's available.

Use the computer without a display
When you select these settings, they will automatically start each time you log on.

Hear text read aloud

☐ Turn on Narrator
    Narrator reads aloud any text on the screen. You will need speakers.

☐ Turn on Audio Description
    Hear descriptions of what's happening in videos (when available).

Set up Text to Speech

Adjust time limits and flashing visuals

☐ Turn off all unnecessary animations (when possible)

How long should Windows notification dialog boxes stay open?
[7.0 seconds ▼]

See also

Audio Devices and Sound Themes
Learn about additional assistive technologies online

[Save] [Cancel] [Apply]

And although there are many other options, perhaps the most helpful is the option 'Get recommendations to make your computer easier to use'. Clicking this option (∗) opens a wizard that asks questions about your abilities (and disabilities), and helps you decide what accessibility options are best for you.

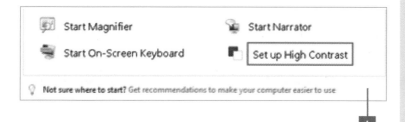

Statements you can select include but are not limited to:

- I am blind.
- I have another type of vision impairment (even if glasses correct it).
- A physical condition affects the use of my arms, wrists, hands or fingers.
- Pens and pencils are difficult to use.
- Conversations are difficult to hear (even with a hearing aid).

Explore additional ease of access options (cont.)

- I am deaf.
- I have a speech impairment.
- It is often difficult for me to concentrate.
- It is often difficult for me to remember things.
- I have a learning disability, such as dyslexia.

After filling out the questionnaire, you'll receive information regarding the settings recommended for you.

Last, but certainly not least, is Vista's speech recognition software. This program does a good job of allowing you to control your computer with your voice. From the options you can set up your microphone, take a speech tutorial, train your computer to understand you, and more.

With speech recognition you can:

- Start programs.
- Open menus.
- Click on buttons.
- Click on objects.
- Dictate documents.
- Write and send email.
- Do almost anything you can do with a keyboard and mouse.

You have to work through a wizard before you can use the software, and that takes a bit of time, so let's start there.

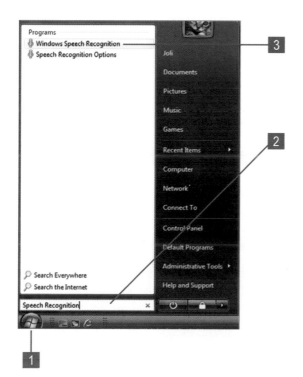

Using speech recognition

Setting up Windows speech recognition

1 Click on Start.

2 In the Start Search box, type Speech Recognition.

3 Select Windows Speech Recognition from the results.

7

Using speech recognition (cont.)

4 Read the introductory page and click on Next.

5 Select your input device. Choose from Headset Microphone, Desktop Microphone, or Other. Click on Next.

Set up Speech Recognition

Welcome to Speech Recognition

Speech Recognition allows you to control your computer by voice.

Using only your voice, you can start programs, open menus, click buttons and other objects on the screen, dictate text into documents, and write and send e-mails. Just about everything you do with your keyboard and mouse can be done with only your voice.

First, you will set up this computer to recognize your voice.

Note: You will be able to control your computer by voice once you have completed this setup wizard.

Next | Cancel

4

Set up Speech Recognition

Select the type of microphone you would like to use

Headset Microphone
Best suited for speech recognition, you wear this on your head.

Desktop Microphone
These microphones sit on the desk.

Other
Such as array microphones and microphones built into other devices.

Next | Cancel

5

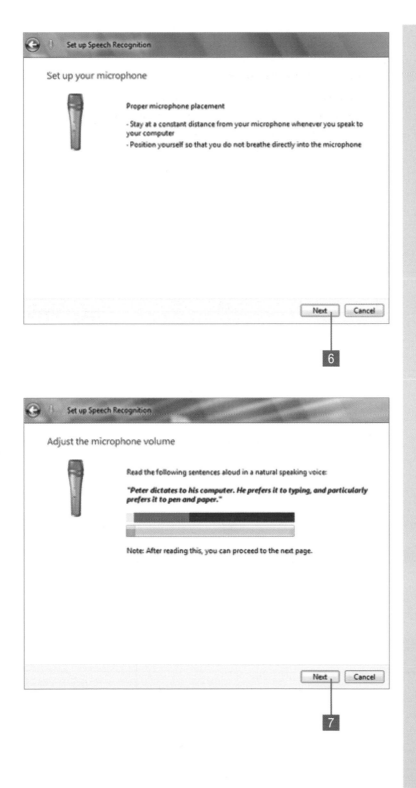

6 Read the information, and if necessary, place your microphone at the suggested distance, and click on next.

7 Read the sentence as suggested, in a natural speaking voice. Reposition the microphone if necessary, so that when you speak the bar appears in the green area. Click on next to continue.

7

Configuring accessibility options 135

Using speech recognition (cont.)

---

8 Click on next to continue setting up. (There is no screenshot of this here.)

9 Click on 'Enable document review'. This will help the computer understand your words and phrases. Click on next.

10 Click on View Reference Sheet to see a list of commands the computer can respond to. Read the information provided and print it if desired. (There's a print button at the top of the page.) Click on next to continue.

Set up Speech Recognition

Improve speech recognition accuracy

You can improve the computer's ability to recognize spoken words by allowing the computer to review documents and mail. The computer will learn words and phrases to better understand you when you speak.

Note: These words and phrases are not revealed to other users or sent to Microsoft.

More information on Windows Privacy Policy

○ **Enable document review**
○ **Disable document review**

Next   Cancel

9

Windows Help and Support

Search Help

▸ Show all

Common commands in Speech Recognition

You can print this topic for quick reference while you're using Windows Speech Recognition.

▸ How do I use Speech Recognition?

▸ Common Speech Recognition commands

▸ Dictation

▸ Keyboard keys

▸ Punctuation marks and special characters

Speech Reference Card

The Speech Reference Card is a list of commands the computer can resp...

Print out the list and keep it with you for a quick reference to the comma... you can use with the computer. When you encounter a program or some... part of the computer that's difficult to control by voice, this list of comm... can be very useful.

View Reference Sheet

Next

10

Run Speech Recognition every time I start the computer

☑ **Run Speech Recognition at startup**

Next   Cancel

11

You can now control this computer by voice.

We strongly recommend that you take the interactive speech recognition tutorial. You will learn and practice the commands that will let you successfully control your computer by voice.

Click Start Tutorial to begin taking the tutorial.

Start Tutorial   Cancel

12

11 If you want speech recognition to run every time you start your laptop, accept the defaults and click on next. Otherwise, remove the tick before clicking on next.

12 Click on Start Tutorial or Cancel. We suggest you choose Start Tutorial, and work through it now.

Did you know?

If you want to run the speech tutorial later, you can. When you're ready, click Start, and in the search box, type Speech Recognition Options. Click Speech Recognition Options in the results to access the speech tutorial.

Important

The speech recognition tutorial will not run unless your screen resolution is set to 1024 by 768 pixels or higher.

Okay, training the speech tool using the tutorial is fun. Once your microphone is set up, you're ready to rock and roll. In fact, the first page of the tutorial offers the option to click on next or to *say* it! Make sure to say the word 'next', that's the whole purpose!

Using speech recognition (cont.)

Training the speech recognition system

1. Click on next to start the tutorial. If you clicked on Cancel in the last section, you'll need to locate the tutorial again.

2. Say 'next' to start the tutorial.

3. Read the information on each page as it appears, and say next to continue.

4. Continue through the tutorial until it ends. Note that you may have to say the command several times for the program to recognise your voice, tone and accent. As you work through the training, the program will get better at recognising the words you speak.

Did you know?

You can spend the better part of an afternoon working through all of the tutorials. Just keep at it.

1

1 Say 'start speech recognition'.
Verify speech recognition is
'listening'.

2 Say Start.

3 Say Internet Explorer. (Internet
Explorer opens.)

4 Say close that. (Internet
Explorer closes.)

5 Say start.

6 Say control panel.

7 Say change desktop
background.

8 Say browse.

9 Say img36.

10 Say open.

11 Say 4.

12 Say OK. Say OK.

13 Say close that.

7

Safety and security

Introduction

Windows Vista comes with built-in features to keep you and your data safe from Internet ills, nosy children and download-happy grandchildren. Vista also offers help in avoiding email and web criminals whose only purpose in life is to steal your data, get your bank account or credit card numbers, or steal your identity. Mail even informs you if it thinks an email is 'phishing' for information you shouldn't give out.

To protect you, Vista has a firewall, the ability to create user accounts and passwords, use parental controls, use Windows Defender, and obtain help and support. In this chapter you'll learn about these features and others, and additional ways you can protect yourself and your laptop.

Your laptop was not sent to you with all of the available safety measures in place. While many measures are enabled by default, which you'll learn about later, some require intervention from you.

Here's an example. If you have grandchildren who use your computer, they can probably access or delete your personal data, download harmful content, install applications, or change settings that will affect the entire computer, all very easily. You can solve this problem by creating a computer account just for them. In conjunction, every account you create should be password-protected, especially yours. It wouldn't do much good to create accounts and not assign passwords!

What you'll do

Add a new user account

Require passwords

Enable system restore

Configure Windows update

Use Windows Firewall

Use Windows Defender

Resolve security warnings

Set up parental controls

Create a back-up

View and clear Internet Explorer history

Use help and support

Locate and watch a demonstration video

Beyond creating user accounts, here are some other ways to protect your laptop, which we'll discuss in depth in this chapter:

- System restore: if enabled, Vista stores 'restore points' on your laptop's hard drive. If something goes wrong you can run a system restore utility, choose one of these points and revert to a pre-problem date. The program only deals with 'system data', so none of your personal data will be affected (not even your last email).

- Update Windows: if enabled and configured properly, when you are online, Vista will check for security updates automatically and install them. You don't have to do anything, and your laptop is always updated with the latest security patches and features.

- Firewall: if enabled and configured properly, the firewall will help prevent hackers (people whose job it is to get into your computer and do harm to it) from accessing your laptop and data. The firewall blocks most programs from communicating outside the network (or outside your laptop). If you want to allow a program to communicate outside your safety zone you can 'allow' a program by adding it to an 'exceptions' list. This is all very easy to do.

- Defender: you don't have to do much to Defender except understand that it offers protection against online threats. It's enabled by default and it runs in the background. However, if you ever think your computer has been attacked (by a virus, worm or malware) you can run a manual scan.

- Security warnings: the Security Center is a talkative application. You can be sure you'll see a pop-up if your anti-virus software is out of date (or not installed); if you don't have the proper security settings configured; or if Windows Update or the firewall is disabled. You'll also get a user account control prompt each time you want to install a program or make system wide change. You'll learn about warnings and what to do about them in this chapter.

- Parental controls: if you have grandchildren, children, or a forgetful or scatterbrained spouse who needs limitations imposed, you can apply them using Parental Controls. These put you in charge of the hours a user can access the computer, which games they can play and what programs they can run (among other things).

- Backup and Restore Center: this feature lets you perform back-ups, and in the case of a computer failure, restore them (put them back). However, there are other options too, including copying files to a CD or DVD, copying pictures and media to an external hard drive, USB drive or memory card, or storing them on an online server.

8

User accounts and passwords

If every person who accesses your laptop has their own standard user account and password, and if every person logs on using that account and then logs off the laptop each time they're finished using it, you'd never have to worry about anyone accessing anyone else's personal data. That's because when a user logs on with his own user account, he can only access his data (and any data other users have elected to share).

Additionally, every user account is provided with a 'user profile' that tells Vista what desktop background to use, what screen saver, and preferences for mouse settings, sounds and more. Each user also has their own web bookmarks and email settings, address books and personal folders. User accounts help all who access the computer keep their personal data, well, personal.

Also, by creating standard accounts for users (yes, even yourself) instead of administrator accounts, you can keep the computer safe by requiring administrator credentials to make system-wide changes such as installing applications, changing security settings and accessing certain files on your laptop. Even if you are the only person who accesses the computer, you should still create a standard account for yourself and use it. If someone does steal your laptop, they won't be able to use it without your password. And, if they try to do something that may harm the laptop, they'll also have to know your administrator credentials and administrator password. That being the case, hackers won't be able to get in as easily either.

Adding a new user account

1 Click on Start.

2 Click on Control Panel.

3 Click on 'Add or remove user accounts'.

4 Click on 'Create a new account'.

8

User accounts and passwords (cont.)

5 Type a new account name. This should be the user's name. If you are creating an account for yourself, stop. Read the section **The administrator account dilemma** before continuing. The steps here are for creating an account for someone else, like a child, grandchild or spouse.

6 Check 'Standard user' is selected.

7 Click Create Account.

8 Click the new account.

9 Click 'Create a password'.

10 Type the new password, input it again to confirm it, and provide a password hint.

11 Click 'Create password'.

12 Click the X in the top-right corner to close the window.

The administrator account dilemma

It's very likely you're logging on to your laptop using an administrator account. That's because when you set up Vista, it made you create an administrator account! Nowhere did it tell you to create a standard account later, or otherwise inform you of the importance of it. That said, all of your personal data, preferences, email settings and other configurations are likely to be in an administrator account, which causes problems with moving to a standard account.

To find out if you're logging on using an administrator account:

- Click on Start.
- Click on Control Panel.
- Click on 'Add or remove user accounts'.
- If the account you log on with says Administrator, as shown here, you're using an administrator account.

Joli Ballew
Administrator
Password protected

As stated, you should be using a standard account exclusively. Unfortunately, if you simply create a new standard account for yourself, when you log on to the laptop using your new account, it's like logging on to the laptop for the first time. You have to reconfigure your desktop background, screen saver, applications, email and web favourites, and find a way to move or copy your personal folders to the new account. Although it's not impossible, it is a royal pain. That being the case, if you really want to switch from an administrator account to a standard one, you'll have to work through the steps below.

8

User accounts and passwords (cont.)

Important

Only work through these steps if you've read **The administrator account dilemma** above and are sure you currently log on using an administrator account.

Move from an administrator to a standard account

1. Click on Start.
2. Click on Control Panel.
3. Click on 'Add or remove user accounts'.

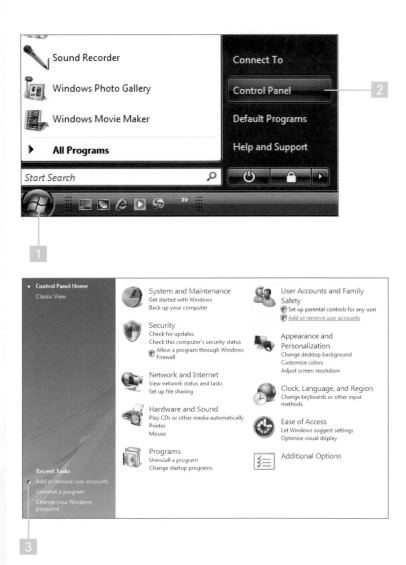

Choose the account you would like to change

Joli Ballew
Administrator
Password protected

Guest
Guest account is off

Create a new account
What is a user account?

4

5

Name the account and choose an account type

This name will appear on the Welcome screen and on the Start menu.

Admin

○ Standard user
Standard account users can use most software and change system settings that do not affect other users or the security of the computer.

◉ Administrator
Administrators have complete access to the computer and can make any desired changes. To help make the computer more secure, administrators are asked to provide their password or confirmation before making changes that affect other users.

We recommend that you protect every account with a strong password.

Why is a standard account recommended?

Create Account   Cancel

6

Admin ——— 7
Administrator

User accounts and passwords (cont.)

4 Click on 'Create a new account'.

5 Type 'Admin' for the account name. Select Administrator.

6 Click on Create Account.

7 Click on the new Admin account.

8

User accounts and passwords (cont.)

8 Click on 'Create a password'.

9 Type the new password, type it again to confirm it, and type a password hint. It's best to create a password that contains upper and lower case letters and a few numbers. Write the password down and keep it someone out of sight and safe. Each time you need to make a system-wide change, you'll need to input Admin and the password to obtain access.

10 Click on 'Create password'.

11 Click the back arrow to return to the previous screen.

Make changes to Admin's account

Change the account name

Create a password ——————————————— **8**

Change the picture

Set up Parental Controls

Change the account type

Delete the account

Manage another account

Note that you can also click on items to change the picture; change the account name; and remove the password. These and other options can be used to personalise the account.

Choose the account you would like to change

 Joli Ballew
Administrator
Password protected

 Admin
Administrator
Password protected

 Guest
Guest account is off

Make changes to Joli Ballew's account

Change the account name

Change the password

Remove the password

Change the picture

Set up Parental Controls

Change the account type

Delete the account

Manage another account

User accounts and passwords (cont.)

12 Click on your old administrator account, not the new Admin account.

13 Click on 'Change the account type'.

8

!

Important

Write down your user name and password and keep it in a safe place.

User accounts and passwords (cont.)

14 Click on 'Standard user'.

15 Click on 'Change Account Type'.

16 Click on Start.

17 Click on the right arrow.

18 Click on Log Off.

19 Log back in using your new standard account (which is your old user name and credentials).

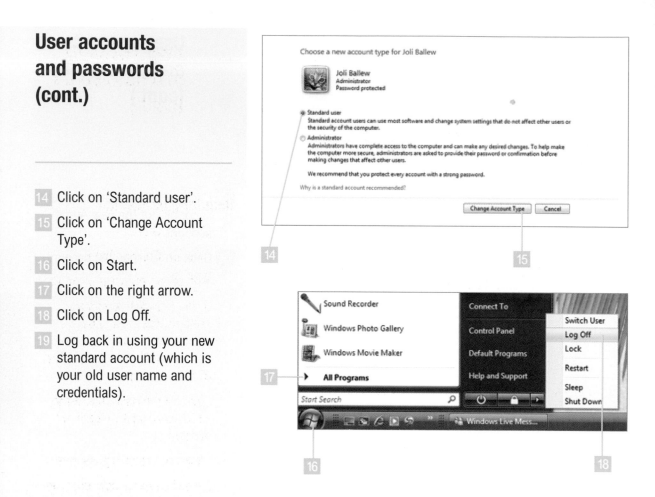

For your information

When logged on as a standard user, and when you need to make a change to the system that affects everyone, you will either be prompted to insert the Admin password, or simply be told you are not allowed to make this change. If prompted that you don't have access, you'll have to log off and log back on as Admin to complete the change. It's much more likely you'll be prompted to input the Admin password. What you see depends on how other security features are configured. Whatever happens though, the protection you get by using a standard account outweighs the nuisance of the occasional security message.

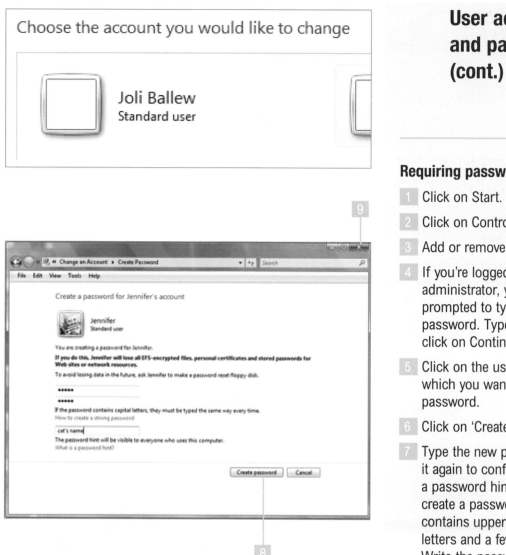

Choose the account you would like to change

Joli Ballew
Standard user

Create a password for Jennifer's account

Jennifer
Standard user

You are creating a password for Jennifer.

If you do this, Jennifer will lose all EFS-encrypted files, personal certificates and stored passwords for Web sites or network resources.

To avoid losing data in the future, ask Jennifer to make a password reset floppy disk.

•••••

•••••

If the password contains capital letters, they must be typed the same way every time.

How to create a strong password

cat's name

The password hint will be visible to everyone who uses this computer.

What is a password hint?

Create password   Cancel

Note there are options to change the picture, change the account name, remove the password, and otherwise personalise the account.

Requiring passwords

1. Click on Start.
2. Click on Control Panel.
3. Add or remove user accounts.
4. If you're logged on as an administrator, you'll be prompted to type the Admin's password. Type it. Otherwise, click on Continue.
5. Click on the user account to which you want to apply a password.
6. Click on 'Create a password'.
7. Type the new password, type it again to confirm it, and type a password hint. It's best to create a password that contains upper and lower case letters and a few numbers. Write the password down and keep it someone out of sight and safe. Each time you need to make a system wide change, you'll need to input Admin and the password to obtain access.
8. Click on 'Create password'.
9. Click the X in the top right of the window to close it.

8

Protecting your laptop

You learned a little about restoring the system, updating the firewall and Defender in the introduction. Now it's time to look at each of these more closely, and to verify they are set up properly and running as they should be.

System restore

System Restore is a utility that lets you return your computer to an earlier time without affecting your personal files, including documents, spreadsheets, e-mail and photos. You'll only use System Restore if and when you install a program or driver that produces error messages or causes problems for the computer, and uninstalling the problematic application or driver doesn't resolve the issue.

System Restore, by default, regularly creates and saves restore points that contain information about registry settings and system information that Windows uses. Because System Restore works only with its own system files, it can't recover a lost personal file, email or picture. In the same vein, it will not affect this data either. It's important to verify that System Restore is enabled and configured properly.

Enabling System Restore

1 Click on Start.

2 In the Start Search box, type 'System Restore'.

3 Click on System Restore under the Programs results.

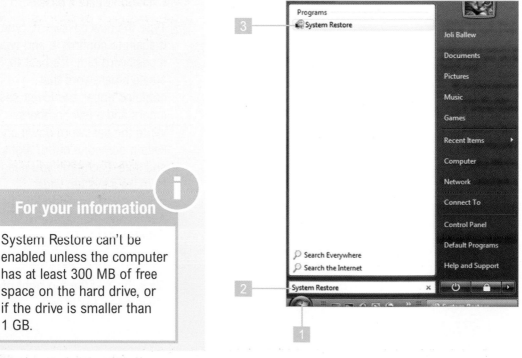

For your information

System Restore can't be enabled unless the computer has at least 300 MB of free space on the hard drive, or if the drive is smaller than 1 GB.

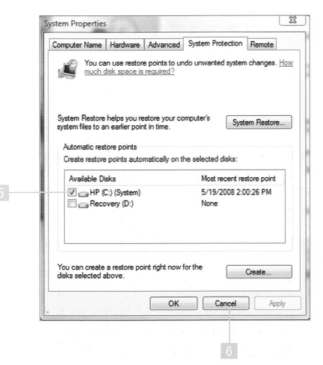

4 Click on 'open System Protection'.

5 Check that the C drive, or the system drive, is selected. If it is not, select it.

6 Click on OK.

7 In the System Restore window, click Cancel.

8

For your information

You can create a restore point manually by clicking Create.

For your information

To run System Restore, open it as noted in steps 1–4, and click Next to start the wizard.

Safety and security 155

Protecting your laptop (cont.)

Updating Windows

It's important to configure Windows Update to get updates automatically. This is the easiest way to ensure your computer is as up-to-date as possible, at least as far as patching security flaws Microsoft uncovers, having access to the latest features, and obtaining updates to the operating system. I propose you verify that the recommended settings are enabled as detailed here, and occasionally check for optional updates manually.

When the software is configured as recommended here, updates will be downloaded automatically when you are online, installed, and if necessary, your computer will be rebooted automatically. You can configure the time of day you want this to happen. Once updates are installed, you'll see a pop-up as shown here.

Windows installed new updates
Your computer was restarted to finish installing updates.
Click to see which updates were installed.

For your information

The Windows Help and Support Center offers pages upon pages of information regarding Windows Update, including how to remove them or select updates when more than one is available. I think the above paragraphs state all you need to know as an average 50+ computer user, and that you need not worry about anything else.

Configuring Windows Update

1. Click on Start.

2. Click on Control Panel.

3. Click on Security.

4. Click on Windows Update.

5. You may see here that Windows is fine, or you may see that there are available updates. Anything else means that Windows Update is not configured using recommended settings. Whatever the case, click on Change settings.

6. Check the settings are configured to 'Install updates automatically (recommended)' as shown here. (You can choose another setting, but I don't recommend it.)

7. Notice the default time of 3 AM. Change this to a time when your laptop is online but is not being used.

8. Check the two items ticked here are ticked on your laptop.

9. Make changes if needed, and click on OK.

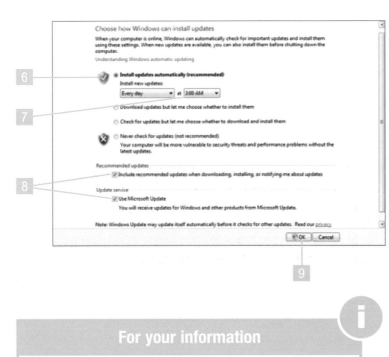

For your information

If the computer is not online at 3 am, it will check for updates the next time it is.

Protecting your laptop (cont.)

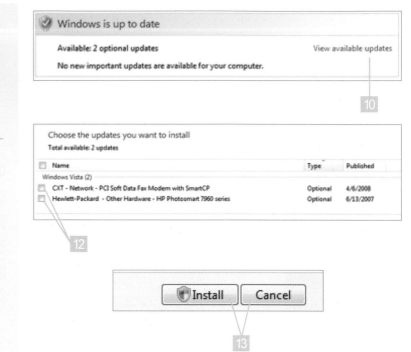

10 Back at the Update window, if you see that optional components are available (or any other updates for that matter), click on 'View available updates'.

11 Install any required updates, critical updates or security updates. To do this, tick the update and click on Install.

12 Read the optional update descriptions, and if desired, tick and download those. Optional updates may not be necessary: for instance, I no longer own the HP Photosmart 7960 printer, so there is no reason to get the update.

13 Click on Install or Cancel.

14 Click the X in the top right corner to close the window.

Windows security features

There are two more security features to explore: the firewall and Defender. There isn't much you need to do with these features except to make sure they are both enabled and are protecting your laptop. By default, both are enabled.

Windows Firewall checks the data that comes in from the Internet (or a local network) and decides whether it's good data or bad. If it deems the data harmless, it will allow it to come though the firewall, if not, it's blocked. You have to have a firewall to keep hackers from getting access to your laptop, and to help prevent your computer from sending out malicious code if it is ever attacked by a virus or worm.

Sometimes the firewall will block programs you want to use, such as:

- Live Messenger
- Office Outlook
- Remote Assistance
- Media Player
- Wireless Portable Devices.

These and others are blocked by default, and the first time you try to use them you'll be prompted to unblock them. There is reasoning behind this, and it has to do with protecting you from online ills. A hacker may try to come through the Internet to your laptop using an application you don't normally use, such as Remote Assistance. It can't come through unless you 'allow' it too. (When unblocking a program you can ask not to be prompted again regarding that application.)

Defender protects your laptop against malicious and unwanted software. Generally this is a type of data called spyware, malware or adware. Spyware can get on your laptop without your knowledge and can wreak havoc by causing these types of problems:

- Adding toolbars to Internet Explorer.
- Changing your web browser's home page.
- Taking you to websites you do not want to visit.
- Showing pop-up advertisements.
- Causing the computer to perform slowly.

Defender helps protect this type of data from getting on to your laptop.

It's up to you to make sure that the firewall and Defender are running and configured properly. That's what you'll do in the next two sections. Additionally, you'll have the option of changing a few of the parameters, such as when scans are completed and what happens when potentially dangerous data is detected.

8

Important

!

If you work through the steps for the firewall and it is turned off, it may be turned off because you have a third-party firewall software installed; such as McAfee, Zone Alarm or Norton. If you aren't sure, go ahead and enable Windows Firewall. If you have a third-party firewall, my advice is don't enable it because running two firewalls can cause problems for the laptop.

Protecting your laptop (cont.)

Using Windows Firewall

1. Click on Start.

2. Click on Control Panel.

3. Click on Security.

4. Under Windows Firewall, click on 'Turn Windows Firewall on or off'.

5. Verify the firewall is On. If not, select On.

6. Click on the Exceptions tab. Notice the exceptions already enabled. You can enable exceptions manually here or wait until you're prompted when trying to use the application.

7. Click on OK.

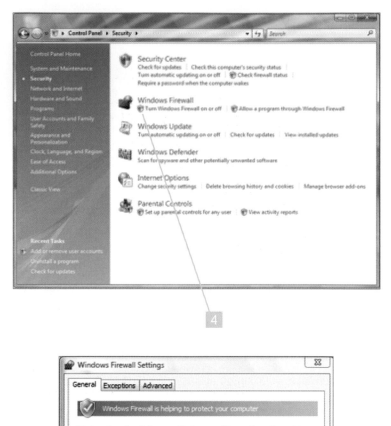

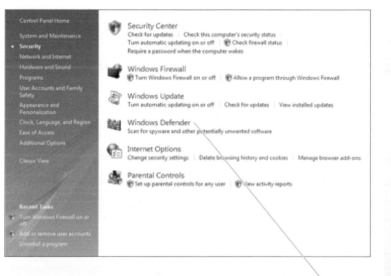

Windows Firewall Settings

General | Exceptions | Advanced

Exceptions control how programs communicate through Windows Firewall. Add a program or port exception to allow communications through the firewall.

Windows Firewall is currently using settings for the private network location.
What are the risks of unblocking a program?

To enable an exception, select its check box:

Program or port

- ☐ BITS Peercaching
- ☑ Connect to a Network Projector
- ☑ Core Networking
- ☐ Distributed Transaction Coordinator
- ☑ File and Printer Sharing
- ☑ HP Connections
- ☑ HP Connections
- ☑ Internet Connection Sharing
- ☐ iSCSI Service
- ☐ Media Center Extenders
- ☑ Microsoft Office Outlook
- ☐ Netlogon Service
- ☑ Network Discovery

Add program... | Add port... | Properties | Delete

☑ Notify me when Windows Firewall blocks a new program

OK | Cancel | Apply

Using Windows Defender

1 Click on Start.

2 Click on Control Panel.

3 Click on Security.

4 Click on Windows Defender. Hopefully, you'll see that no unwanted or harmful software has been detected. If something does come up, you'll be prompted regarding what to do next. (This is highly unlikely.)

Control Panel Home

Control Panel Home
System and Maintenance
• Security
Network and Internet
Hardware and Sound
Programs
User Accounts and Family Safety
Appearance and Personalization
Clock, Language, and Region
Ease of Access
Additional Options

Classic View

Recent Tasks
Turn Windows Firewall on or off
Add or remove user accounts
Uninstall a program

Security Center
Check for updates | Check this computer's security status
Turn automatic updating on or off | Check firewall status
Require a password when the computer wakes

Windows Firewall
Turn Windows Firewall on or off | Allow a program through Windows Firewall

Windows Update
Turn automatic updating on or off | Check for updates | View installed updates

Windows Defender
Scan for spyware and other potentially unwanted software

Internet Options
Change security settings | Delete browsing history and cookies | Manage browser add-ons

Parental Controls
Set up parental controls for any user | View activity reports

Protecting your laptop (cont.)

5

5 Click on Tools.

6 Click on Options.

7 Verify that Automatic Scanning is enabled.

8 If desired, change the approximate time of the scan. It's best to leave the other defaults as they are.

9 Click on Save if you've made changes, or Cancel if not.

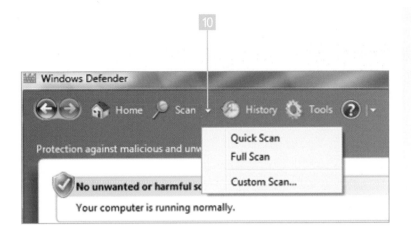

Resolving security warnings

Last but not least, you need to visit the security centre occasionally to check for any warnings. If you see anything in red or yellow, the problem needs to be resolved. In this example, two problems exist. First, there's no virus protection and second, the firewall is disabled. To be protected, these items must be taken care of.

10 Click on the arrow next to Scan (not the Scan icon). Note that you can perform a quick scan or a full scan manually. Do this if you think the computer has been infected.

11 Click the X in the top right corner to close the Defender window.

8

Protecting your laptop (cont.)

Resolving security warnings

1. Click on Start.

2. Click on Control Panel.

3. Click on Security.

4. If there's anything in red or yellow, click on the down arrow (if necessary), to see the problem.

5. Note the fix and perform the task. For the firewall, click on 'Turn on now'.

6. For virus protection, click on 'Show me my available options'.

7. Select from the two choices shown here. Ideally, you should have an anti-virus program such as Windows Live OneCare, Norton, McAfee or Zone Alarm. (If you have an anti-virus application, Vista will probably find it automatically after installation.)

8. Continue in this manner to resolve all any other security issues.

9. Click the X in the top right corner of the window to close it.

There are two other things you can do to protect your family, your laptop and data. First, protect children with parental controls. These aren't a cure-all, but they do help. You still have to find a way to protect your kids from bad influences online when they're away from home, but at least while they're under your roof (or in your car) you can look after them. Second, learn how to create back-ups of your data and settings. Although it's unlikely something will happen in the immediate future that is so bad it would destroy your laptop and all of your data, it could happen (and it does). It's best to be prepared.

Parental controls

As noted in the introduction, these controls can be applied to children, grandchildren, guests and even spouses. You can configure controls to set limits on when a person can use the computer (and for how long), what games they can play, what websites they can visit, and what programs they can run.

As you can see here, there are options to set time limits, games, access to programs, and to set up family safety features in Live OneCare (if you've signed up for Live OneCare). There is also an option to view reports.

◄ **Protecting your family and your data**

> **!** **Important**
>
> You can only apply parental controls to users with a standard user account. All other user accounts should have passwords.

8

Set up how Jennifer will use the computer

Parental Controls:
- ⦿ On, enforce current settings
- ○ Off

Activity Reporting:
- ⦿ On, collect information about computer usage
- ○ Off

Windows Settings

Time limits
Control when Jennifer uses the computer

Games
Control games by rating, content, or title

Allow and block specific programs
Allow and block any programs on your computer

More Settings

Windows Live OneCare Family Safety
Set up the Family Safety web filter

Current Settings:

Jennifer
Standard user
No Password

View activity reports

Web Restrictions:	Windows Live OneCare Family Safety
Time Limits:	Off
Game Ratings:	Off
Program Limits:	Off

OK

Protecting your family and your data (cont.)

Setting up controls

1. Click on Start
2. Click on Control Panel.
3. Under User Accounts and Family Safety, click on 'Set up parental controls for any user'.

You can review 'activity reports' that let you see what that person has been doing on the computer. You can also see what content has been blocked, which will allow you to see how far the user has been testing the limits of the controls you've set.

On an activity report you can view the following:

- Top 10 websites visited.
- Most recent 10 websites blocked.
- Web overrides.
- File downloads.
- File downloads blocked.
- Logon times.
- Applications run.
- Application overrides.
- Games played.
- Email received, sent and contact list changes.
- Instant Messaging conversations, webcam, audio, game play, file exchange, link exchange, SMS message and contact list change.
- Media played.

 User Accounts and Family Safety
Set up parental controls for any user ——— 3
Add or remove user accounts

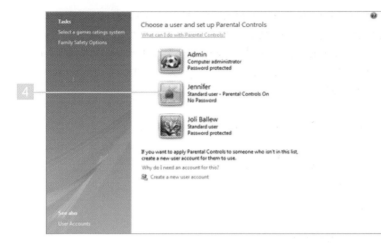

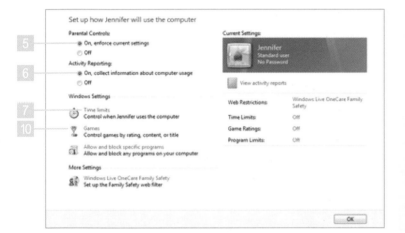

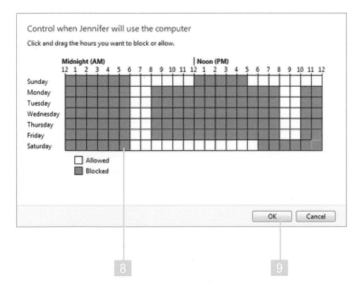

Protecting your family and your data (cont.)

4 Click on the standard user account for which you want to set controls (in this case, Jennifer). It's OK if this account doesn't have a password, but you should still consider setting one up.

5 Under Parental Controls, click on the On button.

6 Under Activity Reporting, click on the On button.

7 Click on Time Limits.

8 Click and drag to set times to block and allow. Blue is blocked.

9 Click on OK.

10 Click on Games.

Protecting your family and your data (cont.)

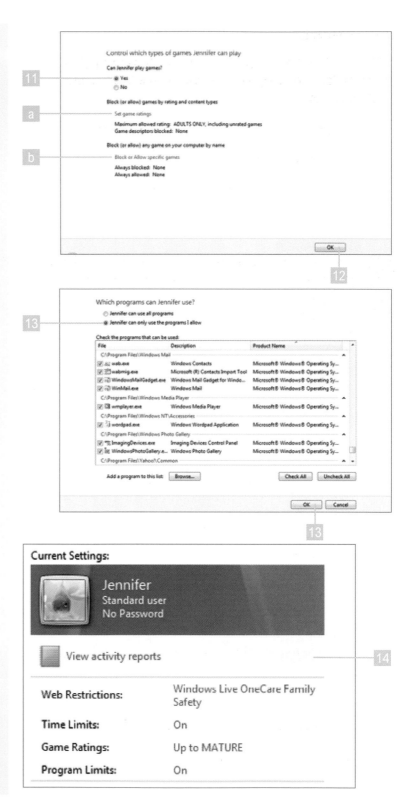

11 Click on Yes to allow games to be played, or No to disallow it. If you click on Yes:

a Click on 'Set game ratings' and select an age group from the resulting list, and configure additional settings. Click on OK.

b Click on 'Block (or Allow) specific games' and for each game listed, the configuration for each. By default, it's based on user ratings. Click on OK.

12 Click on OK to close the game controls windows.

13 Click on 'Allow or block specific programs'. If the user can access all programs, select '<user name> can use all programs'. Otherwise, choose '<user name> can only use the programs I allow'. For the latter, select and deselect programs the user can run. Click on OK.

14 Come back to the Parental Controls Window to monitor activity reports.

15 Click on OK.

Backing up data

Vista comes with a program you can use to back up your personal data. The program is located in the Backup and Restore Center.

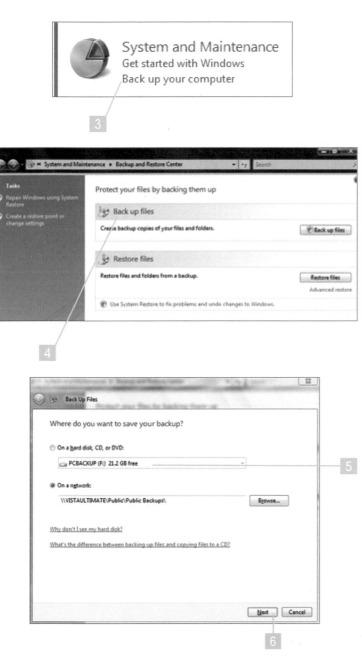

Creating your first backup

1. Click on Start.

2. Click on Control Panel.

3. Click on 'Back up your computer'.

4. Click on 'Back up files'.

5. Choose a place to save your back-up. Since back-ups can be large, consider a USB drive, external hard drive or DVD. You can also choose a network location. For the first one, if possible, select a location that has several GB of space, such as an external hard drive or network location, just to be safe.

6. Click on Next. (If prompted for any other information, such as a hard-drive partition, to insert a blank DVD or insert a USB drive, do so.)

8

Did you know?

You can't create a back-up on the hard drive of the computer you are backing up.

Protecting your family and your data (cont.)

7 Select what to back up. First timers should select everything. Click Next.

8 Choose settings for how often, what day, and what time future repeats should occur.

9 Click on 'Save settings and start backup'.

Follow the same procedure to restore data from a backup if and when necessary.

Which file types do you want to back up?

All files on this computer of the type that you select will be backed up, including files that belong to other users of this computer. We recommend that you back up all of the file types selected below.

☑ Pictures
☑ Music
☑ Videos
☑ E-mail
☑ Documents
☑ TV shows
☑ Compressed files
☑ Additional files

Category details

Move the mouse pointer over a category on the left or select it with the keyboard to see what types of files will be backed up.

Only files on NTFS disks can be backed up. System files, executable files, and temporary files will not be backed up. What other file types are not included in the backup?

How often do you want to create a backup?

New files and files that have changed will be added to your backup according to the schedule you set below.

How often: Weekly
What day: Sunday
What time: 7:00 PM

Because this is your first backup, Windows will create a new, full backup now.

Vista comes with Internet Explorer, a web browser you can use to surf the Internet. Internet Explorer has everything you need, including a pop-up blocker, zoom settings and accessibility options, as well as tools you can use to mark web pages, set home pages, and sign up for read RSS feeds. Internet Explorer now has a feature called 'tabbed browsing'. With tabs, you can have several web pages open at one time, without having more than one copy of the browser open and running.

You can find the browser from the Windows Start button.

While we won't go into how to use every aspect of Internet Explorer, there are a few things to note in regard to safety. You'll find all of the tools required in the browser's Tools menu.

As you can see, there's a lot going on behind the scenes, and a lot of it is security-related and enabled by default. There's a pop-up blocker to keep unwanted ads from appearing when you visit web pages configured with them, there's a 'phishing' filter to stop you accessing websites that have been reported to Microsoft as suspicious, and there are preconfigured security

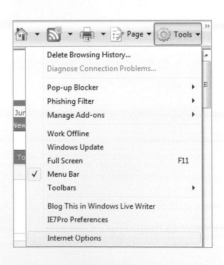

Staying safe online (cont.)

zones and privacy settings to help protect against any other threats you may run across while surfing the web. Since much of this is preconfigured, there's really no need to go into the details a lot here regarding those features. Just make sure you leave everything enabled, and you'll be protected.

There is one item you must use manually and that's the tool to delete your browsing history. With it, you can delete files that can be used to trace where you've been on the web. If your grandchildren use your computer, and do not have their own user account, you'll want to do this before they start surfing the web. Additionally, before leaving the laptop in a hotel room or car, consider deleting these files before you go. If someone did steal your PC, and if they were somehow able to log on (which would be difficult if you enabled a user account), they'd be able to access information regarding your web travels, including saved passwords and information you've used to fill out forms online.

So, if you don't want people to be able to snoop around on your computer and find out what sites you've been visiting, first, create a password-protected user account for yourself. If you're worried beyond that, or if you don't always log off when you have finished using the computer (or if you're doing something online you shouldn't be) you'll want to delete your browsing history.

Delete Browsing History lets you delete the following files:

- Temporary Internet files: these files that have been saved in a temporary Internet files folder. A snooper could go through these files to see what you've been doing online.

- Cookies: these are small text files that include data that identifies your preferences when you visit particular websites. Cookies are what allows you to visit, say, www.amazon.com and be greeted with 'Hello <your name>, We have recommendations for you!' Cookies help a site offer you a personalised web experience.

- History: this is the list of websites you've visited and any web addresses you've typed. Anyone can look at the list to see where you've been.

- Form data: information that's been saved by Internet Explorer to complete form data automatically. If you don't want forms to be filled out automatically by you or someone else who has access to your PC and user account, delete this.

- Passwords that were saved using Internet Explorer autocomplete password prompts.

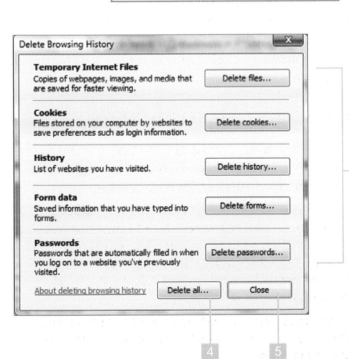

Viewing and clearing history in Internet Explorer

1 Click the Alt key.

2 Click on Tools.

3 Click on Delete Browsing History.

4 To delete any or all of the listed items, use the Delete button.

5 Click Close when finished.

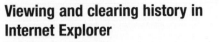

Help and support

Sometimes, things happen that you don't understand. Perhaps your laptop starts showing pop-up messages with security warnings, or it slows down to a crawl. When that happens, you'll need answers fast, and you can find them using Vista's Help and Support feature. One sure way to stay safe and secure is to know what you're doing! You can access Help and Support from the Start menu.

When you open it, you'll have several options, as shown here. If you have time, select each option to see what it offers. You'll be surprised how much information is available. For instance, Windows Basics offers articles on everything from using your mouse to setting up a wireless network. If you want help on something in particular, such as Internet Explorer or Mail, type what you're looking for in the Search Help window and articles that apply will appear.

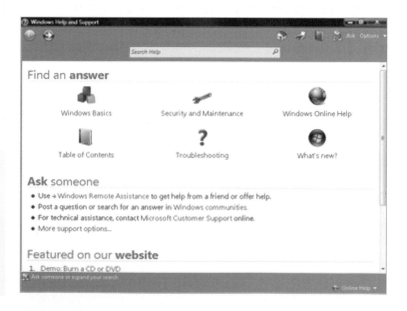

If you're looking for something in particular, click on Table of Contents. From the contents page, just go to the option that most closely matches what you're looking for. If you don't find what you want on the page, just use the Back button to try again. Additionally, you can type anything in the search window if you'd rather go that route.

You can access the Help and Support Center from almost anywhere in Vista. You only need to locate the round blue question mark that you'll find on most windows and dialogue boxes.

Help and support (cont.)

Finally, almost all programs offer a help menu. For help regarding an open program, click on Help and select an option in the drop-down list.

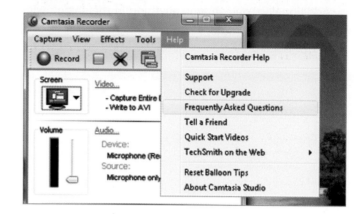

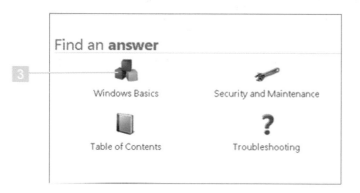

Getting help and support

1. Click on Start.
2. Click on Help and Support.
3. Click on Windows Basics.

Did you know?

If you have a printer installed, you can click on the printer icon to print any help topic.

Help and support (cont.)

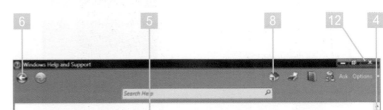

4 Use the scroll bar to browse through the topics.

5 Select any topic to read more about it.

6 Use the Back button to return to the previous screen.

7 Repeat steps 4 to 6 as desired.

8 Click the Home icon in the Help and Support Center to return to the first page of Help and Support.

9 Click on Options.

10 Click on Text Size.

11 Select the desired text size.

12 Click the X in the top right to close the window.

Locating and watching a Vista demonstration video

1. Click on Start.

2. In the search window, type Welcome.

3. Under Programs, click on Welcome Center.

4. In the Welcome Center, under 'Get started with Windows', click on Show all ___ items…

5. Double-click on Windows Vista Demos.

8

Help and support (cont.)

6 Maximise the screen if necessary.

7 Note that you can select any video title, but in this exercise, click on 'Understanding the parts of your computer'.

8 Click on 'Watch the demo'.

9 To stop, or to close Media Player, click on the X.

Adware: Internet advertisements (which are also applications) that often include additional code that can be used to track a user's personal information and pass it on to third parties, without the user's authorisation or knowledge.

Internet server: a computer that stores data that is connected to the Internet. Hotmail offers Internet servers to hold messages and data, so you do not have to store it on your laptop. Such servers allow you to access information from any computer that can access the internet.

Malware: malicious software. Malware includes viruses, worms and spyware.

Phishing: an attempt by a unscrupulous website or hacker to obtain personal data such as bank account numbers, social security numbers and email addresses.

Virus: a self-replicating program that infects computers with intent to do harm. Viruses often come in the form of an attachment to an email.

Worm: a self-replicating program that infects computers with intent to do harm. However, unlike a virus, it does not need to attach itself to a running program.

8

Connecting to the Internet

Introduction

If you aren't online already, now's the time to take the plunge. There are a few things you'll need to do before you can start surfing the web including selecting an Internet service provider (ISP), subscribing to it, installing the necessary hardware and software, and obtaining the required configuration settings. You may also need to choose a user name, password and email address. Once you have all of that, you'll be ready to go.

If you do not want to pay a monthly fee for online access, you can visit free or minimal cost 'hot spots' where you can access the Internet, provided you have a wireless network adapter installed in your laptop. If you have a new laptop, you probably do. If you want to try free service, take your laptop to a hotel, coffee chain or pub and ask if they have free WiFi. If you have the required hardware, you can connect easily.

In this chapter we need to talk about two specific situations. The first is that you are a home user, and you happen to be using a laptop. If this is the case, you can choose a dial-up, DSL or broadband connection. But in this situation, the laptop is your main PC and you use it at home.

The second scenario is that you purchased and will use your laptop for travel, and want to have web access wherever you are. For this type of connection, you'll use a wireless card to connect to the Internet.

What you'll do

Creating a connection to the Internet

Find out if you have wireless hardware

Connect at a free 'hot spot'

Choose among dial-up, broadband, mobile, wireless and satellite

▶

There are a several options for connecting to the Internet. If you use your laptop at home and rarely travel, you are likely to want to connect using your phone line (dial-up) or cable modem (broadband or ADSL). These options are less expensive than wireless options, but you must remain physically connected to the signal.

It would not make sense to pay for a dial-up connection if you travel with your laptop, because locating a phone line to plug your laptop into to connect to the Internet would be difficult. You would also have to pay long distance fees if there's no dial-up server close to where you are. Cable and ADSL offer the same problem. With cable and ADSL connections you have to connect physically to a modem, which in turn is physically connected to a wall outlet, and since a laptop is best used for travel and mobility, this would inhibit its usefulness. So, if you use your laptop for travel, you'll want to choose a provider that allows you to connect wirelessly (or via satellite) from anywhere.

?

Did you know?

Even if your laptop does not come with a wireless card or wireless capability, you can still sign up for wireless Internet. Wireless Internet providers offer hardware that connects to a USB port to acquire a wireless signal.

Almost all Internet options offer varying rate plans which can be calculated based on how often you go online, whether or not you have an existing service with a mobile phone operator, cable TV or digital phone, and/or how much 'bandwidth' you use, which has to do with the amount of data you send and receive. To make the best choice, read on.

Call your cable, satellite, and/or mobile phone providers

If you already have service with a land-line phone company, mobile phone provider, and/or a cable or satellite company (for television service), give those companies a call. Most offer bundled services and offer discounts if you sign up for their Internet service.

The telecoms regulator, Ofcom, offers advice on choosing an ISP:

Ofcom
Riverside House
2a Southwark Bridge Road
London SE1 9HA
Tel: 020 7981 3000
Textphone: 020 7981 3043
www.ofcom.org.uk

Ask friends and neighbours what they use too.

Consider speed and connectivity limits

While you're researching, consider how fast you want to be able to surf the web, and how often. If you don't travel with your laptop, only want to get online once a week to check email from your family and really don't care if that process is fast or slow, consider dial-up. Dial-up is inexpensive, and you can opt for a pay-as-you-go plan. If you want unlimited access to the Internet, and you want a fast connection, consider broadband through a cable company. Finally, if you want to be online wherever you are, get a satellite connection. If you go wireless, you can get a USB adapter or a wireless network card that goes where you go, if your laptop doesn't already have the necessary hardware. Satellite connections are great if you have a laptop and you travel. No matter where you are, you can get online.

Decide on a monthly budget

After you've decided what your ISP options are and have done a little research into cost and speed, decide on a monthly budget. Go to a friend's house if necessary and visit one of the comparison websites to compare prices and services.

Choose among dial-up, broadband, mobile, wireless and satellite (cont.)

For your information

If you don't have any existing services or are unhappy with your television or mobile phone provider, start cold calling ISP providers. You might try Clara.net, Pipex, Be Unlimited or Tesco, among others. There are broadband comparison websites such as www.moneysupermarket.com and www.uswitch.com.

Important

Don't pay a set-up cost. There are too many companies that will set up your connection for free, making this an unnecessary expense. Note that you may have to purchase hardware though.

Configuring your home Internet connection

With hardware (and possibly software) at hand, it's time to configure your home connection. You'll first need to install any hardware you received. If you're setting up using a physical connection, this may mean connecting a cable modem, wireless access point or ADSL modem. If you've selected satellite, you will probably only need to insert a wireless network card or other hardware. Additionally, there may be a router or driver software involved. You'll have to follow the directions that came with the hardware and software to set it up, but don't panic. If you get in a bind, call the ISP. They are there to help; it's their job. They will walk you through the set up process – and will stay on the phone with you until all is set up properly.

Once the hardware is configured, and if the ISP does not walk you through the process of configuring the connection in Vista, you'll need to access the Network and Sharing Center to create the connection yourself. Once inside the Network and Sharing Center, you'll select 'Set up a connection or network'.

During the process you'll need to input the following information, which you can acquire from your ISP. If you don't have it, call them. Write this information down and keep it in a safe place:

- User name.
- Email address.
- Password.

- Incoming POP3 Server Name.
- Outgoing SMTP Server Name.
- Account name (may be the same as user name).

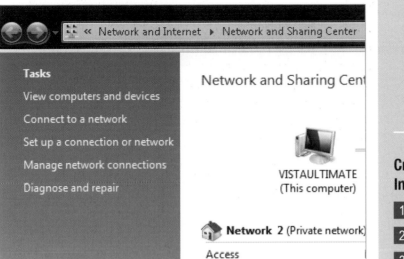

Creating a connection to the Internet

1 Click on Start.

2 Type 'Network and Sharing'.

3 Under Programs, select Network and Sharing Center.

9

Configuring your home Internet connection (cont.)

4 Under Tasks, click on 'Set up a connection or network'.

5 Click 'Connect to the Internet' to set up a wireless, broadband or dial-up connection to the Internet.

6 Click on Next.

7 Select either broadband or dial-up, based on the ISP's connection option.

8 Click on Next (it will appear after you make a selection in step 7).

9 For broadband:

   a. Type your user name and password

   b. Select 'Remember this password' (otherwise you'll have to type the password each time you use the connection).

   c. If desired, type a connection name.

   d. If you have a home network and want to share this computer with others on the network tick 'Allow other people to use this connection'.

   e. Click Connect.

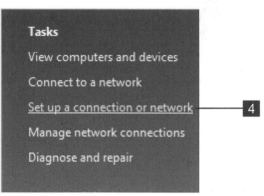

Configuring your home Internet connection (cont.)

10 For dial-up:

a Type the phone number. It should be a local number, otherwise you'll incur high phone charges. If it is not a local number, call your ISP and ask for one.

b Click Dialing Rules. Input the proper information and click OK.

c Type your user name and password

d Select 'Remember this password' (otherwise you'll have to type the password each time you use the connection).

e If desired, type a connection name.

f If you have a home network and want to share this computer with others on the network, put a tick by 'Allow other people to use this connection'.

g Click on Create.

Did you know?

Passwords are case-sensitive.

Creating a wireless satellite connection

If you've chosen satellite Internet, you'll need to install the wireless hardware and software your ISP sent you (or that you purchased). For the most part, when you connect the hardware, you'll be prompted to install a program from a CD-Rom, as see here. The installation program will launch.

During set up, you'll need to follow any prompts and input data as instructed. Once the hardware and software has been installed, click Connect. You'll be prompted to choose a network type. Select Home or Work.

9

Viewing and managing network connections

Once your Internet connection is set up, you can check its status in the Network and Sharing Center. You can also see and access your networked computers (if you have any) and the hardware you've installed to connect to the Internet in the network window.

The network window also offers a link to the Network and Sharing Center. Click on it. You need to go here if you need to diagnose and repair connectivity problems or manage your Internet connection. As you can see here, a connection to the Internet has been configured and is working properly. (You would see a red X on the line between 'Network 4' and 'Internet' if the laptop was not connected to the Internet.)

You can also click on 'manage network connections'. Here, you can see a wireless connection to the Internet, and that it also has a strong signal.

jory	Owner	Type	Phone # or Host Ad...
			∧
			∧

Local Area Connection 3
Network 2
Sierra Wireless HSDPA Netw...

9

Using a free WiFi hot spot ▶

Find out if you have wireless hardware

1 Click on Start.

2 In the search box, type 'device manager'. Click on Device Manager under Programs.

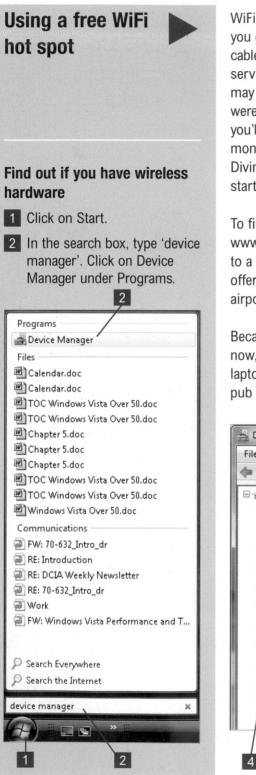

WiFi hot spots are popping up all over the world. Hot spots let you get online without having to be tethered to an Ethernet cable or tied down with a monthly wireless bill. Sometimes this service is free, provided you have the required hardware. (You may also have to buy a drink for the privilege, but hey, you were going to anyway, right?) More often than not though, you'll need a subscription or membership, which can include a monthly or a pay-as-you go fee. The Cloud, BT Openzone, Divine Wireless and iPass are all options, and you can get started from around £6.99 a month for a single device.

To find a WiFi hotspot close to you, go to www.maps.google.com.uk and search for WiFi hotspots, or go to a website such as www.totalhotspots.com. A quick search offers almost 70 in Aberdeen, in various places including airports, hotels, pubs, cafes and restaurants.

Because almost all new laptops come with wireless capabilities now, it's worth trying out. First, you need to find out if your laptop has wireless hardware before you take a trek to a nearby pub or hotel.

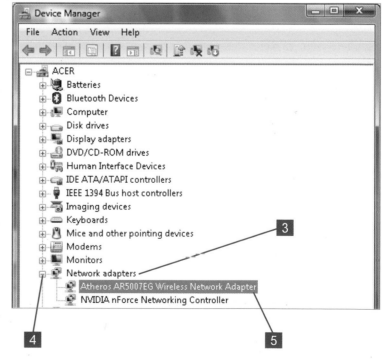

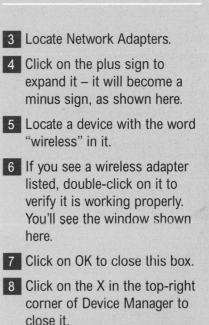

3 Locate Network Adapters.

4 Click on the plus sign to expand it – it will become a minus sign, as shown here.

5 Locate a device with the word "wireless" in it.

6 If you see a wireless adapter listed, double-click on it to verify it is working properly. You'll see the window shown here.

7 Click on OK to close this box.

8 Click on the X in the top-right corner of Device Manager to close it.

9 Note that you may find you do not have a wireless network adapter, as shown here. If you do not have one, I suggest you buy one. Take a look at the options at the start of this chapter.

9

Atheros AR5007EG Wireless Network Adapter Properties

General | Advanced | Driver | Details | Resources | Power Management

Atheros AR5007EG Wireless Network Adapter

Device type: Network adapters
Manufacturer: Atheros Communications Inc.
Location: PCI bus 5, device 0, function 0

Device status

This device is working properly.

6

No wireless device is listed **9**

Using a free WiFi hot spot (cont.)

Connecting at a hot spot

1 Turn on your wireless laptop within range of a wireless network. Generally, this will mean going into the building that offers the wireless connection, or sitting right outside.

2 You'll be prompted from the notification area that wireless networks are available.

3 Click on 'Connect to a network'. If you don't see anything, click on Start and click on Connect To.

4 If more than one wireless network is available, locate the one that you want to use. Often, this is the one with the most green bars, showing a strong signal. If you aren't sure, ask someone who is already connected, or an employee.

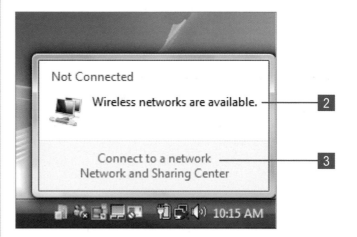

Connect to a network

Type the network security key or passphrase for ZEZ83

The person who setup the network can give you the key or passphrase.

Security key or passphrase:

☐ Display characters

If you have a USB flash drive with network settings for ZEZ83, insert it now.

Connect   Cancel

6

5

5 Click on Connect.

6 You should be connected automatically, but if you aren't, type in the required password. You'll need to ask an employee for the credentials if it's a free hot spot, or you'll need to type in your own credentials, offered by your wireless provider.

9

Jargon buster

Network adapter: hardware that lets your computer connect to a network, such as the Internet or a local network.

Working with media and media applications

Introduction

When you're on the go with your laptop, you can do more than just 'compute'. You can use your laptop as a media centre, where you can listen to music, import digital pictures, fix and email them, watch DVDs, and create your own films from footage you've taken with a digital video camera. If you have the proper hardware, you can even watch and record live TV. That said, the next time you take a holiday, bring along this book, and let your laptop replace your television, stereo and picture frame!

In this chapter we'll briefly discuss the media applications in Vista, and detail how to perform the most common tasks. Note that each application offers many more features and options; this is just enough to get you started with them.

What you'll do

Rip your CD collection in Media Player

Listen to music

Burn a CD

Import pictures from a digital camera, media card or USB drive

Fix pictures

Add picture information (tagging)

Send pictures by email

Watch a DVD in Media Player

Watch a DVD in Media Center

Burn a simple data DVD

Explore Movie Maker

Import video

Basic editing

Save your own videos

Watch live TV

Record a TV programme or series

Rip a CD in Media Player ▶

'To rip' means to copy. When you rip a CD, you copy the tracks to your laptop's hard drive. If you have a large CD collection, this could take some time, but it will be worth it. Once music is on your laptop, you can listen to it in Media Player, burn compilations of music to other CDs, or put the music on a portable music player.

Before you head off on your next trip, take time to rip your music CD collection to the laptop. To rip a CD, simply put it in the CD drive, close any pop-up boxes, and in Media Player, click on the Rip button. During the copy process, you can watch the progress. By default, music will be saved in your Music folder.

Ripping your CD collection in Media Player

1 Insert a music CD into the CD drive.

2 If any pop up boxes appear, click the X to close them. You can select to rip a CD in Media Player from the dialogue box shown here, but I'd like to introduce ripping from Media Player, not from a dialogue box, so that you can access all the options.

Rip a CD in Media Player (cont.)

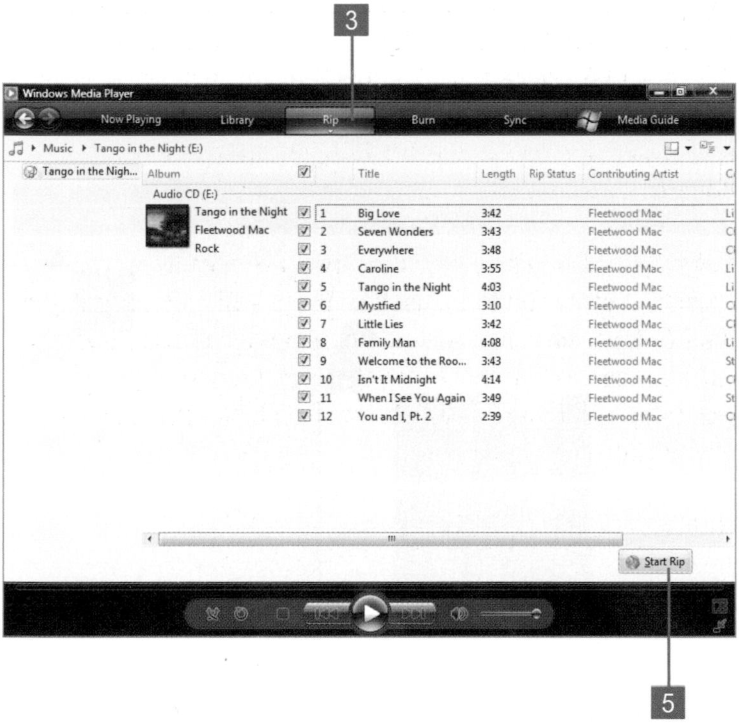

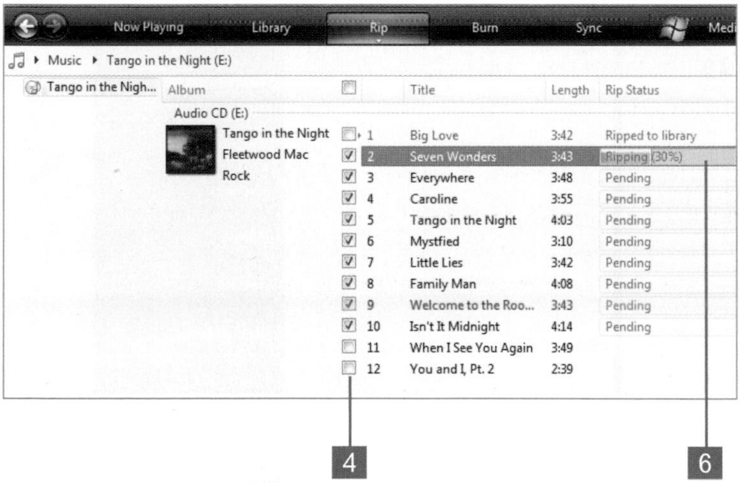

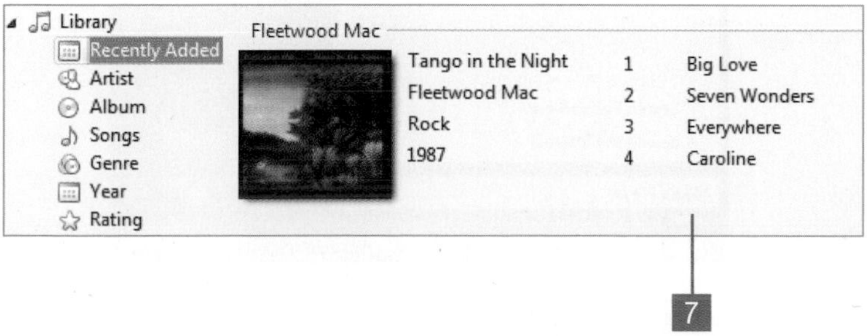

10

3. In Media Player, click on the Rip button.
4. Deselect any songs you do not want to copy to your laptop.
5. Click on Start Rip.
6. Watch as the CD is copied; you can watch the progress, as shown here.
7. The ripped music will now appear in your music library under Recently Added, as well as being listed by artist, album, songs, genre and year.

Playing music in Media Player

To play music, simply navigate to Media Player and double-click on it. Depending on what you choose, Media Player may switch to the Now Playing tab. Here, I'm playing the *Best of Beethoven* album.

Listening to music

1. Click on Start and in the search box type 'Media Player'.

2. Click on Windows Media Player in the results, listed under Programs.

Playing music in Media Player (cont.)

10

3 If necessary, click on the Category button (on the toolbar to the far right) and choose music.

4 Click on Album. (You can also click on any other category to locate a song.)

5 Double-click on any album to play it.

6 Note the control icons at the bottom of the interface. From left to right: shuffle (to play songs in random order), repeat, stop, previous, play/pause, next, mute and a volume slider. Use these controls to manage the song and to move from one song to the next.

Burn a CD in Media Player

▶

Did you know?

You can right-click on any song in the Burn List to access more options, including the option to delete the song from the list (not the laptop), or to move up or move down in the list order.

There are two ways to take music with you when you are on the road or on the go. You can copy the music to a portable device like a mobile phone or other music player (and keep it synchronised using Media Player), or you can create your own CDs, choosing the songs to copy and placing them on the CD in the desired order. CDs you create can be played in car stereos and portable CD players, as well as lots of other CD devices. A typical CD can hold about 80 minutes of music, but don't worry, Media Player will keep track of the songs you select and will let you know when you're running out of space on the CD.

The Burn tab can assist you in creating a CD. Burn is media-speak for copying music from your laptop to a CD. Clicking on Burn brings up the List pane, where Media Player will tell you to insert a blank CD if one is not in the drive, and allow you to drag and drop songs into the List pane to create a Burn List. As music is added, the progress bar at the top of the List pane shows how much space you've used.

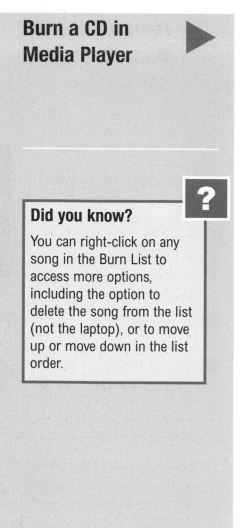

Once you've added music, the Start Burn button becomes active. Here, I'm dragging and dropping music to the List pane, something you'll learn to do in the next exercise.

Notice what's going on in this image:

- There is a CD in the drive.
- There is still 46 minutes and 23 seconds remaining on the disc.
- Songs have been added to the Burn List.
- I Ka Barra (Your Work) is being dragged to the List pane to be added to the Burn List.
- Start Burn is active, and is ready to be clicked on once all songs are added.
- Songs is selected in the Library list, making dragging and dropping simpler.

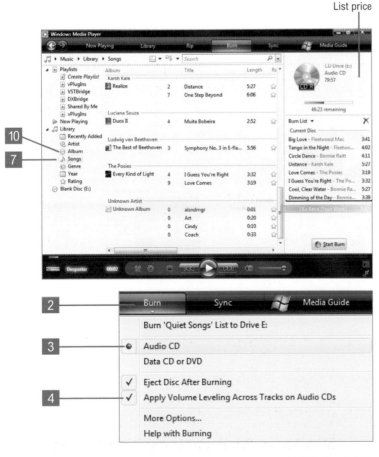

List price

Burn a CD in Media Player (cont.)

Burning a CD in Media Player

1 Open Media Player.

2 Click on the arrow under the Burn tab.

3 Check the audio CD has a dot by it. If it does not, click on it once.

4 Check that 'Apply Volume Leveling Across Tracks on Audio CDs' has a tick by it. This will make sure all songs on the CD are the same volume, and that some tracks are not louder than others.

5 Click outside the drop-down list to close it.

6 Insert a blank CD in the CD drive. (Close any pop-up boxes.)

7 Click Library, click on Songs.

8 Click on any song title to add, and drag it to the List pane.

?

Did you know?

To listen to music in a car or portable CD player, you have to burn a CD, not a DVD.

10

Burn a CD in Media Player (cont.)

9. Drop the song in the List pane to add it to the Burn List.

10. Click on Album.

11. Drag any album to the List pane to add the entire album.

12. Look at the slider in the List pane to verify there is room left on the CD.

13. Right-click on any entry to access additional options including Remove from List, Move Up, Move Down.

14. When you've added the songs you want, click on Start Burn.

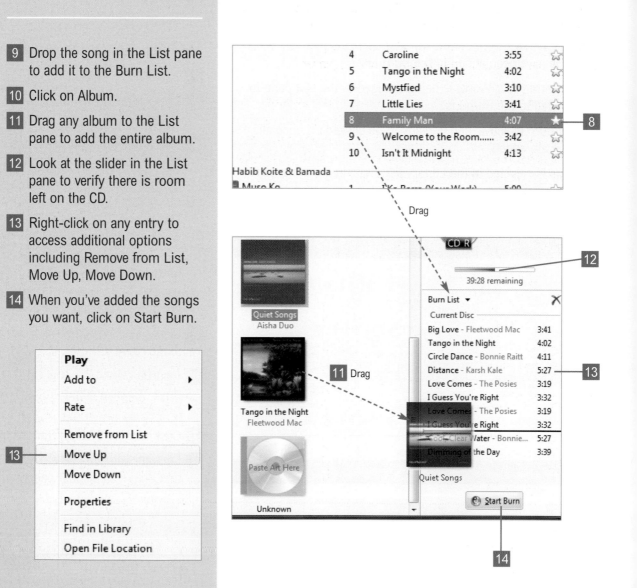

4	Caroline	3:55	☆
5	Tango in the Night	4:02	☆
6	Mystfied	3:10	☆
7	Little Lies	3:41	☆
8	Family Man	4:07	★
9	Welcome to the Room......	3:42	☆
10	Isn't It Midnight	4:13	☆

Habib Koite & Bamada

Muso Ko

Drag

CD R

39:28 remaining

Burn List ▾

Current Disc

Big Love - Fleetwood Mac	3:41
Tango in the Night	4:02
Circle Dance - Bonnie Raitt	4:11
Distance - Karsh Kale	5:27
Love Comes - The Posies	3:19
I Guess You're Right	3:32
Love Comes - The Posies	3:19
I Guess You're Right	3:32
Cool Clear Water - Bonnie...	5:27
Dimming of the Day	3:39

Quiet Songs

Start Burn

Quiet Songs
Aisha Duo

Drag

Tango in the Night
Fleetwood Mac

Paste Art Here

Unknown

Play

Add to   ▸

Rate   ▸

Remove from List

Move Up

Move Down

Properties

Find in Library

Open File Location

There are lots of options for taking digital pictures, including mobile phones, smart phones, digital cameras, webcams and video cameras. And there are even more ways to store and carry pictures with you, including USB drives, music players and iPods and iPhones. Finally, there are many ways to get pictures onto a laptop, including using digital cameras, media cards and scanners. In this section we'll talk about importing pictures from a device to your laptop. Remember, the device doesn't necessarily have to be something that takes the pictures; it can be a scanner, USB drive, media card or music player.

When you connect a camera or other device that contains pictures, you'll be prompted to select a way to import them. You may see several options, as shown here, or only three or four. Whatever the case, choose Import Pictures. This will take you through the Import Pictures and Videos wizard, outlined on the next page.

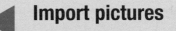

Import pictures

10

AutoPlay

Removable Disk (G:)

☐ Always do this for pictures:

Pictures options

📷 **Import pictures**
using Windows

🖼 **View pictures**
using Windows

View pictures
using Windows Media Center

Acquire image
using PowerProducer

Transfer pictures
using Media Import

Copy Disc
using Sonic Creator Copy

Import pictures and videos
using Windows Live Photo Gallery

View pictures
using Windows Live Photo Gallery

Set AutoPlay defaults in Control Panel

Import pictures (cont.)

Importing pictures from a digital camera, media card, USB drive or an iPhone

1 Connect the device. If applicable, turn it on.

2 When prompted, choose Import Pictures using Windows.

3 Type a descriptive name for the group of pictures you're importing. (For now, accept the default settings, which includes the date imported, so type a name only.)

4 Click on Import.

5 If desired, tick – 'Erase after importing'. This will cause Vista to erase the images from the device after the import is complete.

6 Open Windows Photo Gallery.

7 Click on Recently Imported. You'll see the imported images there. (See the screen here.)

Windows won't recognise all devices, but it does a pretty good job. In fact, it will import pictures from many kinds of mobile phones, including the iPhone. However, on the slim chance your device isn't recognised, you can click on File, then click on Import and you'll be given access to devices attached to your laptop such as a scanners.

Edit photos

Fixing pictures

1. Open Photo Gallery.

2. In the View pane, select Pictures.

3. Use the scroll bar to locate the picture to edit.

4. Double-click on a picture to edit. (Don't use the sample pictures because they've already been optimised.)

With pictures now on your laptop and available in Windows Photo Gallery, your next step is likely to be editing. As noted earlier, Photo Gallery offers editing options, including the ability to correct brightness and contrast, colour temperature, tint and saturation, as well as crop images and fix red eye. You may find, after a bit of time with Photo Gallery though, that you need more options. If that turns out to be the case, consider Photoshop Elements. It's great for beginners and offers all you'll probably need.

To begin editing a picture, first double-click on it. From the Edit pane that appears you can choose from:

- Auto adjust: automatically assesses the image and alters it, which, most of the time results in a better image. If not, there's always the Undo button.

- Adjust exposure: offers slider controls for brightness and contrast. You move these sliders to the left and right to adjust as desired.

- Adjust colour: sliders control the temperature, tint and saturation of the photo. Temperature runs from blue to yellow, allowing you to change the 'atmosphere' of the image. Tint runs from green to red, and saturation moves from black and white to colour.

- Crop picture: removes parts of a picture you don't want.

- Fix red eye: lets you draw a rectangle around any eye that has a red dot in it, and the red dot is automatically removed.

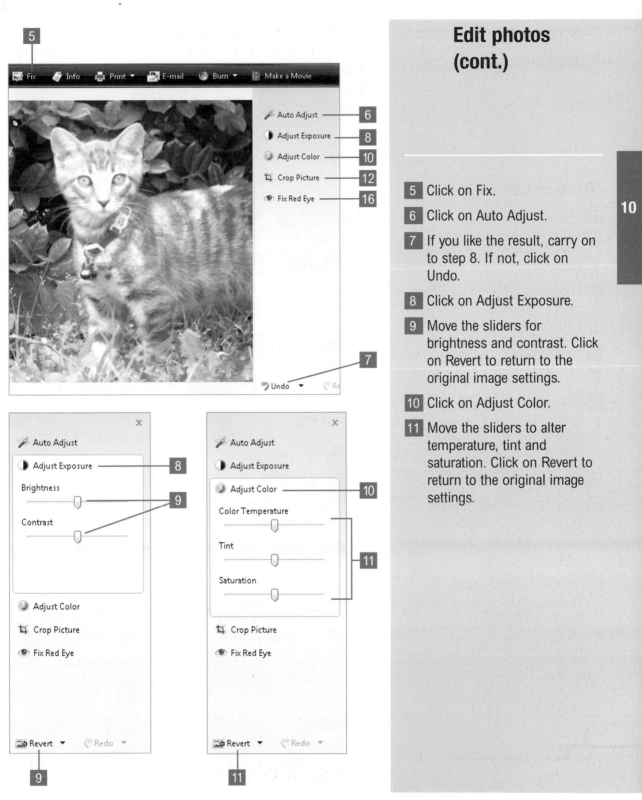

Edit photos (cont.)

5 Click on Fix.

6 Click on Auto Adjust.

7 If you like the result, carry on to step 8. If not, click on Undo.

8 Click on Adjust Exposure.

9 Move the sliders for brightness and contrast. Click on Revert to return to the original image settings.

10 Click on Adjust Color.

11 Move the sliders to alter temperature, tint and saturation. Click on Revert to return to the original image settings.

Edit photos (cont.)

12 Click on Crop Picture.

13 Drag the corners of the box to resize it, and drag the entire box to move it around in the picture.

14 If desired, under Proportion, select any option. (Note you can also rotate the frame.)

15 Click on Apply or Revert.

16 Click on Fix Red Eye.

17 Drag the mouse over the red part of the eye. When you let go, the red eye in the picture will be removed.

18 Click on Undo if desired.

19 To save the changes to the original file, i.e. write over the existing file, click on Return to Gallery.

20 To revert to the original picture, click on File, and then Revert to Original.

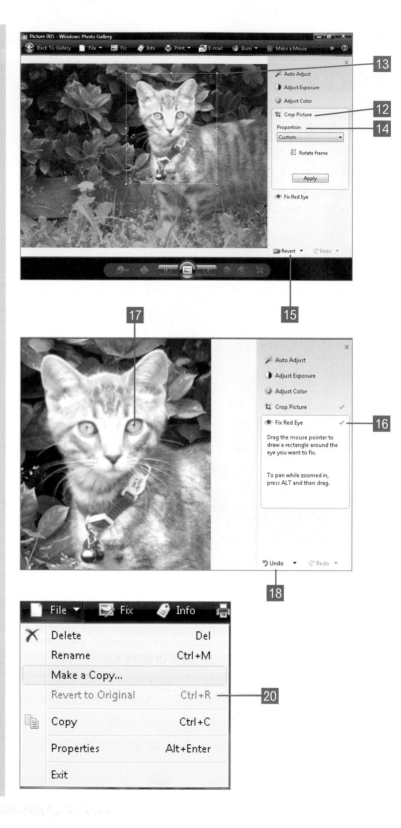

Tags

Tags are useful for organising your photos. Tags are words you assign to pictures that tell you something about them. You have to apply tags to your photos though, which can take time, but once added, tags can be used to group pictures. Some tags are applied automatically when you import pictures from a digital camera, including the date they were uploaded, along with any name you applied to the imported group. While the date is important, tagging a photo (or a group of photos) with a label such as wedding, cat, Italy trip, or similar is a great addition.

Edit photos (cont.)

Adding picture information (tagging)   10

1 Open Photo Gallery.

2 Double-click on any picture.

3 Click on Add Tags.

4 Type a tag name.

Although there are several ways to add tags to photos, the easiest, in my opinion, is to create the tag in the View pane, and then select a photo or a group of photos, and drag those photos to the new tag name. The tag will be applied to those photos. Alternatively, you can select a photo, and in the Info pane click on Add Tags, or right-click on any photo or group of photos and select Add Tags.

Edit photos (cont.)

5 Press Enter on the keyboard.

6 To remove the tag (or any other tag), right-click on the tag.

7 Click on Remove Tag.

8 Click on Back to Gallery.

Back To Gallery

9 Right-click on tags.

10 Click on Create Tag.

Pictures can have several tags. You might tag a photo as 'holiday', but also apply tags that name the people in the picture. To remove a tag, select the picture or pictures that have the tag, and in the Info pane, right-click on the tag and select Remove Tag.

Another type of tag is a rating. You can rate pictures from one to five stars, and then filter the pictures as desired. You can add captions too. All of this can be done from the Info pane, among other places.

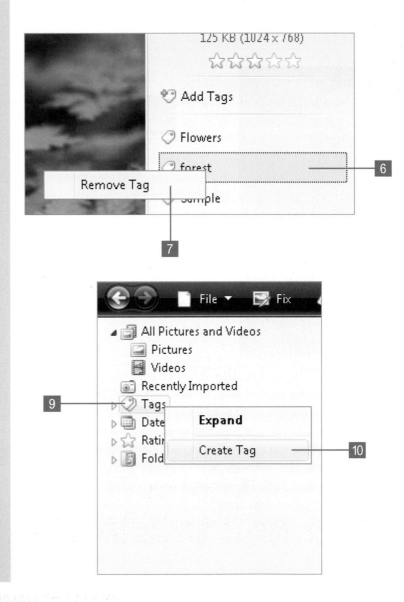

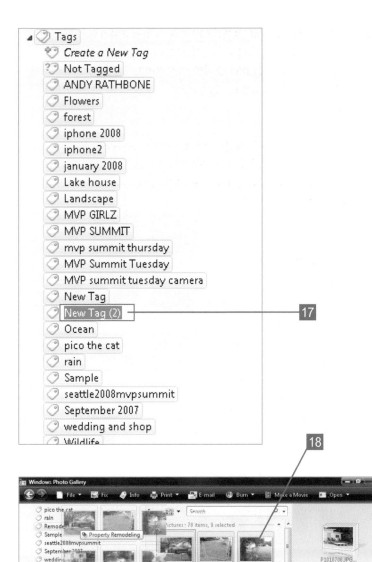

10

17 Type a tag name. (To rename a tag, right-click on the tag and choose Rename.)

18 Locate an image to apply the tag to. Select several images if desired. Hold down the Shift key to select images next to each other, and hold down the Ctrl key to select images dotted around the screen.

19 Drag the selected image(s) to the new tag in the Tags list.

Working with media and media applications 215

Edit photos (cont.)

20 Click on the tag name under Tags, to see the images.

21 To apply a rating, double-click on any picture, or select a group of pictures. In the Info pane, click on the rating.

22 Repeat step 21 to add a caption. (Click on Add Caption.)

There are many ways to show your photos. You can look at them on your laptop, send them to others and burn them to CDs and DVDs, to name a few. And, you know (if you've worked through this book from the beginning) how to do most of this already. Here are a few ideas:

- Use a photo as a Desktop background: in Photo Gallery, right-click on any photo and choose Set as Desktop Background.

- Use a slideshow of your photos as a screen saver: open Appearance and Personalization, and choose Screen Saver. For the screen saver, select Photos. Click on Settings to choose the folder to use.

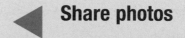

Share photos (cont.)

- Print pictures using a photo printer: click on Print in Photo Gallery. Note you can also order prints from websites, such as Boots and Jessops.

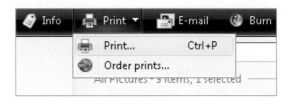

- Add pictures to a video using Movie Maker: from Photo Gallery, click on Make a Movie. You can also browse for pictures from an existing Movie Maker project.

- Burn a DVD of pictures with the DVD tools: from Photo Gallery, click on Burn and Video DVD.

- Send photos by email: in Photo Gallery, select the files to send, click on E-mail, and when prompted, choose either small or medium (for best results). Click on Attach.

Sending pictures by email

1 Open Photo Gallery.

2 Select pictures to send.

3 Click on E-mail.

4 Select a picture size. For email, generally 800 x 600 is best. It's small enough to be sent and received quickly, even on dial-up. The larger the image, the longer it will take to send and receive.

5 Click on Attach.

6 Type the recipient's name(s).

7 Consider rewriting the subject.

8 Consider deleting the text and writing your own in the body of the email.

9 Click on Send.

10

Watch DVDs

You can watch a DVD on your computer just as you would at home. In fact, some people now use their laptops as a 'media centre' connected to a large flat-screen TV. Laptops built as media computers have television, DVRs, DVD players, music players, speakers, surround sound and more, installed and ready to use. That said, it's certainly possible to watch a DVD on your laptop; it's one of the most basic entertainment options.

The first time you insert a DVD into the drive, you'll be given at least one of the options shown here: Play DVD movie using Windows Media Player; and Play DVD movie using Windows Media Center. You'll see more options if you have software installed on the laptop that can also play DVDs. Here you can see a third option, Play Movie using Play Movie (that came with this laptop and has nothing to do with Vista).

To watch a DVD, simply make a choice. Once the video has started, you'll have access to controls such as fast forward, pause, rewind, stop, resume and volume. Here you can see an exercise video that's just about to start in Media Player.

Here's the same film in Windows Media Center. The controls are very similar to Media Player's controls, except there are options for changing the channel, and a few more fast-forward and rewind controls.

If you have Home Premium or Ultimate, start out with Media Center the first time you watch a DVD. If not, Windows Media Player will do just fine.

Watch DVDs (cont.)

Watching a DVD in Media Player

1. Find the button on the outside of the laptop that opens the DVD drive door. Press it.

2. Place the DVD in the tray and press the button again to close it. (Often you can lightly push the door, but not always, so it's best to use the button.)

3. When prompted, choose 'Play DVD movie using Windows Media Player'. If you are not prompted, and the DVD opens in another application, that's fine if that's what you want to use. If not then:

a. Press the Stop button in the application, the Esc key on the keyboard, and/or click the X in the right corner of the window to close the application. There may also be a File menu, where you can select Close.

b. Click on the Start button.

c. Click on Computer.

d. Right-click on the DVD drive icon and click on Open AutoPlay.

Important

If you inserted the DVD and it simply began to play, and were not offered a choice regarding what program to use, click on Start, click on Computer, right-click on the DVD drive icon and click on Open AutoPlay. You'll be offered the choices you saw earlier.

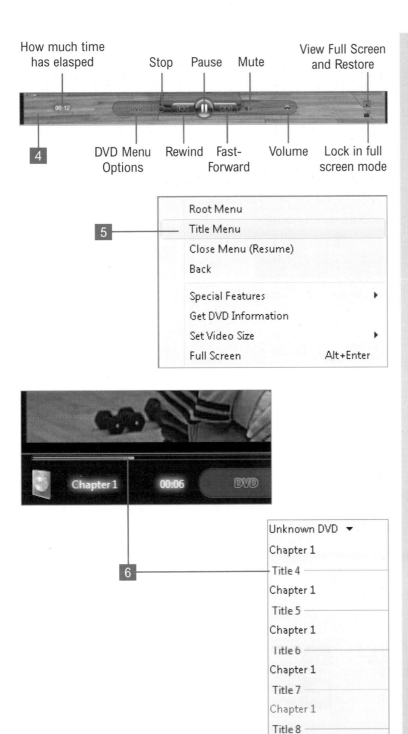

How much time has elasped

Stop

Pause

Mute

View Full Screen and Restore

4

DVD Menu Options

Rewind

Fast-Forward

Volume

Lock in full screen mode

5

Root Menu

Title Menu

Close Menu (Resume)

Back

Special Features ▶

Get DVD Information

Set Video Size ▶

Full Screen   Alt+Enter

Chapter 1   00:06   DVD

6

Unknown DVD ▼

Chapter 1

Title 4

Chapter 1

Title 5

Chapter 1

Title 6

Chapter 1

Title 7

Chapter 1

Title 8

Chapter 1

Title 9

Chapter 1

e When prompted, choose 'Play DVD movie in Windows Media Player'.

4 The film may start automatically, or you may be prompted to choose from a menu. Options may include play movie, and view special features. Use the controls to manage the film. Media Player controls are outlined here.

5 To return to the Title menu, or the menu shown when you input the DVD, click on DVD and chose the title menu.

6 To skip around in the DVD, either move the slider or choose a title from the Media Guide pane.

Watch DVDs (cont.)

Watching a DVD in Media Center

1 Find the button on the laptop that opens the DVD drive door. Press it.

2 Place the DVD in the door and press the button again to close it.

3 When prompted, choose 'Play DVD movie using Windows Media Center'. If you are not prompted, and the DVD opens in another application, that's fine if that's what you want to use. If not then:

a Press the Stop button in the application, the Esc key on the keyboard, and/or click the X in the right corner of the window to close the application. There may also be a File menu, where you can select Close.

b Click on the Start button.

c Click on Computer.

d Right-click on the DVD drive icon and click on Open AutoPlay.

e When prompted, choose 'Play DVD movie using Windows Media Center'.

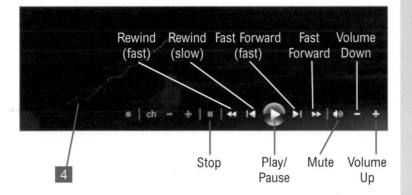

Rewind (fast) Rewind (slow) Fast Forward (fast) Fast Forward Volume Down

Stop Play/ Pause Mute Volume Up

4

4 The video will start automatically. The controls that you need to understand to manage DVD playback are outlined here.

10

Burn a data DVD

If you want to copy data from your computer to a DVD, you can do so in virtually any window that contains data. Here is a Pictures folder, and you can see the Burn icon on the toolbar. To burn a DVD, simply select the data you want to copy and click this icon. When prompted (and the DVD door will open automatically), insert a blank DVD, type a title for it, and click on Next. If anything else is required, you'll be prompted.

Burning a DVD is a great way to back up the data on your laptop when you're away from home. If anything happens to the laptop, at least you'll have your holiday snaps on a DVD!

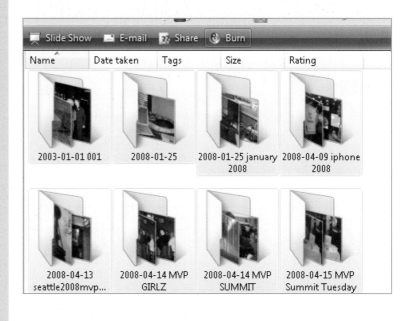

This process is normally reserved for backing up data (vs. creating a DVD you will share with others), because there are no options to create menus, scenes or otherwise give the DVD a professional look. If you want to create a DVD to watch on a TV set using a DVD player, it's best to use Windows DVD Maker. We won't cover that program in this book, but there's information in the help pages in Vista if you want to use it.

4

Name	Date modified	Type
Accessibility	5/17/2008 10:05 AM	File Fol
Attachments	5/16/2008 10:44 AM	File Fol
Calendar	5/16/2008 10:44 AM	File Fol
Create new Email Addr...	5/16/2008 10:44 AM	File Fol
Delete Browsing History	5/17/2008 9:48 AM	File Fol
Favorites	5/17/2008 9:18 AM	File Fol

3

E-mail   Share   Burn

Burn a Disc

Prepare this blank disc

Disc title: May 22 2008

7

○ Live File System - Allows you to add and erase files, like a USB flash drive. Might not be readable on operating systems before Windows XP.
Change version

○ Mastered - Readable on all computers and some CD/DVD players. Requires you to write all files at once, and individual files can't be erased afterwards.

Which CD or DVD format should I choose?

Hide formatting options   Next   Cancel

8

Burning data to a DVD

10

1. Click on Start.

2. Click on Documents (or select Pictures, your personal folder or any other folder that contains data you need to back up).

3. Select the data to burn to the DVD. To select a continuous run of files or folders in a list, hold down the Shift key while selecting. To select several files or folders spread around the screen, hold down the Ctrl key and click on each one.

4. Click on Burn.

5. Insert a writeable disk into your DVD drive.

6. Click on the arrow next to 'Show formatting options'.

7. Depending on the type of DVD burner you have and the type of disk you inserted, you may be prompted to select a file system type, as shown here.

8. Click on Next.

Burn a data DVD (cont.)

9 For the most part, that's it. If a window pops up and says that files are waiting to be burned to a DVD, click on the message and click on Burn again. Otherwise, simply wait for the process to complete. (The DVD will eject when the burn is complete.)

10 You can also insert a blank, writeable or rewriteable DVD, and wait for a prompt to burn data to it. You can burn data to a disk using Media Player, Windows, DVD Maker, and any programs you have installed.

If you choose to burn data using Windows, you'll work through the same process detailed here. If you choose Media Player, you'll be prompted to drag music from your music, picture or video libraries to the Burn List. And if you choose Windows DVD Maker, the application will open where you can select the data to add to the DVD.

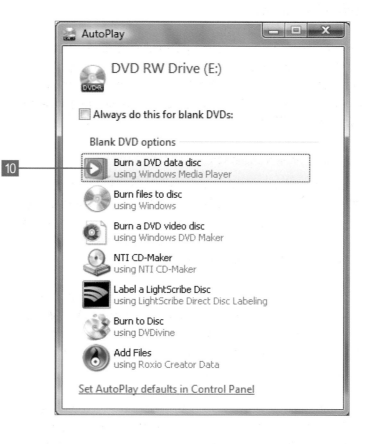

For your information

You'll have to decide what kind of DVD you want to burn. I prefer the default, Live File System for backing up data if it's offered, because I can add data on the fly to the same disk later. I use Mastered for creating DVDs I'll play using CD and DVD players.

If you have a digital video camera, it probably came with an installation CD-Rom and perhaps a program for uploading and editing footage you take with the camera. If you bought a new laptop from a manufacturer with Vista installed, you may have other movie-making software as well. Vista comes with its own software for working with video you shoot yourself too; it's called Movie Maker.

With Movie Maker, you can import video footage you take yourself, photos, music, audio files and TV shows you recorded in the media centre. With the data imported, you can then edit the video, add transitions and effects, and create your own films on DVD.

The Movie Maker interface

You open up Movie Maker from the Start, All Programs list. You can also type Movie Maker into the search window. As with DVD Maker, your laptop will have to meet some minimum requirements to use the program, and you can be certain you'll be prompted if your laptop doesn't meet them.

Movie Maker is divided into three sections: menu and toolbars, the panes in the middle, and the storyboard/timeline at the bottom. Several menus sport common title names, including File, Edit, View and Help, and some that are not so common, such as Tools, Clip and Play.

Interestingly, you don't have to use the menus as often as you'd think; you can do almost anything you want from the Tasks pane. As you can see here, there's an Import section where you can take in footage from a digital video camera, videos already on your laptop, pictures, and audio or music. Once data is imported, you then work through the editing options to add effects, cut footage, or add titles and credits. With the editing complete, you move to the publishing options.

You'll learn more about the interface features, including the storyboard (and timeline), preview pane and menus, as we move through this part of the chapter. First, you need some data to work with, then the additional interface features will be more intuitive and easier to understand.

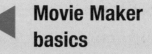

Movie Maker basics

10

Movie Maker basics (cont.)

Did you know?

You can also drag media files into the Imported Media pane from any open window that contains the data.

Importing data

Importing data is the first step in Movie Maker. However, you can't just use anything. You can't import data from certain television channels, such as pay-per-view channels, or data you've 'rented' or purchased from iTunes or similar sources. You can't import data from a DVD, and there are a few types of data Movie Maker doesn't like at all, such as Apple QuickTime. However, there are plenty of data types you can import, including video you take with your own video camera and TV shows you record on non-premium channels and sources. As you might guess, you click the Import Media button to do this.

Editing data

Storyboard mode is the default for Movie Maker, and it's great for adding transitions and effects (once editing is complete), but for editing data, for example, removing unwanted footage from imported video or commercials from a TV show, you're going to want to use Timeline mode. To switch from Storyboard to Timeline mode, you click the Storyboard button and choose Timeline from the menu.

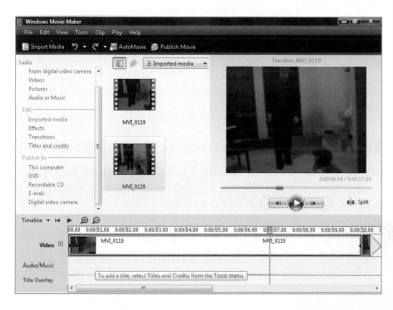

Here's what the timeline looks like. Imported data must be dragged here. (No video has been imported in this clip.)

With the timeline selected, you'll drag the imported video into it. Once it's on the timeline, you can edit its length, by removing video from the beginning, middle or end. You can even add more video as desired.

Movie Maker basics (cont.)

Here are some tips to enhance your video:

- Use the timeline and the play button to move to the beginning of the footage you want to use. Then, click on Split to mark the video, select the first part of the split, and delete the unwanted footage.

- Remove adverts from a recorded TV programme (or unwanted footage from the middle of a home video) using a similar technique. Use the play button to locate the beginning of the unwanted footage, click on Split, and repeat for the end of the unwanted video. Then delete the entire block of video just split from the others.

- Use a transition to move between clips. Fading in and out are often used for the beginning and end of videos, while dissolve, heart, page curls and others are common for moving among pictures.

- Add special effects to your videos, such as fade out to end a wedding video, or any of the zoom effects to focus on a part of the image before moving to the next.

- Add titles and credits at the beginning and ends of your films. You can also add titles before clips you designate.

Publishing the film

Until you publish it, your film is just a project. Once published, it becomes a film. (Then it can't be edited. It's done.) The publishing options are located in the Publish To section in the Task pane. No matter what options you choose, Movie Maker will help you with a wizard.

There are four publishing options, the first is 'Publish to this computer'.

1 Publish to a computer

Select this option when you want to save your video so it can be watched on a laptop or a portable media device. There are two formats:

- AVI (Audio Video Interleave): a high quality, highly compatible format that requires a lot of disk space. Choose this when you have plenty of disk space and for archival purposes (it's the more compatible of the two options).

- WMV (Windows Media Video): for viewing on Microsoft-compatible devices only. Users of iPods and iPhones won't be able to watch the final product. On the upside, it offers lots of video setting options and uses less space than AVI. Choose this option when sharing the video with people who you know have Microsoft-compatible mobile devices, or for viewing using Microsoft XP, Media Center and Vista laptops. Note that since you have more video options, you have a better chance of fitting the data on the desired media (like a DVD or CD).

Without going into every publishing option, note that the setting you choose should reflect who you want to watch it with, and how. The default settings for 'Publish to this computer' is 'Best quality for playback on my computer (recommended)'. Note though, you can choose to compress to a specific amount of MB, or you can choose from the More Settings options, especially if you are limited regarding the amount of hard disk space your video can consume.

'More settings' options differ depending on what edition of Vista you're running, and as you click on each one, the settings for that option appear underneath the choice. Here I've selected Windows Media Portable Device, and you can see the display size (640 x 480), aspect ratio (4:3), estimated space required (1681 KB), and estimated disk space on the laptop I'm working on (30.08 GB).

The setting you select determines the quality and file size of your movie:

- Best quality for playback on my computer (recommended)
- Compress to: 3 MB ▾ •
- More settings: Windows Media Portable Device (1.0 Mbps) ▾

Movie settings

File type: Windows Media Video (WMV)
Bit rate: 1.0 Mbps
Display size: 640 x 480 pixels
Aspect ratio: 4:3
Frames per second: 30

File size

Estimated space required:
1681 KB

Estimated disk space available on drive C:
30.08 GB

Movie Maker basics (cont.)

Importing video, pictures and music to Movie Maker

1 Connect your digital video camera and set it to the playback setting (or something similar), if applicable. If you do not have a digital camera or footage, you can work through this exercise using sample video included with Vista, or video already saved to your laptop.

2 Click on Import Media.

3 Under Favorite Links, browse to the location of the video to add. (You can repeat these steps to add still pictures later if you want to. Still pictures are often used at the beginning and end of videos, but you can add them anywhere.)

Consider saving the file on your hard drive in AVI, if you have enough hard drive space to do so. Save it again to send it to others on DVD, and perhaps a third time for adding to an email. Although, for email, you'll have to shorten the video drastically, because they can be large.

2 Publishing to DVD or CD

If you want to publish directly to DVD, Movie Maker will save the project and close Movie Maker, and open DVD Maker for burning the DVD. You learned how to use DVD Maker earlier, so if that's the route you want to go, refer to that section as necessary.

Publishing to CD isn't a great option. First, CDs only hold 700 MB or so of data, which isn't much video. The quality isn't great either, and many DVD players don't play CDs anyway. However, if you only have a CD burner and your recipient has a CD player on their laptop, it can be done.

3 Publishing for email distribution

You can send your video via email, but remember, ISPs set limits on how large a file you can send, and how large a file your recipient can receive. That said, Movie Maker will make sure the final video is 10 MB or less, so the quality of the video will suffer unless it's really short. Also, you can only attach the movie to an email, play the movie in Media Player, or

For your information

In the first image, I've browsed to video taken with my digital video camera. It's connected to the laptop and turned on. In the second image, I've browsed to the Sample Videos folder in my personal videos folder. Note that you can also browse to data on a memory card.

save a copy of it to the computer when it's finished, not giving you a lot of options. But, if you want to send a clip of your dog playing dead after you shoot it with a pretend gun, and send it to your kids, it may just be the ticket.

4 Writing back to a digital video camera

You can copy the film back you your video camera. You may want to do this to create a back-up copy, or if you want to take

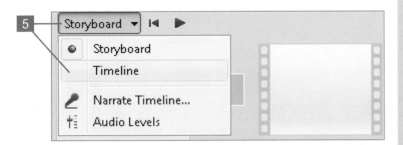

4 Verify that Imported Media is selected in the middle pane, and locate the imported media. There are two imported videos here, one from my digital camera and the Bear video from the Sample Videos folder.

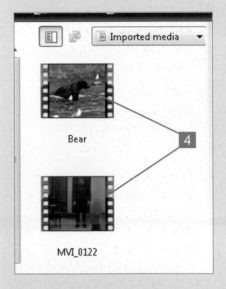

5 Click on Storyboard, and select Timeline at the bottom of the Movie Maker interface.

Movie Maker basics (cont.)

the camera with you and show the film on a TV that is not also equipped with a DVD player. DV cameras connect to TVs easily, and playing them on a laptop only requires you browse to the correct input on the remote control, usually Video 1 or Video 2.

6 Drag the video from the middle pane and drop it on the timeline.

7 Repeat steps 4–6 to add other pictures and video.

8 To add music to your video, click Import Media again.

9 In the Favorites Links pane, select Music.

10 In the Music folder, select the song to add.

11 Drag the music track to the audio/music part of the timeline.

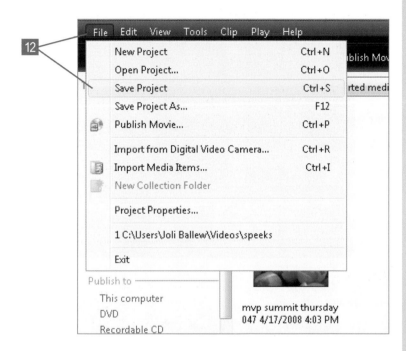

12 Click on File, and click on Save Project.

13 Type a name for the project and click on Save.

10

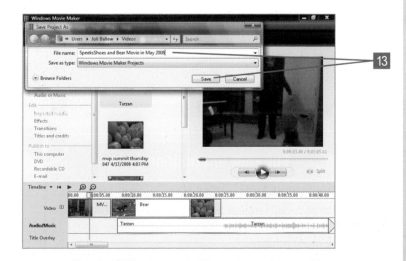

Working with media and media applications 237

Movie Maker basics (cont.)

Editing basics

1. After importing the media file and dragging it to the timeline, click on the beginning of the video footage. The green bar should appear at 00.00 if a video is the first clip on the timeline.

2. To remove video from the beginning of a clip:

   a. Click on the Play button until you reach the point in the Preview window where you want the actual film to begin.

   b. Click on the same button to stop at the exact point where you want the film to begin.

   c. Click on Split.

   d. Click on the first part of the split on the timeline.

   e. Hit the delete key on the keyboard. That part of the video will be removed.

For your information

To remove unwanted video in a video clip that appears in the middle of a clip, repeat the steps here, creating a split before and a split after the unwanted video, and delete the middle clip.

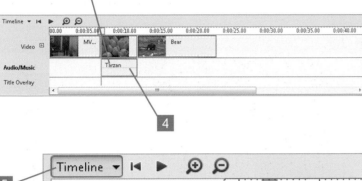

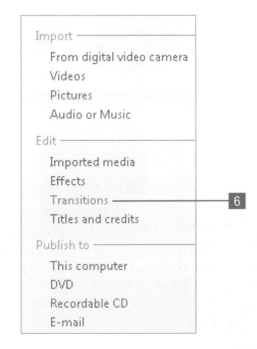

10

3 If you added music, drag the music clip on the timeline so it starts at the exact point in the video you desire. For instance, you may not want music over a clip that contains its own music, or when people are talking. Here, I've put music over a picture clip.

4 Drag the music clip to shorten it.

5 Click on Timeline, and select Storyboard.

6 Under Edit, click on Transitions.

Movie Maker
basics (cont.)

7 Select a transition and drag it to the area between two clips on the Storyboard.

8 Notice the transitions in between clips. You can remove any transition by right-clicking this area.

9 If you added a picture, click it. If not, select a video clip. We'll add an effect (which you can later remove if desired).

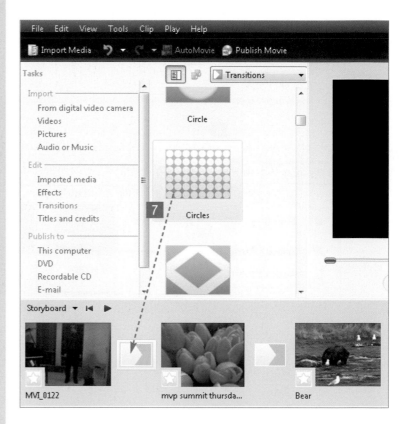

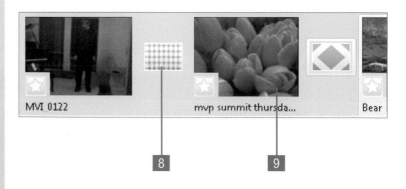

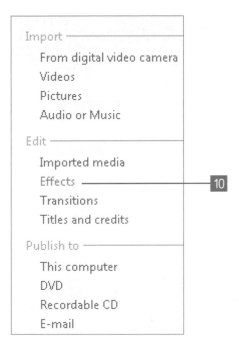

Import
  From digital video camera
  Videos
  Pictures
  Audio or Music

Edit
  Imported media
  Effects ——————————— 10
  Transitions
  Titles and credits

Publish to
  This computer
  DVD
  Recordable CD
  E-mail

10 Under Edit, click Effects.

11 Drag any effect on to a picture or video clip. As with transitions, you can right-click to remove. (Right-click, click on Effects, select the effect to remove, and click on Remove.)

12 Click on Play in the Preview pane. Use the slider to move to the beginning of the video if necessary. Preview the video.

13 Repeat any steps here to edit the video further. Note you may need to switch to timeline mode again.

14 Click on File, Save Project when complete.

10

Movie Maker basics (cont.)

Adding titles and credits

1 Click on 'Titles and credits'.

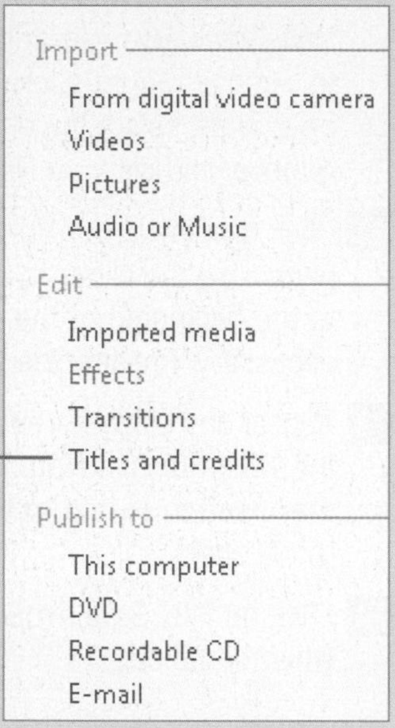

Import ─────────
   From digital video camera
   Videos
   Pictures
   Audio or Music

Edit ─────────
   Imported media
   Effects
   Transitions
1 ─── Titles and credits

Publish to ─────────
   This computer
   DVD
   Recordable CD
   E-mail

2 To add a title to the beginning of a video, click on 'Title at the beginning'.

3 Enter the text that should appear for the title. You must do this or the option to Add Title will remain in grey and you won't be able to proceed.

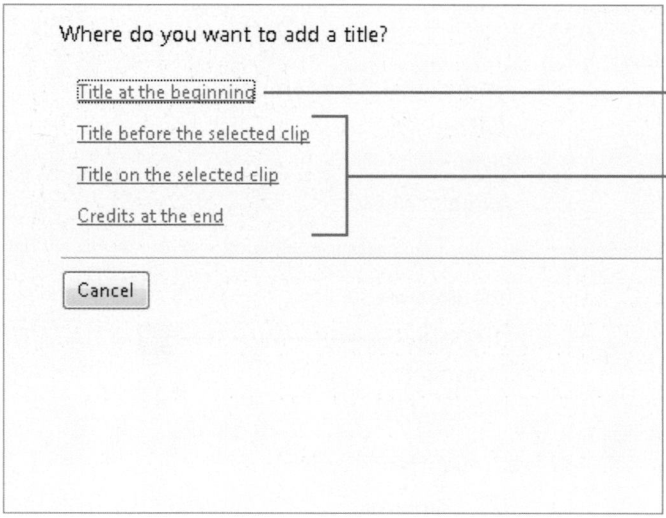

Where do you want to add a title?

Title at the beginning ─── **2**

Title before the selected clip
Title on the selected clip ─── **9**
Credits at the end

Cancel

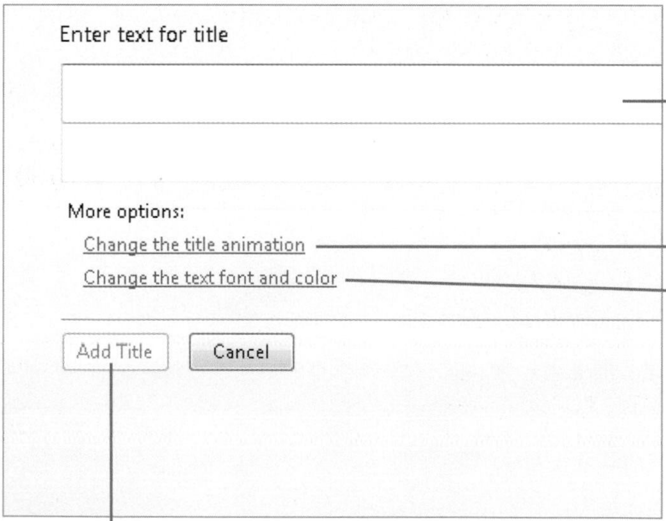

Enter text for title

─── **3**

More options:
   Change the title animation ─── **4**
   Change the text font and color ─── **6**

Add Title   Cancel
8

10

4 If desired, click on 'Change the title animation'.

5 Select an animation from the choices offered.

6 If you want, click on 'Change the text font and color'.

7 Configure the font, colour, transparency, position and other options as desired.

8 Click on Add Title.

9 To add additional data, such as a title before a selected clip, on a selected clip, or to add credits to the end of the film, repeat these steps.

7

8

Movie Maker basics (cont.)

Publishing videos

1 With a video project open, imported, edited and saved, click on Publish Movie.

2 Make a publishing choice.

3 Click on Next.

4 If you selected 'This computer':

a Type in a file name.

b Select a folder to publish to. By default it's the videos folder. It may be best to leave it that way.

c Click on Next.

d Select a video setting. Refer to the information earlier in this chapter to make the proper choice.

e Click on Publish.

5 If you selected DVD:

a Click on OK when prompted to save your video and close Movie Maker, and open DVD Maker.

b Work through DVD Maker as outlined earlier in this chapter.

File   Edit   View   Tools   Clip   Play   Help

Import Media   AutoMovie   Publish Movie

Publish Movie

Where do you want to publish your movie?

This computer
Publish for playback on your computer

DVD
Publish for playback on your DVD player or computer

Recordable CD
Publish for playback on your computer or device that supports WMV files

E-mail
Send as an e-mail attachment using your default e-mail program

Digital video camera
Record to a tape in your DV camera

How do I publish a movie?

Next   Cancel

Publish Movie

Name the movie you are publishing

File name: SpeeksShoes May 2008 Roger has not called back about board meeti

Publish to: Videos   Browse...

Next   Cancel

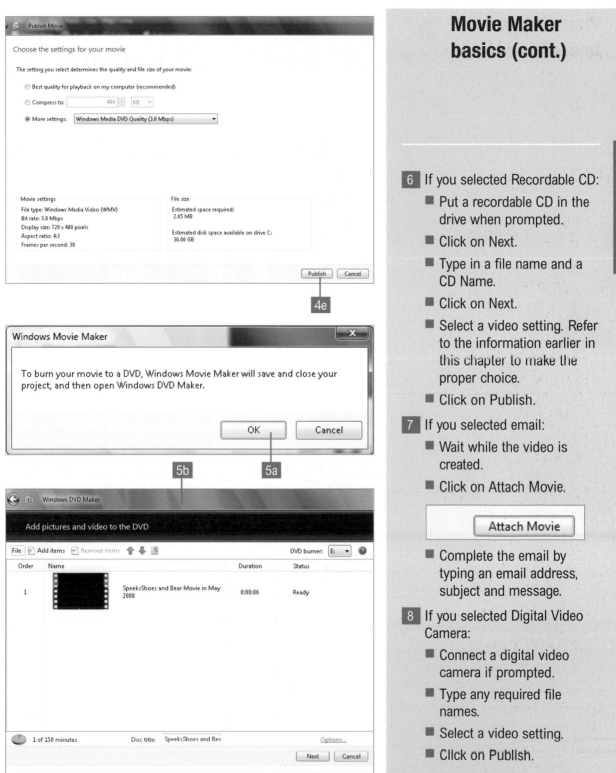

Movie Maker basics (cont.)

6 If you selected Recordable CD:
- Put a recordable CD in the drive when prompted.
- Click on Next.
- Type in a file name and a CD Name.
- Click on Next.
- Select a video setting. Refer to the information earlier in this chapter to make the proper choice.
- Click on Publish.

7 If you selected email:
- Wait while the video is created.
- Click on Attach Movie.

> **Attach Movie**

- Complete the email by typing an email address, subject and message.

8 If you selected Digital Video Camera:
- Connect a digital video camera if prompted.
- Type any required file names.
- Select a video setting.
- Click on Publish.

Watching live television

When you're watching TV, you'll see the broadcast, of course, but other items will appear and disappear, seemingly at will. As you can see here, the channel number as well as the show's name (among other things) appear, as do familiar controls. The show's broadcast information appears when you change to the channel, and you can also bring it up by right-clicking in that area of the screen. When you right click you'll not only get the show information but other options as well.

As you can see, there are six options:

■ Program Info: displays a screen where you can record the programme, the series and see information about the show.

■ Record: starts recording the current programme.

■ Record Series: starts recording the current programme and schedules the series to be recorded.

■ Zoom: changes the way the picture is displayed.

■ Mini Guide: information about the programme in a minimal format (compared with Program Info).

■ Settings: opens Media Center settings.

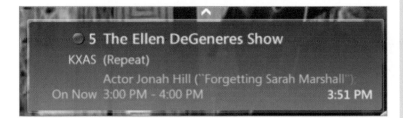

5 The Ellen DeGeneres Show
KXAS (Repeat)
Actor Jonah Hill (`Forgetting Sarah Marshall`)
On Now 3:00 PM – 4:00 PM   3:51 PM

There are also TV controls. These appear when you move your mouse to the bottom of the screen, if you press specific buttons on a remote control or keyboard, and in a few other instances. With these buttons you can:

■ Record the show you are watching.

■ Change the channel using the minus and plus buttons.

■ Stop watching TV.

■ Rewind quickly or more slowly using one of the two rewind buttons.

■ Pause (and then play) live TV.

■ Fast forward slowly or more quickly.

■ Turn the sound off. Mute the TV by clicking the Mute button.

The X here next to the speaker symbol means the volume is muted.

■ Decrease or increase the volume using the minus and plus buttons next to the speaker.

You can pause up to 30 minutes of Live TV. After 30 minutes, the broadcast becomes unpaused and starts playing again – from where you paused it. When you close Media Center or change the television channel, the 30 minutes of saved television is deleted. Pausing is great for skipping through commercials. Just pause the TV for a while at any point, and when commercials come on, simply fast-forward through them.

Watching live television (cont.)

Watching live TV

1 Open Media Center.

2 Click on TV + Movies

3 Click on Live TV.

4 Experiment with the channel up and down buttons.

5 Click on Pause. Wait a few minutes.

6 Click on Play.

7 Turn the sounds on and off.

8 Change the volume.

9 Fast-forward and rewind.

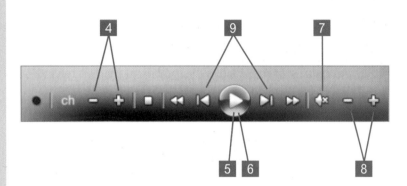

There are a lot of ways to access the commands to record a programme or series. As you learned in the previous section, you can right-click on the bottom left of a live TV show to access these commands. You won't always want to record what you're watching though; you will probably want to record something that is coming on later in the week. That's what the guide is for. And while there are several ways to access the guide, the most straightforward is from the TV + Movies menu you're already familiar with. (You can also open the guide using a remote control or media keyboard if you have one.)

You move through the guide using the arrow keys on your keyboard, using a scroll wheel on a mouse, or using a remote control. You can click with the mouse on these arrows to move through the guide as well. The arrow will appear when you hover the mouse over that particular area of the screen.

Record television (cont.)

You can access more options for a programme by clicking on it. Clicking on a programme offers the options shown here, including the option to record.

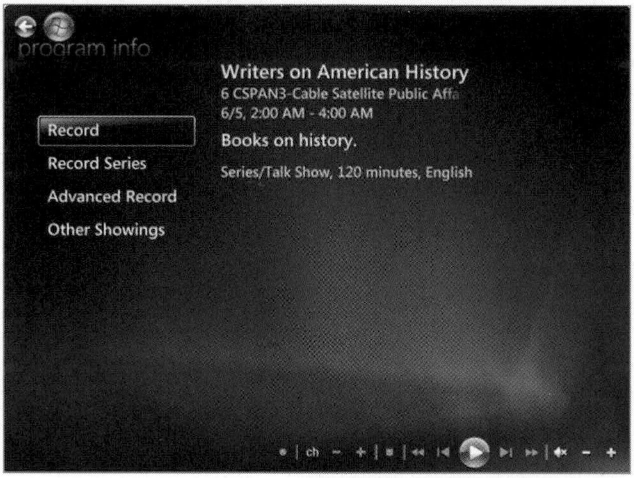

The four settings shown here offer the following options:

- Record: schedule a television show to record the next time it is broadcast. Once scheduled to record, a red dot will appear in the guide for that programme.
- Record series: schedule an entire series to record. As with record, a red dot will appear in the guide for that programme.
- Other showings: this offers future broadcasts of the show.
- Advanced record: sets advanced recording settings including frequency, stop, quality and keep.

Important

Remember, you can always click the back arrow (it will appear when you hover the mouse over the top left corner) to return to the previous screen.

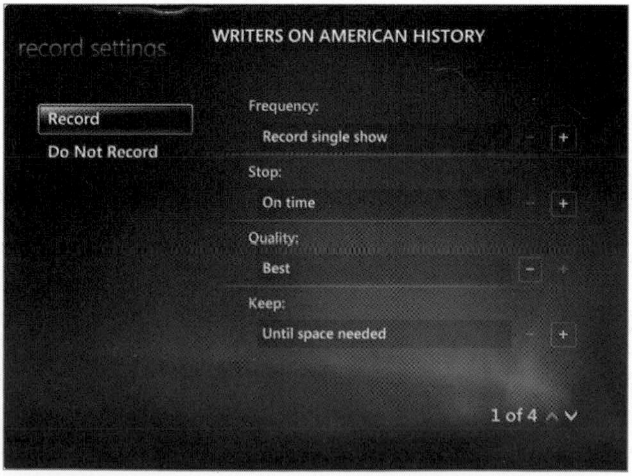

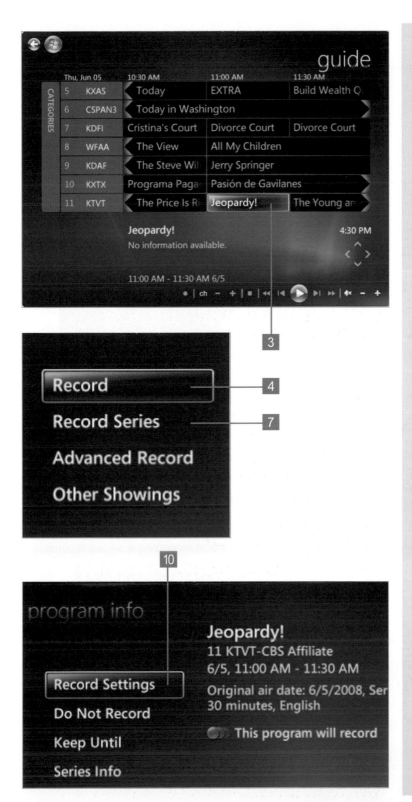

Recording a TV show or series

1. Click on TV + Movies and scroll right to the guide.

2. Use your mouse, arrows on the keyboard, or another method to locate the show to record.

3. Click on the programme.

4. Select Record.

5. To record a series, locate the series to record.

6. Click on the programme.

7. Select Record Series.

8. To configure advanced settings, look for the show that's scheduled to record. It will have red dot by it.

9. Click on the programme.

10. Click on Record Settings.

Record television (cont.)

11 To change the setting for a specific episode, click on 'Settings for this episode only'. To apply changes to a series, use 'Settings for the entire series'.

12 Work through the options to configure them. Here you can see settings for a series. Click on the plus and minus signs to change a setting.

13 Click on the Back arrow (it will appear when you hover the mouse over the top left corner) to return to the previous screen. Repeat as needed.

There are additional options that you'll see from time to time:

■ 'Do Not Record' cancels the scheduled recording or series.

■ 'Keep Until' lets you choose how long to keep a recording and when to record over it.

■ 'Series Info' shows information regarding a series recording.

■ 'Recording Conflicts' appears when two shows are scheduled to record at the same time. (When a conflict occurs during the recording process, you'll be prompted to choose one or the other.)

Important

When in doubt, right-click a recording or programme. You can almost always access options to record, stop a recording or access information.

Watch a recorded TV show

To watch a television show you've recorded, simply browse to TV + Movies, Recorded TV, and click on the recorded show you want to watch! As you can see here, you can also add a recording, view scheduled recordings and browse by title.

Jargon buster

Clip: a piece of video footage.

DV: digital video, generally used as DV camera.

Import: to bring files on to the computer from another source, such as a digital video camera.

Publish: to change a video project in progress into a film that can be viewed by others in its final form.

Split: to turn one clip into two or more smaller clips.

Transition: a way of moving from one clip to another, such as fading in or out.

Video format: the video file type, such as AVI or WMA.

Instant and video messaging

Introduction

You've probably heard about text messaging, instant messaging and video messaging, but have yet to explore these technologies. All three offer a way to communicate quickly with others. Text and instant messaging require you to type your message and click on a send button. It's similar to email, but it's instantaneous; the recipient gets the message right after you send it. Instant messaging generally means text communications between two or more computers; text messaging is between two mobile phones. That said, in this chapter we'll use the term instant messaging when discussing all these types of communications.

Video messaging is like instant messaging, but one or both users also offer live video of themselves during the conversation. This is a great way to communicate with grandchildren who live far away, because you can see them and they, you. As such technology becomes more widespread, you may soon be able to talk to your doctor using a web camera and live video feed, a pharmacist, a travel agent, or even a computer technician. It's best to jump on this bandwagon now, so you'll be ready when anyone else is.

Regarding instant messaging, you may be wondering why you wouldn't simply send an email or make a phone call. You've probably seen kids texting on their phones and wondered the same thing. Well, email can take a few minutes to arrive, and if you want to the recipient to answer right away (say within the

What you'll do

Download and install Live Messenger

Get a messenger account

Sign in

Add a contact

Instant messaging basics

Set up a microphone

Send a voice clip

Have a PC-to-PC phone conversation

Install a webcam

Have a video conversation

For your information

Instant messaging and video messaging take place over the Internet and do not require a land line (unless you use a dial-up modem to get online). Video quality is directly proportional to the speed of your Internet connection.

next few seconds), instant messaging is the best option. Instant messaging is like a text-based CB radio. You send a message, and the recipient acknowledges and responds instantly. As for mobile phones, well, they aren't all they are cracked up to be. A phone call can be disruptive; the phone may ring while a person is in a meeting, when the recipient has his or her hands full, or when it's awkward to accept a call (like in a restaurant or driving). Teachers aren't fond of mobiles ringing either. Instant messaging lets you get your message across instantly and quietly. (Text messaging is usually done between mobile phones, but you can send text from your computer to a mobile if you like.)

The best option for instant messaging, especially if you want to use video messaging, is Windows Live Messenger. Live Messenger doesn't come with Vista though, but it is a Microsoft product and is fully compatible. It's easy to acquire too, and I'll show you how.

With Live Messenger you can:

- Communicate instantly using text, voice or video with anyone who has compatible software. Your children and grandchildren probably already do.

- If the people you want to reach are not there, whatever you type will be displayed the next time they log on.

- You can set your status when online. You can choose to be online, busy, right back, away, in a call, out to lunch, appear offline, or you can sign out. Anyone who you use instant messaging with will see your status when they go online.

- You can see each other's files, photos and videos using a shared folder. Others can access these to see what you put there.

- You can make phone calls to friends, family and contacts without paying long distance rates. You can make video calls or PC-to-PC calls to anyone with a messenger account.

- You can get instant alerts for sports, traffic, weather, news and just about anything else you can think of.

You can't use these features until you install Live Messenger. If you've never downloaded anything before, fear not. This is one of the easiest downloads around.

◄ **Get Live Messenger**

11

Get Live Messenger (cont.)

Downloading and installing Live Messenger

1. Click on Start.

2. Click on Internet to run your web browser.

3. In the address bar, type www.microsoft.com (the 'http//' will be added automatically: in fact, you can leave out the 'www.' as well).

4. In the search window on the Microsoft home page, type 'Download Windows Live Messenger'.

5. Press Enter on the keyboard.

6. Click on the link to download Live Messenger. It will probably be the first link in the list.

7. Click on Download.

Windows Live Messenger (Version 2008)

Brief Description

Connect, share, and make your conversations count.
Windows Live Messenger has a fresh new look, but it's still got all the features you love.

On This Page

↓ Quick Details
↓ System Requirements
↓ Related Resources

↓ Overview
↓ Instructions
↓ What Others Are Downloading

Download

Quick Details

File Name: WLinstaller.exe

Get Live Messenger (cont.)

8 When prompted, click on Open.

9 Click on Accept.

10 Before clicking on Install, deselect every option, unless you want to change your default search engine, change your home page, or help improve Windows Live.

11 Click on Install.

11

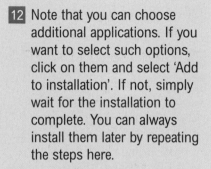

12 Note that you can choose additional applications. If you want to select such options, click on them and select 'Add to installation'. If not, simply wait for the installation to complete. You can always install them later by repeating the steps here.

13 Once Messenger has finished installing, click on Start Messenger.

Select any additional products you want to install.

☑ **Writer** (5 MB) - Easily publish rich content to your blog

☑ **Family Safety** (3 MB) - Help keep your family safe online

[Add to installation]

Learn more about these products

[Close]

12

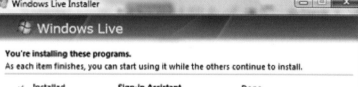

Windows Live Installer

Windows Live

You're installing these programs.
As each item finishes, you can start using it while the others continue to install.

| ✓ | Installed | **Sign-in Assistant** | Done |
| ✓ | Installed | Start Messenger | Done |

For your information

You'll be instructed to start Live Messenger throughout this chapter. You can do this a number of ways: double-clicking on the Messenger icon in the notification area of the taskbar; from the Start>All Programs list; by typing Messenger in the Start Search dialogue box and selecting the program from the results. You may also have a shortcut to the program on your desktop.

To use Messenger you'll need a Windows Live ID. This is an email address that you get from Microsoft. If your email address ends in @hotmail, @msn or @live, you already have one. Also, older MSN accounts are compatible. If you don't have any of these, you'll need to get one. Once you have a Windows Live ID, often called a Passport, MSN or Hotmail account, you will use it to sign in to Messenger.

When you get a Live ID, you have to offer up personal information such as your name, gender, birth year and place, and have to rely on Microsoft to keep this information private. While I am happy to let Microsoft have such details, you should check the company's terms of use and privacy statements for yourself. You can find these, as with most websites, at the bottom of the home page.

Configure Live Messenger

Getting a Live ID

1 Live Messenger should be running from the installation in the previous section. If it isn't, open it up.

2 Click on 'Sign up for a Windows Live ID'. (That is, if you don't already have a Hotmail or Live email address.)

3 Click on Sign In.

4 Type in the required information, and click I Accept when finished. (Make sure to write down the information somewhere.)

5 If prompted for any other information, or to let Microsoft or its partners contact you via email, read carefully and choose the desired responses. I suggest you choose not to receive email from anyone.

11

Configure Live Messenger (cont.)

Signing in

1 Open Messenger.

2 Type your Live ID and password in the designated areas.

3 If you want the laptop to 'remember' you, remember your password, and/or sign you in each time you start your PC, click the desired options. Don't click these on a public computer, such as one at a library or an Internet café, but you can select this on a home PC (if everyone who uses the PC has their own account and your identity and password can remain private).

4 Click on Help.

5 Click on 'Show the menu bar'.

6 Click on Sign In.

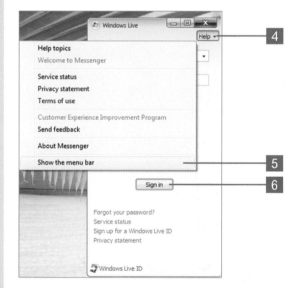

To communicate using Live Messenger, you have to add people as a 'contact'. That means you have to know their instant messaging ID. You won't know their password, and no one will know yours, but this ID is the key to adding people you want to communicate with. That said, you're going to have to know someone with a compatible instant messaging ID and a messenger application to continue with this chapter.

After you've added a contact, a notification will be generated to the person you want to add. If the person agrees to be a contact, he or she will appear in your contact list. If the person rejects your offer, you will not be able to communicate using the program.

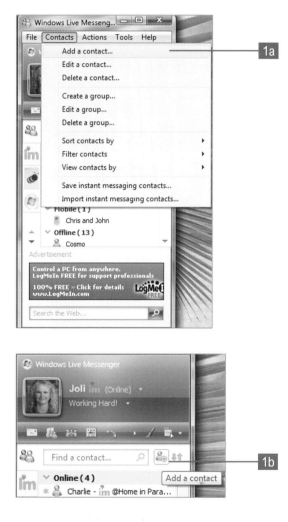

Configure Live Messenger (cont.)

Adding a contact

1 There are two ways to get started when adding a contact:

a Click on the Contacts menu, and then click on 'Add a contact'.

b Click on the 'Add a contact' button.

11

Did you know?

If you are unsure about compatability, email or call the person you'd like to add, and ask them if they use a messenger program that's compatible with Windows Messenger programs. If they say yes, ask for their instant messaging address.

Configure Live Messenger (cont.)

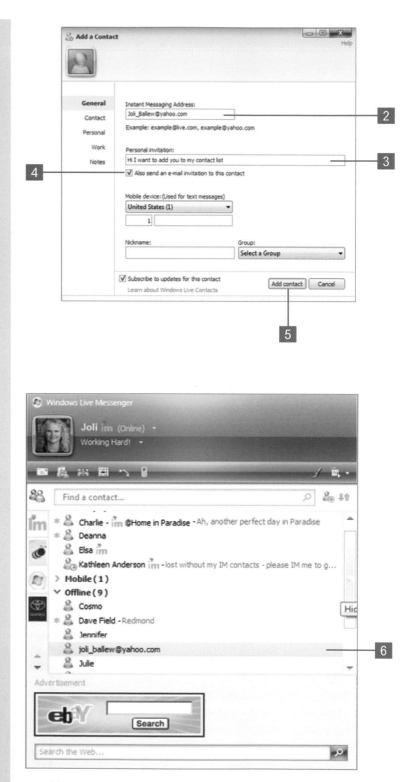

2 Type the contact's instant messaging address. Remember, the address could end in @hotmail, @live, @msn or @yahoo. However, there are other addresses that will work, and there are other programs that are compatible with Windows Live Messenger.

3 Type a personal invitation, if you want.

4 Tick 'Also send an e-mail invitation to this contact'. This is important because if the email address you add is not compatible with Windows Messenger, at least the recipient will receive an invitation through their email.

5 Leave the rest of the data blank and click on 'Add contact'. (You can add more information later if you want to.)

6 Notice the new contact name in the Window Live Messenger interface. The new contact will appear to be 'offline' until the contact approves of your request (sent in step 5).

Windows Live Messenger

Joli "komen (joli_ballew@hotmail.com) has added you to his/her contact list.

Do you want to:

○ Allow this person to see when you are online and contact you

○ Block this person from seeing when you are online and contacting you

Remember, you can make yourself appear offline temporarily to everyone at any time.

☑ Add this person to my contact list.

View Profile   OK   Cancel

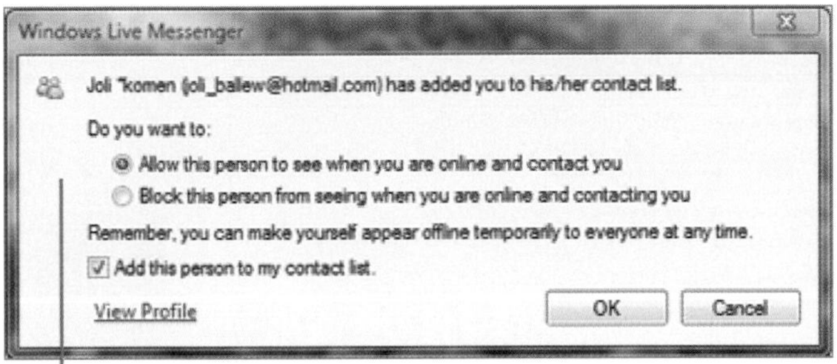

7

7 Your contact-to-be will receive a notification like the one shown here. If the recipient allows it, the next time he or she is online and logged on to their messenger service, you'll see their name in the Live Messenger contact list.

11

Windows Live Messenger

File Contacts Actions Tools Help

Windows Live Messenger

joli_ballew@yahoo.... (Online) ▾
<Enter a personal message> ▾

Find a contact...

① You have 1 pending request.

∨ Online (1)

Joli im - Working Hard!

Advertisement

Free Salary
Calculator »   cbsalary.com

Search the Web...

For your information

When people add you as a contact you will receive a message like the one shown here. You will need to click on Allow if you know the person. Be careful, you won't know everyone who sends you an invitation. Only allow those people you know.

Messaging

Once you've downloaded, installed, signed in and added a contact, you're ready to instant message! To start, simply double-click on a contact in your list. You'll want to choose someone who is 'online', designated in green (vs. grey). This opens a window similar to what's shown here. Just type your message in the bottom pane and click on Send (or press Enter on the keyboard), and wait for the contact to respond.

However, as you might have guessed, all of the menus at the top of this window are full of options. Here are some options you may want to explore:

- File: click on Save to save the conversation. Click on 'Send a single file' to transmit a file via Messenger.

- Edit: click on Cut, Copy, Paste, Delete or Select. Click on Change Font to select a different typeface for the conversation. You can even select a font colour and size.

- Actions: invite someone else to join the conversation (this is not an option when using a webcam). Click on Call to make a phone call to another computer or a phone. Calling a computer is free; calling a land line is charged by the minute and you have to sign up for the service. Click on Video to start a video call, show your webcam in a current conversation or view a contact's webcam. You can personalise Messenger to change the background.

- Tools: to change the size of the text, use audio and video options to set up a microphone and/or webcam, and click on 'Webcam settings' to tweak your installed webcam. Use Options to configure your preferences.

Instant Messaging basics

1 Open Messenger.

2 Click on the down arrow for Show Menu.

3 Click on Contacts.

4 Click on 'Sort contacts by'.

5 Click on Status. (This will group your contacts by who is online and who is not.)

11

Messaging
(cont.)

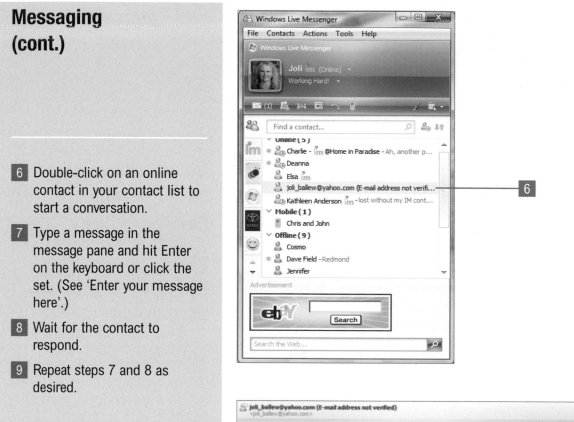

6 Double-click on an online contact in your contact list to start a conversation.

7 Type a message in the message pane and hit Enter on the keyboard or click the set. (See 'Enter your message here'.)

8 Wait for the contact to respond.

9 Repeat steps 7 and 8 as desired.

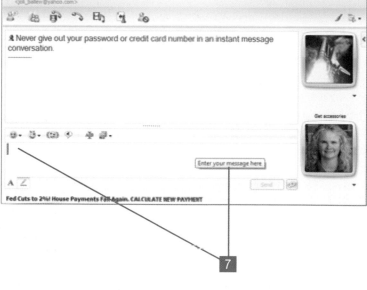

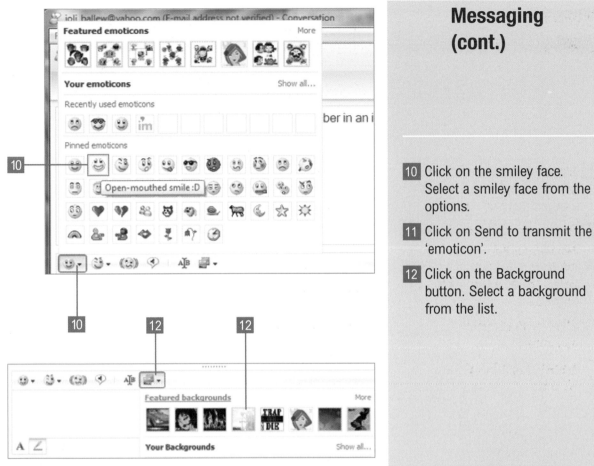

10 Click on the smiley face. Select a smiley face from the options.

11 Click on Send to transmit the 'emoticon'.

12 Click on the Background button. Select a background from the list.

11

Messaging (cont.)

13

13 Click Actions, and click on 'Invite a contact to join this conversation'.

14 Select a contact to add. Note you cannot have several contacts in a video conversation, only a text conversation.

Actions	Tools	Help

Invite a contact to join this conversation...   — **13**

Send a single file...
Create a sharing folder
Send a nudge
Send a wink...
Send an e-mail message
Share the current background

Call   ▶
Video   ▶
Start an activity...
Play a game
Request remote assistance

Personalize Messenger   ▶

Add to contacts
Block

Click on a contact to select it

To invite others to this conversation, select one or more contacts or enter e-mail addresses in the results list.

Find a contact...

14

☐ Charlie - im @Home in Paradise
☐ Deanna
☐ Elsa im
☐ joli_ballew@yahoo.com (E-mail address not verified)
☐ Kathleen Anderson im

OK   Cancel

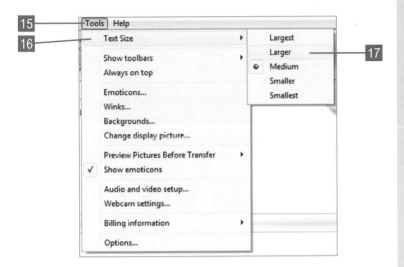

15 Click on Tools.

16 Click on Text Size.

17 Select a text size.

18 Carry on experimenting.

11

Voice and video communications

You can have voice communications with your contacts using a microphone and speakers or a combination headset. Voice communications between PCs are free (calling from your PC to a land line requires a fee). As you know, if you have a webcam you can also include video. For both, quality depends on the speed of your Internet connection. However, even if your connection is too slow to support a high-quality video or voice conversation, you can still send and receive voice clips. If nothing else, a voice clip of your little grandchild saying 'grandma' is pretty cool.

Before you can use voice and/or video with Messenger you'll need to set up a microphone and speakers (note that this may be a headset, or this hardware may be included inside a laptop, among other configurations), and a webcam. That requires you work through the audio and video setup wizard. You can find the link to this from the Tools menu. Once the microphone, speakers and/or webcam is working properly, you can then send voice clips and have voice and video conversations.

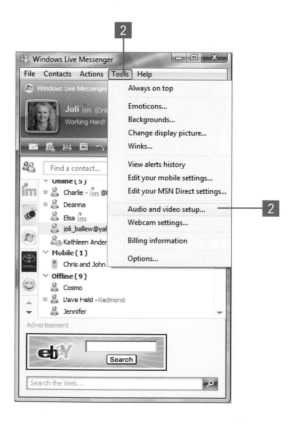

Set up a microphone and webcam

1 Plug in the microphone, speakers, webcam and/or headset, if necessary. The microphone may be built in, or it may be part of a webcam setup, or it could be configured in myriad other ways. If there's any software for these items, you must install it first. For that, you'll need to insert the CD that came with the device(s) and work through the set-up program before continuing. (If you aren't sure, just follow the directions here. You'll know soon enough if the hardware is installed.)

2 Click on Tools, and click on Audio and Video Setup.

3 In the Getting Started page, make sure you've followed the directions to close programs that play sound or display video, and that your speakers, microphone and webcam (if applicable) are plugged in.

4 Click on Next.

11

Instant and video messaging 273

Voice and video communications (cont.)

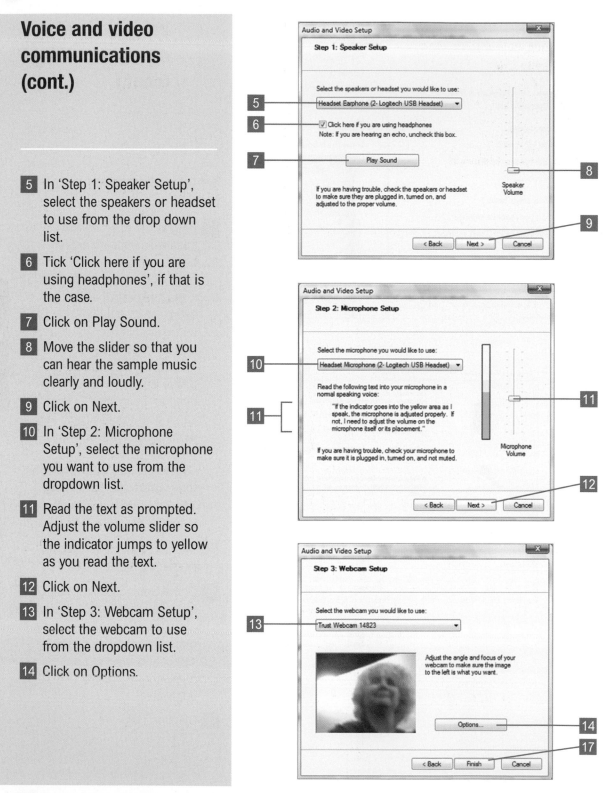

5 In 'Step 1: Speaker Setup', select the speakers or headset to use from the drop down list.

6 Tick 'Click here if you are using headphones', if that is the case.

7 Click on Play Sound.

8 Move the slider so that you can hear the sample music clearly and loudly.

9 Click on Next.

10 In 'Step 2: Microphone Setup', select the microphone you want to use from the dropdown list.

11 Read the text as prompted. Adjust the volume slider so the indicator jumps to yellow as you read the text.

12 Click on Next.

13 In 'Step 3: Webcam Setup', select the webcam to use from the dropdown list.

14 Click on Options.

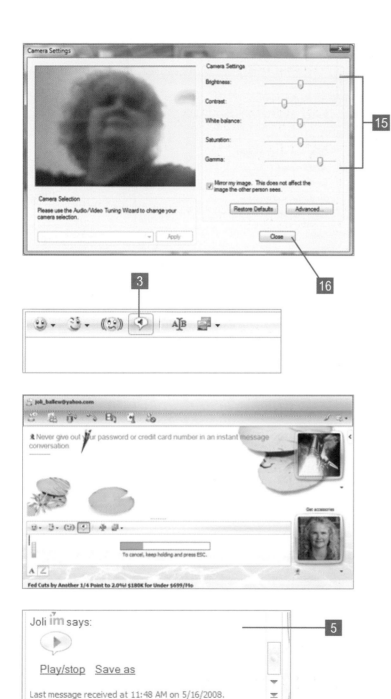

Voice and video communications (cont.)

15 Configure brightness, contrast and other settings to match your needs.

16 Click on Close.

17 Click on Finish.

Send a voice clip

1 Open Live Messenger.

2 Double-click on an online contact in your list to start a conversation.

3 Find the Voice Clip icon. It's next to the smiley faces. But don't click on it.

4 Click on and hold the Voice Clip icon to record your clip. Release when finished. (Alternatively, use the F2 key.)

5 The recipient will be prompted to play the clip to hear it.

11

Voice and video communications (cont.)

Have a PC-to-PC phone conversation

1 Work through the audio and video set-up wizard if you have not already.

2 Double-click on a contact in your list who is online and who has the required hardware to hold a voice conversation (microphone, speakers and/or headphone).

3 Click on Actions.

4 Click on Call.

5 Click on Call computer.

6 You will have to wait for your contact to click on Answer.

7 After your contact has answered the call, you will see 'Call connected' on your screen. Note 'Hang up' is also available.

8 Speak into your microphone and the person on the other end will hear you. They can speak too, and you both can communicate for free, using voice.

9 Click on 'Hang up' when finished.

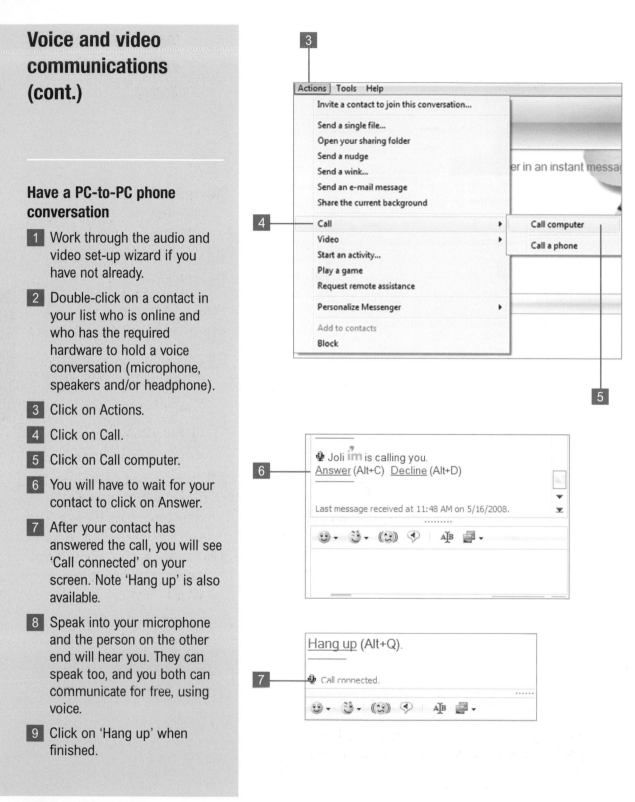

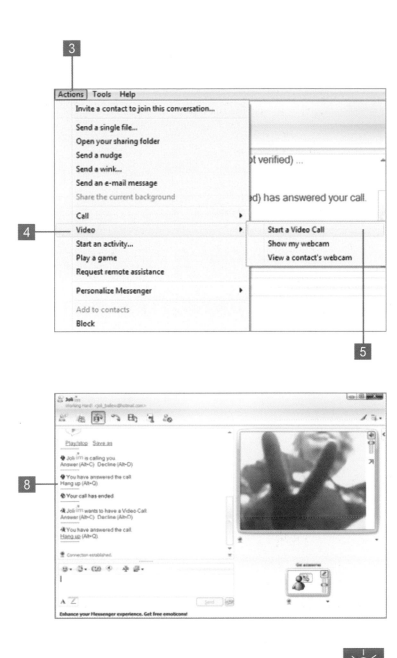

Having a video conversation

1. Work through the audio and video setup wizard if you have not done so already.

2. Double-click on a contact in your list who is online, and, who has the required hardware to hold a video conversation (webcam, microphone, speakers and/or headphone).

3. Click on Actions.

4. Click on Video.

5. Click on Start a Video Call.

6. As with a voice conversation, the contact will have to click on Answer to accept the call.

7. During the call, the contact will see your webcam. If the recipient has a webcam, you will see theirs.

8. As with a voice call, either person can click Hang up to end the call.

11

Jargon buster

Webcam: a camera that can send live images over the Internet.

Emoticon: a graphic used to show emotion such as a smiley face, a face with a frown, etc. Most emoticons are faces.

The Mobility Center

Introduction

Mobility Center is only available on mobile PCs and offers features just for users that are on the go. If you own a laptop or notebook computer, Tablet PC, Smart PC or Ultra-Mobile PC, you've got easy access to power management options, wireless features, presentation capabilities, battery status and synchronisation options.

Many of these features will prove useful, and you'll access them often, including selecting a power plan from the notification area to improve battery life, using presentation settings when playing a slide show or managing some other type of production, and easily turning off wireless capabilities when on an airplane (while still being able to use your computer). All of these options and more are available from the mobility window.

What you'll do

Explore the Mobility Center

Extend e-battery life

Turn on and off wireless connectivity

Turn on presentation settings

Access synchronisation settings

Use the Sync Center

Connect an external display

For your information

In this chapter, I use terms such as portable PC, portable computer, notebook, laptop and even, occasionally, Tablet PC to describe mobile computers running Vista. For the most part, these terms are interchangeable in the context of this chapter unless stated otherwise.

Although Mobility Center was created for business users, you don't have to be at work to take advantage of the features. Say you're on a plane, and the captain comes on the speaker and tells you it's safe to use electronic devices, provided you turn the wireless feature off. You can do that in Mobility Center. While there, you may also want to dim the screen to increase battery life, turn off the speaker so you don't bother the person sitting beside you, and perhaps check updates on a mobile device while you have the time.

When you open the Mobility Center you'll see several squares that contain various features:

- Brightness: use the slider to adjust your display. This will only change the brightness temporarily. It will not change the brightness as it is configured in Control Panel's power settings.

- Volume: use the slider to adjust the volume or the PC speakers, or tick the mute box.

- Battery status: see how much life is left in your battery. You can also change power plans here.

- Wireless network: turn the adapter on or off.

- Screen rotation: if you are using a Tablet PC, you'll have this option. Use it to change the orientation from portrait to landscape, or vice versa.

- External display: if you're giving a presentation, such as a PowerPoint birthday or a slide show, you can connect another monitor to your laptop to show the presentation. With a secondary monitor, people won't have to crowd around your laptop.

- Sync Center: creates a partnership with a device or synchronises files between your laptop and another device.

- Presentation settings: turn off the screen saver, change the speaker volume and select a new desktop background image. You can also access other connected displays.

Did you know?

You may see settings not listed here, supplied by your computer manufacturer. These will be specific to your mobile PC and are not part of the mobility settings in Vista.

12

Explore Mobility Center (cont.)

Exploring Mobility Center

1. Click on Start.

2. In the search dialogue box, type Mobility.

3. Click on Windows Mobility Center under Programs.

4. Move the slider for brightness to the left to dim the display; to the right to brighten it.

5. Tick Mute to turn off all sound, or move the slider to the left to lower the sound.

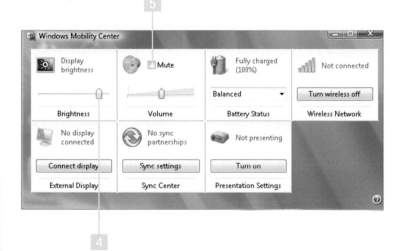

There are lots of ways to improve battery life, although some are more obvious than others. You can lower the display brightness in Mobility Center, opt for a power-saving power plan and turn off animated effects, to name a few. You can change how and when the laptop sleeps or goes into hibernation. You can also choose the Vista Basic rather than Windows theme. The easiest way to conserve battery power and improve battery life though is to use the Power Saver plan, which is available in Mobility Center (among other places).

For your information

Power Saver reduces performance, but if you really need to make your battery last, say for a four-hour flight, this is the option to choose.

Extend battery life

Extending battery life

1 Open Mobility Center.

2 Click on the down arrow for battery status to select the power saver plan.

12

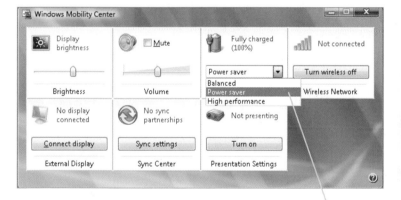

Extend battery life (cont.)

There are other ways to select a power plan and manage battery use. For starters, there's a battery meter icon in the notification area. To see the status of the battery, hover the mouse over the icon. The icon shows a power meter and a plug. Depending on the status of the laptop and its battery, you'll see different variations on the icon.

Using the battery meter

If you want to change the power plan from the notification area, click on the battery icon. If you click the icon once, you can select one of three power plans: balanced, power saver and high performance.

Battery icon ———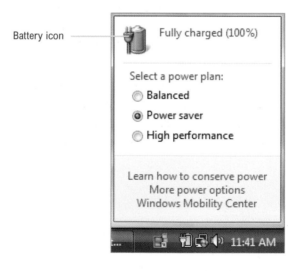

The power plans are:

- Balanced: the default power plan. This is meant to imply that the plan balances power use and computer performance. You won't get the best power savings with this plan, and you won't get the best performance either. You will get something inbetween. While the laptop is plugged into a power source, the display and hard disk are turned off after 20 minutes of inactivity, and after 60, the computer will go to sleep. When the laptop is running on battery power, Windows will turn off the display after 5 minutes and will turn off the hard drive after 10 minutes of inactivity. The PC will go to sleep after 15 minutes of inactivity while on battery power.

- Power saver: this plan is all about lengthening battery charge. That means in all instances, even when the laptop is plugged in, you'll notice decreased brightness and processor levels, and the computer will go to sleep, turn off hard disks and turn off the display within minutes of inactivity.

- High performance: this plan is all about enhancing performance and doesn't worry about battery life. Here, Vista provides all of your CPU's processing power, which is necessary for playing games and performing resource-intensive tasks. The computer will still turn off its display, put the hard drive to sleep and put the computer to sleep after a set amount of idle time.

If you right-click the icon, you'll see a pop-up menu where you can access Power Options (a control window), Windows Mobility Center, or click on Show System Icons. The last option brings up the Taskbar and Start Menu Properties window.

Wireless connectivity ▶

You can make the charged batteries last longer by turning off unnecessary features, including wireless connectivity. If you do not need access to a local network, whether its WiFi or Bluetooth, turning off wireless capabilities will preserve the battery power you have. When wireless connectivity is turned off, Vista does not scan for networks and so saves power.

Turning on and off wireless connectivity

1 Open the Mobility Center.

2 Click on 'Turn wireless off' to disable your wireless adapter. (You'll click 'Turn wireless on' to turn it on again.)

There are some settings in Vista that disable your usual power management settings temporarily, to make sure that your laptop stays awake while you give a presentation.

For instance, you may want to create a PowerPoint presentation or a Photo Gallery slide show for a party, and run that presentation (on battery power) without having the screen dim, the hard drive go to sleep or a screensaver come on.

There are settings you can configure too. These include:

- 'I am currently giving a presentation': tick this option to enable presentation settings.
- Turn off the screen saver.
- Set the volume to.
- Show a particular background temporarily.
- Use an external display.

Exploring presentation settings (cont.)

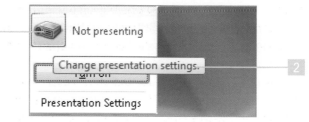

Turning on presentation settings

1. Open the Mobility Center.

2. Click on Turn Off or Turn On to enable or disable presentation settings.

3. To configure the settings, click the projector icon in the settings window in Mobility Center.

   - In the settings window, if desired, click on 'I am currently giving a presentation'.

   - Click on 'Turn off screen saver' to keep this from coming on during your presentation.

   - Click on 'Set the volume to:', to alter the volume settings.

   - Click on 'Show this background:' to select a desktop background during a presentation.

   - Configure the desktop background to appear in the centre, as tiles or to fit the screen.

4. Click OK to apply.

5. Click the X in the window to close it.

Sync Center can help you keep your files, music, contacts, pictures and other data on your laptop in the same state as your mobile devices, network files and folders, and compatible programs such as Outlook. You only need to use Sync Center if you keep files in more than on location, such as on a mobile PC, music player, USB drive, PDA or mobile phone, as well as your computer. As an example, when you take pictures on your mobile phone, you probably want to put those pictures on your PC's hard drive when you get home. That's syncing. Beyond copying though, if you copy files to say, a mobile PC, and then alter the files, you'll want to replicate your changes with the same files on the desktop PC. You do not want to have different versions of the same file scattered across devices. You won't know which file is up to date, and which one is not.

There are two ways to sync devices. The first is called a one-way sync. You could choose this to sync pictures on a mobile phone to your PC. In this process, any time you change information on one device, the same information is changed on the second. It's a one-way street. You take pictures with a mobile, and when you sync to a PC, the pictures you took get copied to the PC. That's it. Nothing gets copied to your mobile phone.

The other process is a two-way sync. You can create a two-way sync between a network folder and a computer. Changes made on the desktop PC will be copied to the network PC, and vice versa. Two-way syncs are generally used at work, where people use more than one PC; one-way syncs are used more often with phones, cameras and music players.

Here's a common situation for a one-way sync. You manage your music collection on your PC and use a portable music player. You want to have a relationship between the PC and music player so that any tracks you add to or delete from your computer are also added to or deleted from your music player. You don't want the process to delete music from the music player though. Therefore, you create a one-way sync.

Jargon buster

Synchronising is the process of keeping files matched, when those files are used on more than one device.

12

Sync Center (cont.)

Here are some sync rules to remember. If, while syncing data:

- The sync utility discovers two versions of the same file that are different, it selects the most recent version to keep by default.

- Sync Center discovers that a file has changed in both locations, it prompts you there's a conflict and lets you to choose which version to keep. You can keep both if you aren't sure.

- Sync Center finds files are identical in both locations, it doesn't do anything.

- Sync Center finds you added a new file in one location but not the other, it copies the file to the other location.

- Sync Center finds you have deleted a file from one location but not the other, it will delete the file from the other location.

Did you know?

You can only sync with network folders if you use Ultimate, Enterprise or Business because those are more work-related editions.

Important

Sync Center is included with Vista but is often not the best solution. If your music player or mobile phone came with its own software, use that.

Sync Center
(cont.)

Accessing sync settings

1 Open the Mobility Center.

2 Click on 'Sync settings'.

12

Sync Center (cont.)

Using the Sync Center

1. With Sync Center open, turn on any device that needs updating. It may be a mobile phone, flash drive or music player, or any other compatible device.

2. Connect the device and the computer using a USB cable.

3. In the Sync Center, click 'Set up new sync partnerships'.

4. Click on the name of the device in the list of available sync partnerships.

5. On the toolbar, click on 'Set-up'.

6. Select 'Sync this device automatically'.

7. Under 'Available playlists', select 'Sync Playlists'.

8. Select any playlists that you want to update, one at a time, and click on Add.

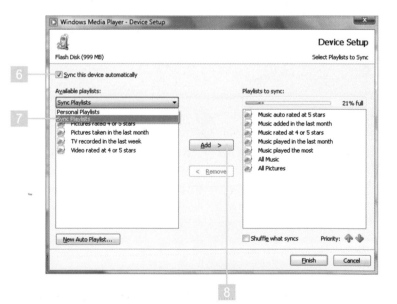

9 To remove a playlist, select it under 'Playlists to Sync'.

10 Click on Remove.

11 Click on Finish.

12 To sync, click 'View sync partnerships'. If you don't see your device, connect it again by turning it off and on. In the worst case, you'll have to restart the PC.

13 Click on your device in the list of sync partnerships.

14 Click Sync.

15 Watch the sync progress bar to see the sync process complete.

Note that you can also choose to 'Shuffle what syncs' and change the priority of a playlist. Shuffling will play the synced music, photos or videos in random order. 'Priority' will make sure the items at the top of the list are synced before anything else.

You can view sync conflicts and sync results by clicking on their links in the Tasks pane.

Sync Center (cont.)

As noted, some devices come with their own software. Here's what happens when you plug in an iPhone. Since the iPhone uses iTunes software, when prompted with this box you'll simply close it and open iTunes. iTunes does all the work and is a much better program than Sync Center. When available, use the software that comes with the device.

As you can see here, iTunes offers its own sync button; a place to check for updates; see how much space is left on the device; shop for music, podcasts and video; and so on. Also, if you install an iPhone and try to set it up in Sync Center, you won't get very far because it's not compatible. You can import pictures though, using the Import Pictures and Videos feature and Photo Gallery.

If you use your laptop for watching TV and DVDs but the screen is small, you can connect an external display. Most laptops offer an external display port. To connect the display, simply link the display to the port on the back of the laptop, plug it in and turn it on. Then, in Mobility Center, you can click on Connect Display and configure settings for it.

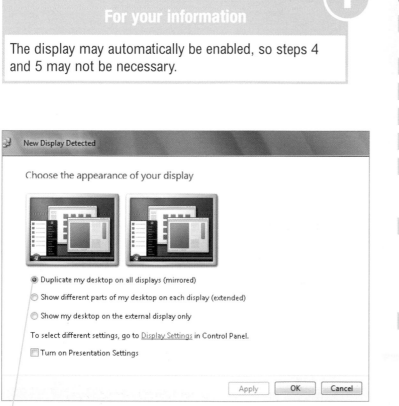

6a

Using an external display

Connecting an external display

1 Connect the external display to the back of the laptop.

2 Plug in the external display.

3 Turn on the external display.

4 Open the Mobility Center.

5 Click on 'Connect display'.

6 When prompted on how to use the display, select one of the options:

a Duplicate my desktop on all displays (mirrored): this option simply duplicates what you see on your laptop on the external display.

b Show different parts of my desktop on each display (extended): this will show what's on your laptop's single display across it and the external monitor. If you choose this, you must also select where the external display is connected, to the left or right of the laptop.

12

Using an external display (cont.)

Choose the appearance of your display

Extend your desktop:
- Right
- Left

Duplicate my desktop on all displays (mirrored)

Show different parts of my desktop on each display (extended)

6b

c Show my desktop on the external display only: this will disable your laptop's monitor and show the display only on the other screen (great for TV and DVD watching).

d To select different settings, go to Display Settings in Control Panel: click on Display Settings to open the Control Panel to configure advanced settings.

7 Click on OK.

Tablet PC features for tablet PCs and laptops

13

Introduction

Although 'slate' tablet PCs have been around for a few years, newer tablet PCs are laptop/tablet hybrids. They have the abilities and look of a laptop and contain a touchpad and keyboard, but also offer the option to write on the screen and have that handwriting recognised and converted to text. This type of screen is called a touch screen. More expensive models offer a screen that can be swivelled around and rotated, which allows you to write on it just as you would a clipboard. Thus, if you have a tablet PC, you have options that 'regular' laptop users don't have. Mainly, the ability to write on the laptop's screen using an input device called a stylus or pen.

If you don't have a tablet PC, but do have Vista Home Premium, Business, Enterprise or Ultimate edition on your laptop, you can still use the Tablet PC tools; your laptop doesn't need to offer the actual functionality of being able to write on the screen. You can use some of these features with a keyboard and mouse, although how useful they will be to you remains to be seen.

What you'll do

Explore the tablet PC input panel

Enter handwritten text using the writing pad

Enter handwritten text using the character pad

Enter text using the on-screen keyboard

Configure tablet PC features

Use the snipping tool

Use sticky notes

Train handwriting recognition

Add web components, numbers and symbols

Add words to the handwriting dictionary

Configure input panel options

Use gestures

Use Windows Flicks

Create a new note with Windows Journal

Tablet PC tools

There are quite a few features and tools designed for tablet PCs and laptop users can access these tools, albeit in many cases, not as effectively. To find out what tools are available and decide which ones you may want to use, let's explore.

Tablet PC input panel

The input panel is at the heart of the tablet PC tools. Here you can write notes in your own handwriting and then enter the converted text anywhere text is accepted. If you have a tablet PC with a touch screen, you can write directly in the Tablet PC Input Panel using the stylus. If you have a laptop, you can write by moving your mouse.

As you write, words are shown under each word you create. If your handwriting is legible, the words will be correct, even if they aren't 'real' words, like my name, shown here.

The input panel also guesses what word you're trying to write before you've finished. If it guesses correctly, you can select the word instead of finishing it yourself.

There's also an input panel tab that appears when the Tablet PC Input Panel is minimised or closed. This tab appears on the screen and you can click on it to bring the input panel to the forefront.

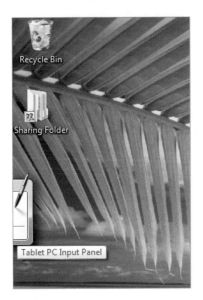

There are a couple of other nice features:

- Back-of-pen erase: if your stylus has an 'eraser' you can turn the stylus over to rub out what you've written.

- Scratch-out gestures: allow you to delete your own handwriting by using strikethrough, and vertical, circular and angled scratch out.

Besides the writing pad shown in these examples, there's a Character Pad. With this, you can write letters one at a time and have them recognised, instead of writing entire words.

If, when you write a letter, the letter seen is not the correct one, you can click the arrow underneath it to select the proper character.

13

Tablet PC tools
(cont.)

Finally, you can input data using a Keyboard on the screen. With this, you'll need to open a program that accepts keyboard input, such as a wordprocesser. The text you type using the keyboard appears in the program's interface.

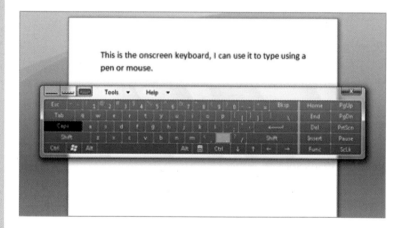

Handwriting recognition

Although you can write notes by hand using the input panel straight out of the box, it's better if you work through the handwriting training tools. Doing so will help Vista recognise your writing more accurately.

One of these is a personalisation tool handwriting recognition. The training takes some time, but it's worth it. You can also turn on automatic learning so that the handwriting recogniser gathers information about the words you write, how you write them and so becomes a better analyser. Finally, you can enable handwriting recognition error reporting, which will send information about the corrections you've made to Microsoft. Your feedback can then be used to improve the system in future versions of Vista. You'll learn more about handwriting recognition later in this chapter.

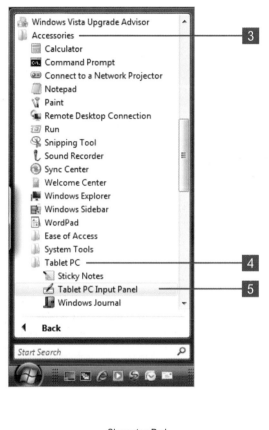

Character Pad

Writing Pad   On-Screen Keyboard

Exploring the tablet PC's input panel

1 Click on Start.

2 Click on All Programs.

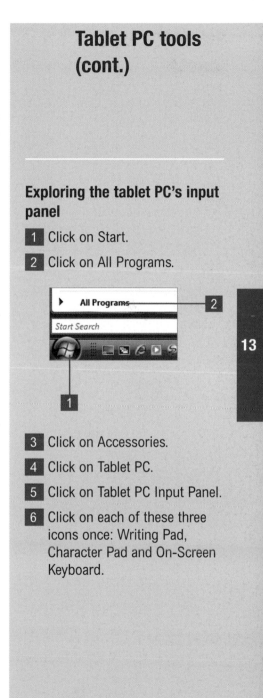

13

3 Click on Accessories.

4 Click on Tablet PC.

5 Click on Tablet PC Input Panel.

6 Click on each of these three icons once: Writing Pad, Character Pad and On-Screen Keyboard.

Tablet PC tools (cont.)

7 Click on Tools. Note that you can allow the input panel to float, or you can fix it at the top or bottom of the screen.

8 Click on the red X in the top right corner of the Tablet PC Input Panel. Notice it closes but is still available on the left of the screen.

9 Click the edge of that input panel to open it.

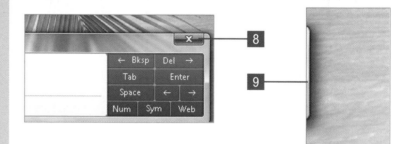

Pen flicks

You can also use your stylus to perform pen flicks. Pen flicks (think about how you look when you flick your wrist) are an easy way to move quickly through web pages and documents, and perform editing tasks such as cut, copy, paste and delete, using nothing but your stylus. To perform a pen flick, move your stylus quickly using a flick motion. You'll learn more about pen flicks later in this chapter, including how to perform them.

Pen cursors

Pen cursors offer visual feedback for actions you perform with your stylus. If you want a visual clue when you single-tap or double-tap with the stylus, or when you perform the equivalent of right-clicking, you can enable pen cursors. You'll learn more about them later in this chapter.

Snipping tool

The snipping tool, although not a tablet PC tool (but perhaps it should be), lets you capture an image by circling an area of your screen using your stylus. With the image created, you can then write on it using your pen. From there, you can post the image, add it to a Windows Journal file, or do any other number of things with it, such as put it in a PowerPoint presentation. You'll learn more about this later in this chapter.

Touch input

Many newer Tablet PCs have screens you can touch with your finger. With this technology you can use your finger instead of a stylus, mouse or keyboard. You'll learn more about this later in the chapter.

13

Using the tablet PC's input panel ▶

Entering handwritten text using the Writing Pad

1 Open the Tablet PC Input Panel.

2 Open a blank document. (If you're unsure how to do this, open WordPad. Click on Start, type WordPad, click WordPad under Programs.)

3 If the Writing Pad is not showing, click the Writing Pad icon.

4 Using the pen, if you have one, write text inside the Writing Pad window. If you do not have a pen, use the mouse.

You will use the input panel in one of three ways to create text: Writing Pad, Character Pad and On-Screen Keyboard. Once text has been created in the first two, you click on Insert to transfer what's been written in the input panel to the open application. When typing with the screen keyboard, text will be entered automatically. The open application may be any application that offers a place to input text, making the input panel a universal place to write with the pen (stylus).

The Writing Pad and Character Pad won't always guess correctly what letter you've written though. That's where handwriting recognition training comes in. When this happens, you will hover your mouse over the incorrect letter to erase it or select the proper letter from a list. As time passes, the input panel will learn your handwriting quirks, and will make fewer mistakes.

Here are some instructions for writing with a stylus:

- Use a tap to place the insertion point anywhere text is accepted. This could include a wordprocessor document, PowerPoint presentation, spreadsheet, email message or the address bar of a web browser (to name a few).

- To open the input panel tab, click it on the left edge of the screen.

- Select from Writing Pad, Character Pad and On-Screen Keyboard.

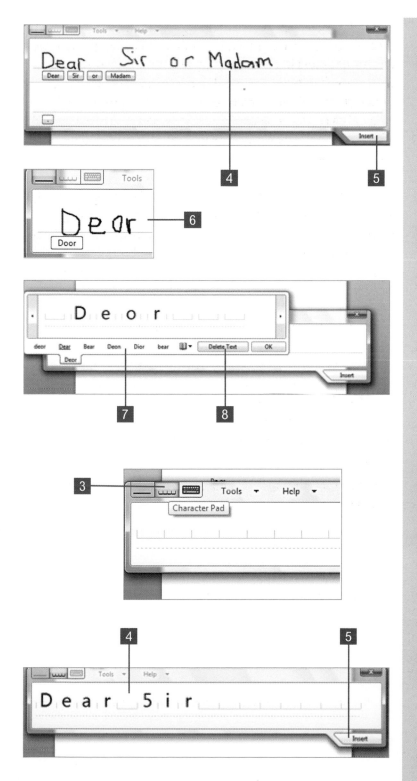

5 If the text is correct, click on Insert.

6 If the text is not correct, click on the incorrect word.

7 Choose the correct word from the list.

8 If the correct word is not in the list, click on Delete Text and try to rewrite the word more neatly.

13

Entering handwritten text using the Character Pad

1 Open the Tablet PC Input Panel.

2 Open a blank document. (If you're unsure how to do this, open WordPad. Click Start, type WordPad, click WordPad under Programs.)

3 Click the Character Pad icon.

4 Using the pen, if you have one, write text inside the Character Pad window. If you do not have a pen, use the mouse.

5 If the text is correct, click Insert.

Using the tablet PC's input panel (cont.)

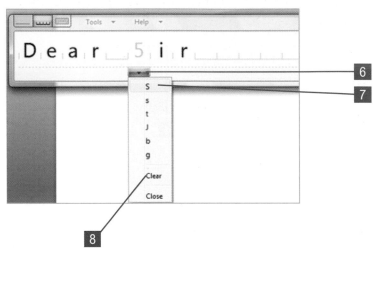

6 If the text is not correct, click the arrow under the incorrect letter.

7 Choose the correct letter from the list.

8 If the correct letter is not in the list, click Clear and try to rewrite the letter more neatly.

Entering text using the screen keyboard

1 Open the Tablet PC Input Panel.

2 Open a blank document. (If you're unsure how to do this, open WordPad. Click Start, type WordPad, click WordPad under Programs.)

3 Click on the On-Screen Keyboard icon.

4 Click the keys on the keyboard. Notice the letters appear in the word document.

5 Note the items on the keyboard, including Home, PgUp, End, PgDn and others. Practise using these keys as you would on a physical keyboard.

6 Continue as desired.

Tablet PC features are configured using a settings option, which you'll find in the control panel under Mobile PC. The dialogue box is shown here.

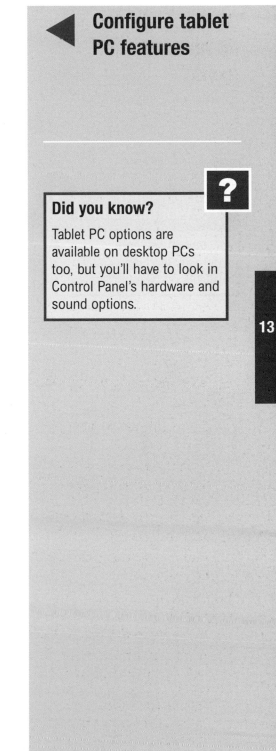

Did you know?

Tablet PC options are available on desktop PCs too, but you'll have to look in Control Panel's hardware and sound options.

13

There are four tabs:

■ General. Here you configure the Tablet PC for right- or left-handed use, select a screen orientation (portrait or landscape), and if desired, run a calibration tool that helps you adjust your touch screen, so that what you mean to touch with your stylus is actually what you touch.

Configure tablet PC features (cont.)

For your information

As you can see here, automatic learning is only available on tablet PCs.

■ Handwriting Recognition. Here you have access to a personalization tool and an automatic learning option.

■ Display. Here you set the default screen orientation. You have four choices: primary landscape, secondary portrait, secondary landscape and primary portrait. You can also change the order in which these choices are implemented when you press the orientation button on the tablet PC.

- Other. Here you can access a link to pen and input devices. When you click on Go to Pen and Input Devices, a window opens where you configure the options.

Pen and input devices settings

When you choose the option to Go to Pen and Input Devices in Tablet PC Settings, a window opens with more configuration options.

Configure tablet PC features (cont.)

There are three tabs:

- Pen Options. Here you set what the pen actions and buttons on the tablet PC do. The defaults are shown here. As you can see, a single-tap is the equivalent of a single-click with a mouse button; a double-tap is the equivalent of a double-click with a mouse button; and press and hold is the equivalent of right-clicking with a mouse button. You can also choose to start the Input Pen using a gesture, such as a flick. You can make changes to these settings by clicking the desired option. Here you can see the options for double-tap settings.

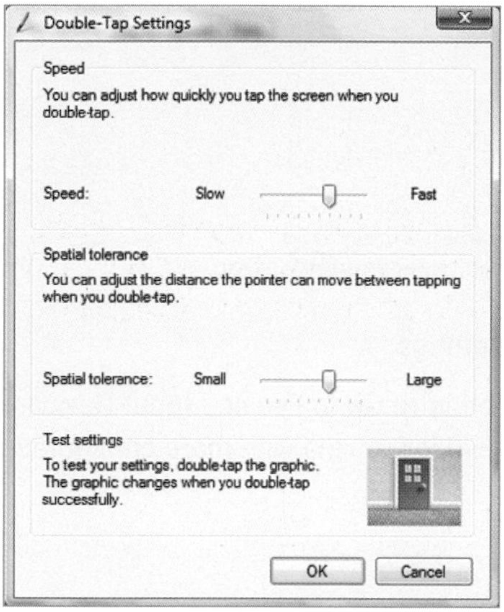

- Pointer Options. Here you can decide whether visual feedback is enabled when you use your pen, and if you want to show the pen cursors instead of the mouse cursor when you use the pen. I like the pointer options because they offer visual proof I've actually performed the task I want to perform with the pen.

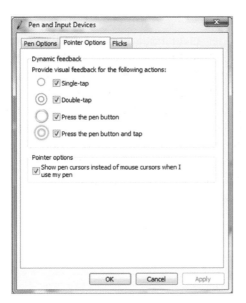

- Flicks. Here you set the flick options, discussed later in the chapter. You can choose to use flicks or not, and you can customise the flicks you do use. You can also change the sensitivity of the flick.

Configure tablet PC features (cont.)

If you have a tablet PC you'll see a fourth tab called Touch. This tab lets you use your finger as an input device. As with other options, you can configure what happens when you double-tap or press and hold, and choose to show or hide a touch pointer.

Configuring tablet PC features

1. Click on Start.
2. In the search dialogue box, type 'Tablet PC Settings'.
3. Click on Tablet PC Settings under Programs.

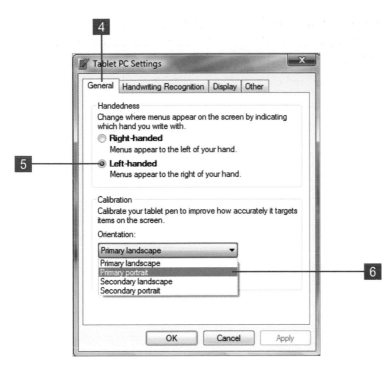

Configure tablet PC features (cont.)

4 Click on the General tab.

5 Choose right-handed or Left-handed.

6 Choose an orientation from the dropdown list.

7 Click on the Handwriting Recognition tab. If you have a tablet PC, turn on automatic learning.

13

Configure tablet PC features (cont.)

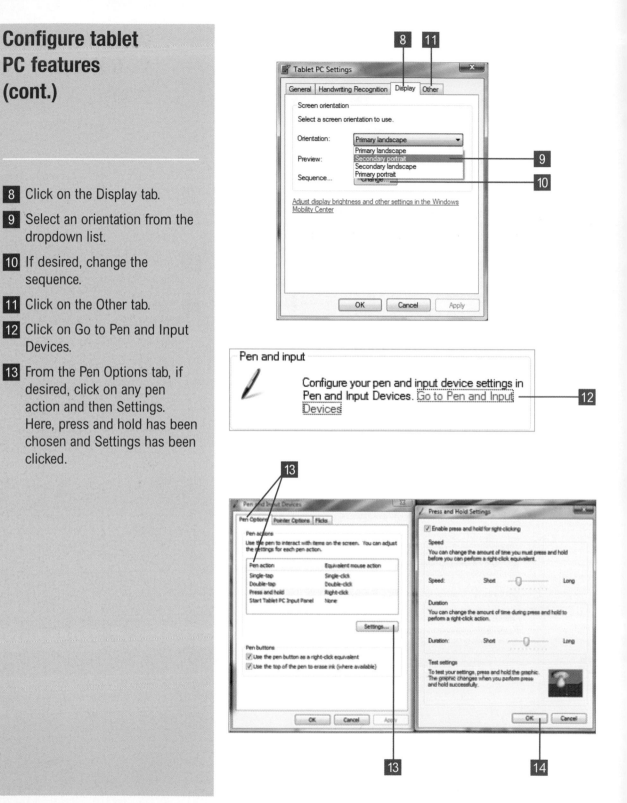

8 Click on the Display tab.

9 Select an orientation from the dropdown list.

10 If desired, change the sequence.

11 Click on the Other tab.

12 Click on Go to Pen and Input Devices.

13 From the Pen Options tab, if desired, click on any pen action and then Settings. Here, press and hold has been chosen and Settings has been clicked.

Pen buttons

- ☑ Use the pen button as a right-click equivalent
- ☑ Use the top of the pen to erase ink (where available)

15

14 If you chose Settings, make the appropriate changes and click on OK.

15 If desired, change what the pen buttons do by deselecting the options.

16 Click the Pointer Options tab.

17 Make changes as desired.

18 Click the Flicks tab.

19 Do not make changes to the Flicks tab; come back here after learning about flicks later in the chapter to change the default settings if desired.

20 Click OK.

13

Snipping Tool ▶

The Snipping Tool is not a Tablet PC tool, but perhaps it should be. Instead, it is located in the Accessories folder, and lets laptop and tablet PC users mark an area of the screen to copy to the Snipping Tool window. Once the image has been created, you can write on the image, send it in an email, or any other number of things. It's great for copying information from web pages, presentations, documents and spreadsheets, but it works well for almost anything, really. Think of it as copy and-paste – but with images.

When you first use the tool, it will ready itself to perform a 'clip'. As you can see here, a grey cloud covers the screen. You use your mouse to draw around the area to copy. By default, the shape created when you drag your mouse is a rectangle.

Press Cancel instead of snipping though, and you can see the available features. Note that you can change the default Rectangular Snip to a free-form shape, window or full-screen.

You can on click Options to see the window here, which is self-explanatory. I suggest you select 'Display icon on the Quick Launch toolbar', which will make the tool easier to locate later.

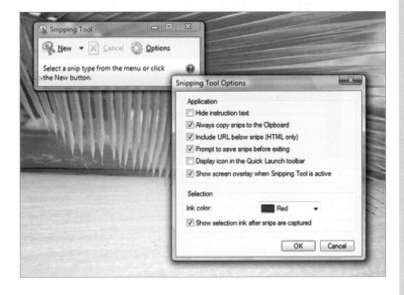

If you've clicked Cancel, you'll need to click the New button to create a snip. Then you'll drag the pen (or the mouse) around the screen to capture the desired area. With that done, you'll see the clip in the Snipping Tool window, where you can then work with it, which includes writing on the snip with your pen, erasing what you've written, and saving it or emailing it, among others.

Snipping Tool (cont.)

Using the Snipping Tool

1 Click on Start.

2 In the search window, type Snip.

3 Click Snipping Tool under Programs results. You may also see this on the Quick Launch area of the taskbar.

For your information

You may see the Snipping Tool icon in the quick launch area if you've already used and configured it.

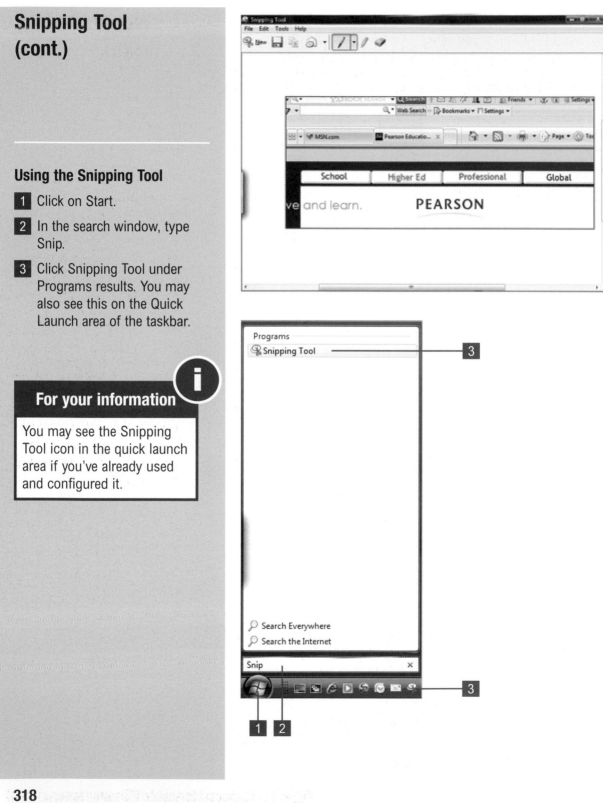

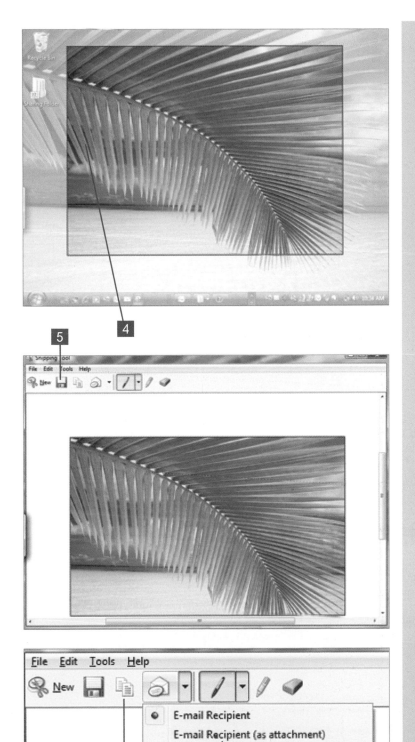

Snipping Tool (cont.)

4 Drag your mouse across any area of your screen. It can even be the Desktop.

5 To save the snip to your hard drive, click the Save icon.

6 To copy the snip so you can paste it into another application, click the Copy icon.

7 To email the snip, click the email icon. By default, this will place the snip inside the body of the email. To send the snip as an attachment, click the arrow under the email icon and select E-mail Recipient (as attachment).

13

Snipping Tool (cont.)

8 To write on the image, select a pen from the dropdown list (if you simply click the Pen icon you'll use the Blue Pen by default).

9 Select Customize from the dropdown list to change the colour, thickness and tip of the pen.

10 Use your stylus or mouse to write on the image.

11 Click the Highlighter to pick out any part of the snip. Drag the pen over the area to highlight.

12 Click on the eraser icon to rub out part of the snip. Drag the pen over the area of the snip you previously wrote on.

Sticky Notes is another option in the Tablet PC folder, and it enables you to create short handwritten or voice notes. You can jot down ideas, reminders, or create lists using the pen or stylus just like on a Post-It note, or create a voice clip by speaking into the microphone. Sticky Notes offers more options than the sidebar Notes gadget too. Sticky Notes offers tools, help and other options. If you use Sticky Notes often, you can have it start automatically when you turn on your laptop.

13

Sticky Notes (cont.)

Using Sticky Notes

1 Click on Start.

2 Click on All Programs.

3 Click on Accessories to expand the list.

4 Click Tablet PC to expand it.

5 Click on Sticky Notes.

6 Use your stylus to write on the note. You can also use the mouse. You cannot use the Tablet PC Input Panel.

7 To delete what you've written and not save the note, click on the Delete This Note button.

Did you know?

You can use the input panel to add notes to the sidebar Notes gadget.

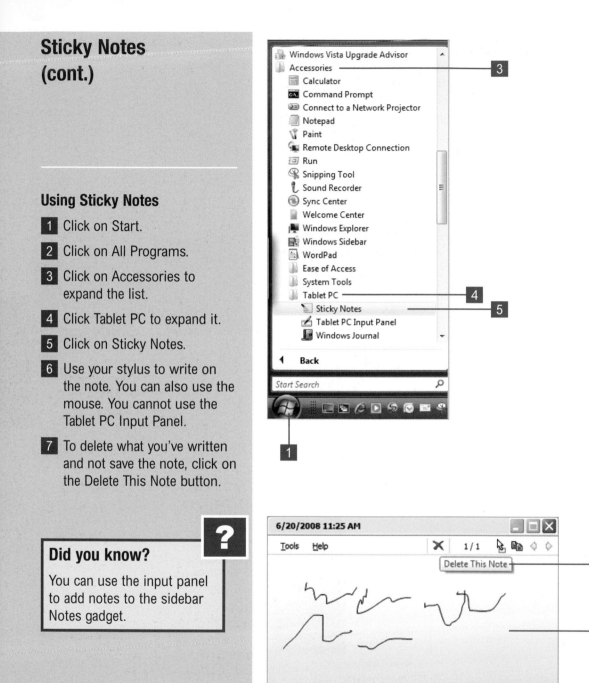

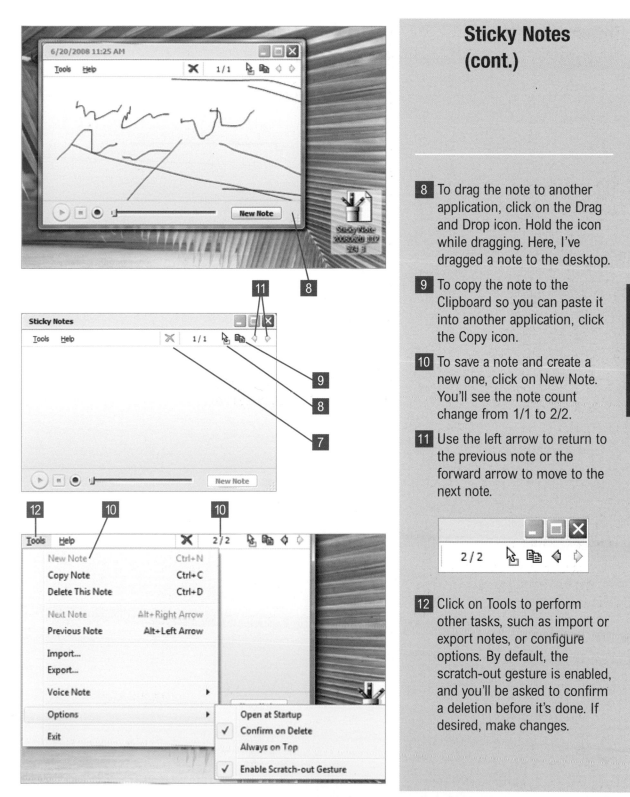

Sticky Notes (cont.)

8 To drag the note to another application, click on the Drag and Drop icon. Hold the icon while dragging. Here, I've dragged a note to the desktop.

9 To copy the note to the Clipboard so you can paste it into another application, click the Copy icon.

10 To save a note and create a new one, click on New Note. You'll see the note count change from 1/1 to 2/2.

11 Use the left arrow to return to the previous note or the forward arrow to move to the next note.

12 Click on Tools to perform other tasks, such as import or export notes, or configure options. By default, the scratch-out gesture is enabled, and you'll be asked to confirm a deletion before it's done. If desired, make changes.

Sticky Notes (cont.)

---

13 To record a voice clip, click on the Voice Note button and then the record control.

14 Speak into the microphone.

15 Click on the Stop button when finished.

16 To play the clip, click on Play.

As mentioned earlier, you can teach Vista how you write using recognition tools. If you have a tablet PC, you can enable automatic learning too, which allows Vista to learn more about you each time you write. To get started, you'll work though the personalisation options. In doing so, you provide samples of your handwriting so Vista can learn your style. (If you want, after that's complete and you've done a bit of handwriting, you can report mistakes Vista has made to Microsoft, so it can improve future versions.) There are also steps you can take to correct errors and make handwriting recognition work better.

13

Handwriting Personalization - English (United States)

Personalize handwriting recognition

Providing samples of your handwriting increases the likelihood of your writing being recognized correctly. For best results, start with specific characters or words that are causing recognition errors for you.

Target specific recognition errors
Provide handwriting samples for specific characters or words that are being recognized incorrectly.

Teach the recognizer your handwriting style
Provide a more extensive set of handwriting samples. Start here if you experience poor handwriting recognition overall.

Related Tasks:
Change automatic learning settings
Learn how to transfer your personalized recognizer to another Tablet PC
Delete handwriting samples that you provided for the current language
Learn more about handwriting recognition personalization

Cancel

Teach the recogniser your handwriting style

When you click on 'Teach the recognizer your handwriting style', you'll be prompted to do two things: write sentences; and write numbers, symbols and letters. You should work though both options as this will offer better accuracy, and lessen the time you spend correcting what Vista thinks you've written. This isn't easy to do though; there are lots of screens to work through, so be prepared to spend some time here. In the long run though, the time spent now will pay off.

Handwriting recognition (cont.)

Training handwriting recognition

1 Open the Tablet PC Input Panel.

2 Tap Tools with your stylus.

3 Tap Personalize Handwriting Recognition.

4 Tap 'Teach the recognizer your handwriting style'.

5 Tap Sentences.

6 Read the information offered and tap Next to continue.

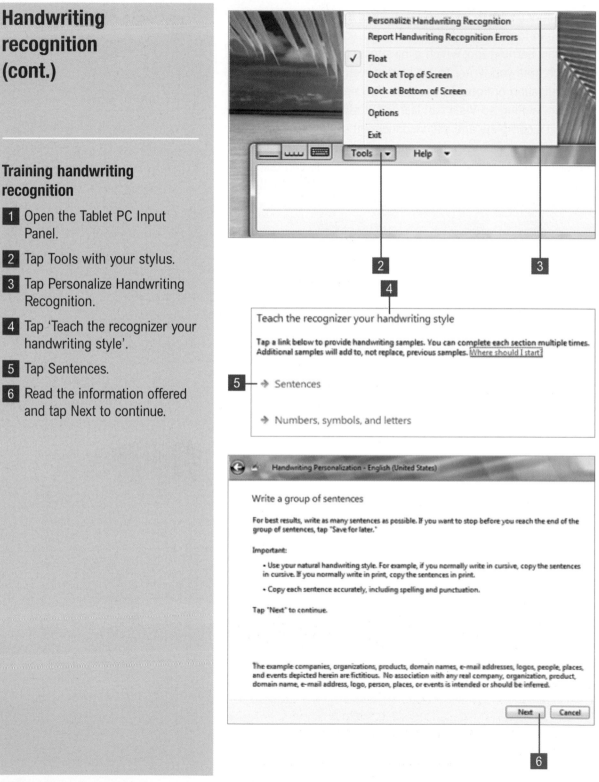

Personalize Handwriting Recognition

Report Handwriting Recognition Errors

✓ Float

Dock at Top of Screen

Dock at Bottom of Screen

Options

Exit

Tools ▾   Help ▾

Teach the recognizer your handwriting style

Tap a link below to provide handwriting samples. You can complete each section multiple times. Additional samples will add to, not replace, previous samples. Where should I start?

→ Sentences

→ Numbers, symbols, and letters

Handwriting Personalization - English (United States)

Write a group of sentences

For best results, write as many sentences as possible. If you want to stop before you reach the end of the group of sentences, tap "Save for later."

Important:

• Use your natural handwriting style. For example, if you normally write in cursive, copy the sentences in cursive. If you normally write in print, copy the sentences in print.

• Copy each sentence accurately, including spelling and punctuation.

Tap "Next" to continue.

The example companies, organizations, products, domain names, e-mail addresses, logos, people, places, and events depicted herein are fictitious. No association with any real company, organization, product, domain name, e-mail address, logo, person, places, or events is intended or should be inferred.

Next   Cancel

Write the sentence once

Write the following sentence one time in your normal writing style.
Be sure to write the sentence exactly as it appears, including any punctuation.

Adventure Works sells good used ski equipment.

Adventure Works

Screen 1 of 50

Next | Save for later | Cancel

Handwriting Personalization - English (United States)

Your handwriting samples have been saved

The writing samples you provided will be used to personalize the recognizer the next time that you update it.

For best results, provide as many writing samples as possible. You can return at any time to provide more. Additional samples will add to, not replace, previous ones. If you are finished for now, tap "Update and exit."

→ Continue to provide handwriting samples

ⓘ It will take a few minutes or longer for the recognizer to be personalized with your handwriting samples. A notification appears when this process is completed.

Update and exit

Handwriting recognition (cont.)

7 Work through as many screens as you have time for.

8 Each time you finish a screen, click on Next.

9 If you get tired, click on 'Save for later'.

10 Click on 'Update and exit'.

11 Repeat as necessary to complete all of the tasks.

13

For your information

Vista's handwriting recognition isn't a mind reader. Unless you have excellent handwriting, it's going to make mistakes. You will have to spend time correcting those mistakes to fix errors in documents and URLs, and while time consuming, this actually minimises future errors.

Handwriting recognition (cont.)

Get better handwriting results

There are tools to help you get better handwriting results, including AutoComplete, Gestures and Back-of-Pen Erase. There are also tools in the Input Panel that make inputting data easier, like the ability to access symbols quickly and web entries you input often, such as .com.

The easiest way to get better results is to take advantage of AutoComplete. You may be familiar with this if you use texts on a mobile phone. As with texting, AutoComplete offers suggestions for the words you've yet to finish writing. Sometimes it offers the right word and sometimes not. If it does offer the right word, simply tap it to select it. You don't have to finish writing the word.

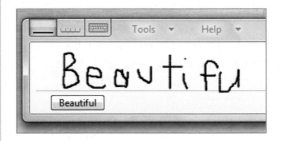

You can also use scratch-out gestures. These are movements you make with your pen to erase what you've written. Just as you would use a pen to scratch out an unwanted mark on a written page, you use your tablet PC pen to scratch out handwritten text in Vista. There's more on gestures in the next section. If your stylus allows it, you can use back-of-pen erase to rub out handwritten text too. All you have to do is flip the stylus upside down, just as you would with a pencil, and move the pen over the text to erase.

The input panel also offers buttons, including Bksp (Backspace), Del (Delete), Tab, Enter, Space and left arrow and right arrow keys, along with Num (Number) and Sym (Symbol). Num opens the Number panel; Sym to open the Symbol panel. To use these, simply tap the pen on any symbol or number to insert it. You use these keys in the same way you'd use them on a physical keyboard.

Click on Web to open the keys that offer common elements of web addresses such as .com (for US websites).

Note that most web browsers automatically put in 'http://www.' for you.

You can configure options for the Writing Pad, Character Pad and other input panel features to suit your handwriting preferences. You can change the thickness of the ink used when you write with the pen; configure how close to the end of the writing line you want to be before a new line is offered in Writing Pad; you can have Vista input characters automatically, after a short or long pause when writing; and you can even change how the panel opens (using a tap or by pointing).

If there are words you write often, such as your name or a company's name, you can add that word to a dictionary. The next time you start to write the word, it may appear as an AutoComplete word you can select.

Finally, the calibration tool should be used if, when you try to touch something on the screen, you don't hit what you want every time.

Handwriting recognition (cont.)

13

Handwriting recognition (cont.)

Adding web components, numbers and symbols

1 Open the Tablet PC Input Panel.

2 Tap Start.

3 Click on Internet to open your web browser.

4 Tap inside the browser's address bar.

5 Tap the web button in the Tablet PC Input Panel.

6 Tap http://.

7 Tap www.

8 Handwrite any website name, such as Google or JoliBallew.

9 Tap Insert.

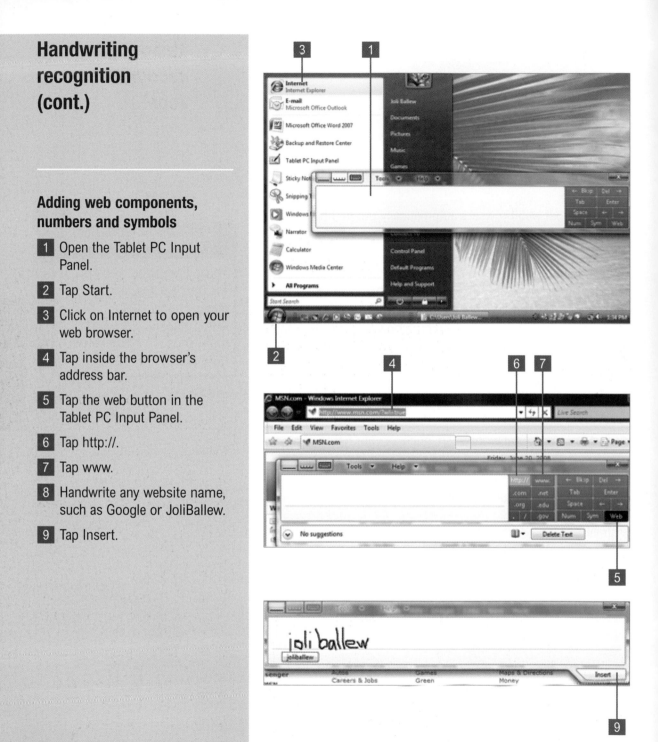

11

http://	www.	← Bksp	Del →
.com	.net	Tab	Enter
.org	.edu	Space	← →
. /	.gov	Num	Sym	Web

12

10

13

msn

Web | MSN | Images | Video | News | Maps

$

Popular Searches: Lil Wayne | Michelle Obama | Taser shootout

Welcome

Sig

Hotmail — Air Tickets/Travel — Election 2008 — Lifestyle — News
Messenger — Autos — Games — Maps & Directions — Real Estat

Tools ▾ Help ▾

← Bksp Del →
Tab Enter
Space ← →
Num Sym Web

15

16 14

1

Joli

Joli

2

J o l i

joli Jot; Jok Jo; Job; Joy | Delete Text | OK

Joli

Add to dictionary
Recognize as ▸

4 5 6 7

10 Tap Web.

11 Tap .com.

12 Tap Enter.

13 With your web browser still open, tap inside any area where text is accepted, such as a search window.

14 On the Tablet PC Input Panel, click Sym.

15 Click any symbol to insert it.

16 Click Num.

18 Click any number to insert it.

19 Continue experimenting.

Adding words to the dictionary

1 In the Input Panel, select the Writing Pad.

2 Input your first name.

3 Correct as needed, by clicking the incorrect word underneath as detailed earlier.

4 Click on the name.

5 In the resulting pop-up box, click on the dictionary icon.

6 Click on 'Add to dictionary'.

7 Click on OK.

13

Handwriting recognition (cont.)

Configuring input panel options

1 Open the Input Panel.

2 Click on Tools.

3 Click on Options.

4 Click on the Settings tab.

5 Change the settings as you want. You can choose where the Insert button goes and how it is activated (by a tap or by a point). Leave AutoComplete selected for now.

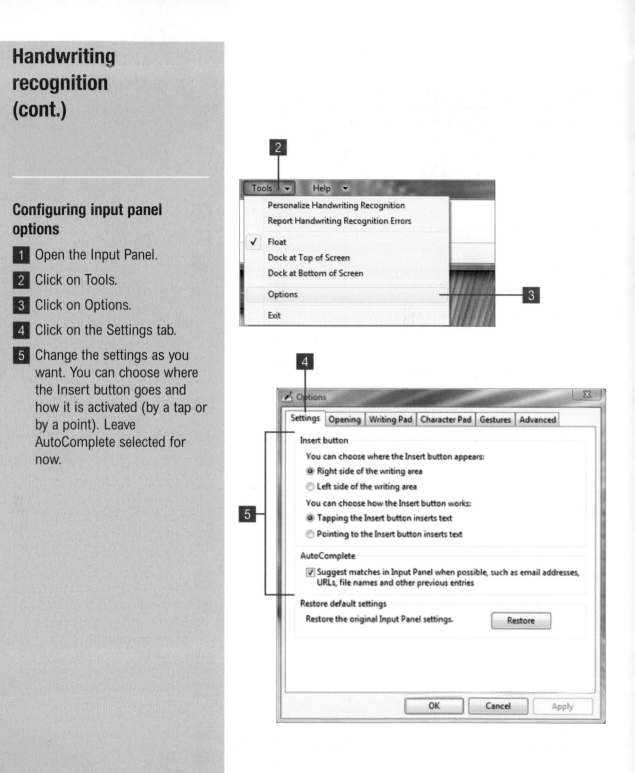

Options

| Settings | Opening | Writing Pad | Character Pad | Gestures | Advanced |

Actions that open Input Panel

You can choose which action opens Input Panel:

◉ Tap the Input Panel icon or the tab to open Input Panel

◯ Point to the Input Panel icon or the tab to open Input Panel

Input Panel icons and tab

☑ For tablet pen input, show the Input Panel icon next to the text entry area when possible

☐ Show the Input Panel icon on the taskbar

☑ Show the Input Panel tab

  ☑ Show the Input Panel tab when the pen is out of range

  ☑ Show Input Panel sliding open from the tab

You can choose where the Input Panel tab appears:

◉ On the left edge of the screen

◯ On the right edge of the screen

Learn more about opening and moving Input Panel

[OK] [Cancel] [Apply]

Options

| Settings | Opening | Writing Pad | Character Pad | Gestures | Advanced |

Appearance

Ink thickness: — Fine Point ▼

Automatic text insertion

You can choose to have Input Panel automatically insert your text in the text entry area.

☐ Automatically insert individual characters after a pause:

Length of pause:

Short pause   Long pause
(0.25 sec)   (10 sec)

New writing line

Choose how close to the end of the writing line you want to write before a new line appears.

Distance:

Less space   More space

[OK] [Cancel] [Apply]

Handwriting recognition (cont.)

6 Click on the Opening tab.

7 Configure settings as desired. You can choose how to open the Input Panel (tap or point), and how the icons and tabs appear. You may want to configure the panel to reside on the right side of the desktop or the left, for instance.

8 Click on the Writing Pad tab.

9 Change the ink thickness by selecting an option from the dropdown list. By default, Fine Point is selected. You can also have Panel automatically insert what you've written after a certain time. I suggest selecting this and experimenting with this feature. If desired, configure the amount of space that must be present before panel creates a new line.

13

Handwriting recognition (cont.)

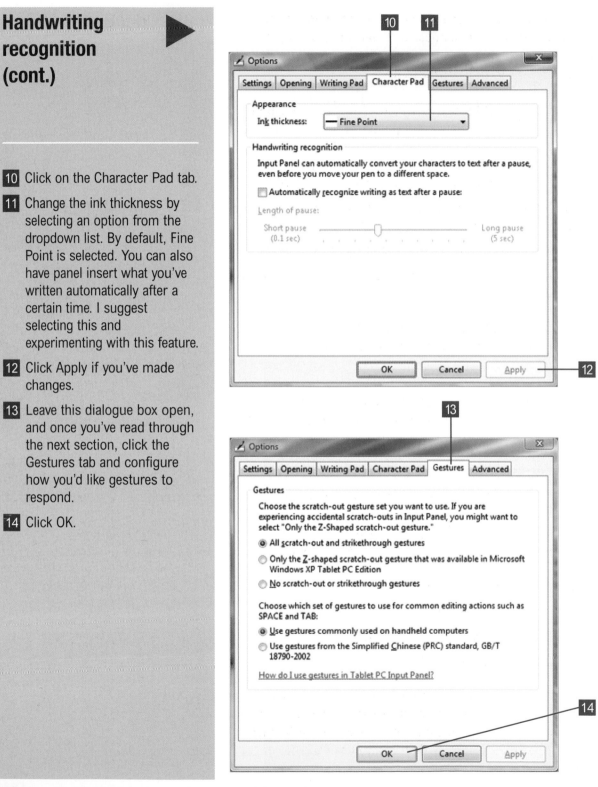

10 Click on the Character Pad tab.

11 Change the ink thickness by selecting an option from the dropdown list. By default, Fine Point is selected. You can also have panel insert what you've written automatically after a certain time. I suggest selecting this and experimenting with this feature.

12 Click Apply if you've made changes.

13 Leave this dialogue box open, and once you've read through the next section, click the Gestures tab and configure how you'd like gestures to respond.

14 Click OK.

10 **11**

Options

Settings | Opening | Writing Pad | **Character Pad** | Gestures | Advanced

Appearance

In_k thickness: ⎯ Fine Point ▼

Handwriting recognition

Input Panel can automatically convert your characters to text after a pause, even before you move your pen to a different space.

☐ Automatically _recognize writing as text after a pause:

_Length of pause:

Short pause   ⬤   Long pause
(0.1 sec)   (5 sec)

OK   Cancel   Apply

12

13

Options

Settings | Opening | Writing Pad | Character Pad | **Gestures** | Advanced

Gestures

Choose the scratch-out gesture set you want to use. If you are experiencing accidental scratch-outs in Input Panel, you might want to select "Only the Z-Shaped scratch-out gesture."

⬤ All _scratch-out and strikethrough gestures

○ Only the _Z-shaped scratch-out gesture that was available in Microsoft Windows XP Tablet PC Edition

○ _No scratch-out or strikethrough gestures

Choose which set of gestures to use for common editing actions such as SPACE and TAB:

⬤ _Use gestures commonly used on handheld computers

○ Use gestures from the Simplified _Chinese (PRC) standard, GB/T 18790-2002

How do I use gestures in Tablet PC Input Panel?

OK   Cancel   Apply

14

There are two ways to use gestures; the first is to rub out unwanted text in the input panel; the second is to edit data. Let's start by applying gestures in the input panel, specifically to remove unwanted handwritten text.

You can use any of the following scratch-out gestures in the Writing or Character Pad in the input panel:

- Strikethrough is a single line you draw through unwanted text. Text can be a single character, word or sentence.
- Vertical scratch-out removes text by moving the pen over the unwanted text in the form of an M or a W.
- Circular scratch-out deletes data by dragging a circle over it.
- Angled scratch-out, like strikethrough, deletes unwanted text when you draw an angle over it.

When using the gesture, simply move the pen or stylus over the unwanted text using any of these movements. The text will disappear.

As noted, gestures can also be used to edit data. There are four gestures: backspace, space, enter and tab. After you've written your text, you can use these gestures to move back a space, create a space, enter the text or tab to the next tab stop.

There are two options for using these gestures: handheld or simplified Chinese. By default, the gestures used for handheld computers are selected. The gesture symbol you'd use then, unless you made changes to the default settings are:

- Backspace: move the pen from right to left.
- Space: move the pen from left to right.
- Enter: move the pen down and then left.
- Tab: move the pen up and then right.

If you change the defaults, the gesture for space changes. In this instance, you move the pen diagonally up and to the right and then down and to the right. You can set the gesture type from the Input Panel's Tools>Options feature, from the Gestures tab.

Gestures

13

Gestures (cont.)

Using gestures

1 Open the Input Panel.

2 Write something using the stylus.

3 Use any of the scratch-out options to delete the handwritten text.

For your information

Practise editing gestures in the Windows Journal section of this chapter.

Here are a few tips for using gestures:

- Make sure the pen touches the screen when you draw them.
- If gestures aren't recognised, try drawing them faster or slower.
- Use 90-degree angles when moving left and right.
- For editing gestures, perform the gesture over an area clear of ink, otherwise Vista may think you're trying to scratch out the text.

Flicks are different from gestures in that you make movements with a stylus by 'flicking' your wrist in a certain direction. You use flicks to navigate web pages, documents and to perform tasks such as copy and paste. While gestures are used to erase data, or tab, space or otherwise manage the placement of data, flicks are used for moving around in a document (or web page) or editing one. When you think about creating a flick, think about flicking your wrist; it's the same motion.

As with gestures, there are two types of flicks: navigational and editing flicks. The former let you perform tasks including scroll up, scroll down, and moving back or forward in a document or web page. Editing flicks include cut, copy, paste, delete and undo. You perform these tasks when you flick the pen in the proper direction. There are eight, including up, down, left, right and the four diagonal.

You will want spend a few minutes configuring how flicks work. You do this in the Pen and Input Devices introduced earlier, under the Flicks tab. There's also an option to practise using flicks, shown here. By default, only navigational flicks are enabled.

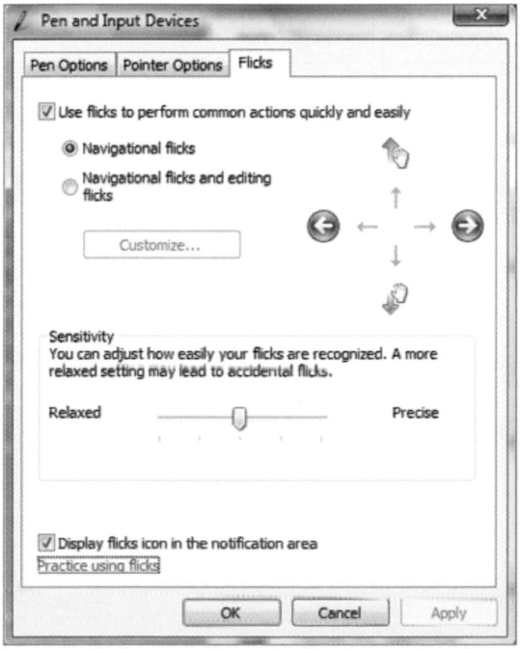

13

Flicks (cont.)

If you want to enable editing flicks you have to click on 'Navigational flicks and editing flicks'. Once selected, you can click on customise to tell Vista what to do when you perform a flick. Here you can see the dialogue box and the default settings.

By default, flicking the stylus using a diagonal flick, which moves from left to right and upward, copies the selected text. You can change this behaviour though. Take a look at the options here. I suggest, for starters, you work with the defaults, and only consider changing the settings after you've done a little experimenting.

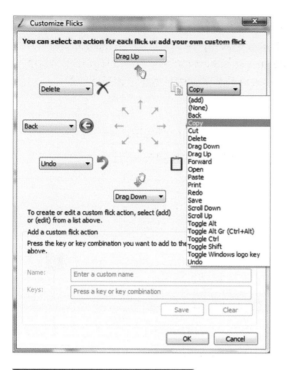

For your information

To customise flicks, return to the task entitled **Configuring tablet PC features** (p. 312).

Using flicks

1 Click on Start.

2 In the search box, type 'Pen and Input Devices'.

13

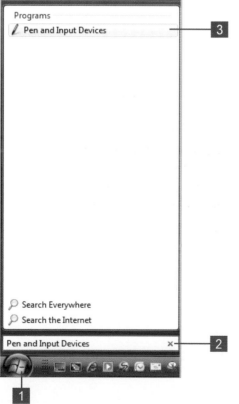

Flicks (cont.)

3 Click on Pen and Input Devices under Programs.

4 Click on the Flicks tab.

5 Click to practise using flicks.

6 Work through the wizard pages to learn how to use flicks.

7 When finished, click on Finish, and then OK.

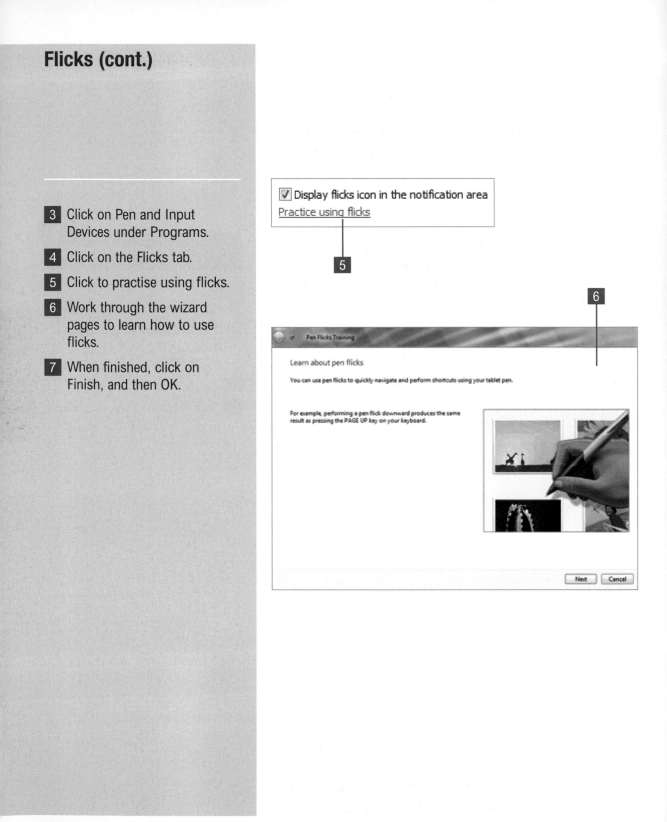

Journal is another tablet PC feature, although you can use it even if you don't have a tablet PC (if you can learn to write with a mouse or buy a handwriting digitiser). Journal lets you create entries using a tablet PC pen. A journal might be just the ticket when travelling, as you can jot down notes, keep a diary or a weekly record of events. You can also use it for taking notes in a class, while on the phone, or even to keep notes about a doctor's visit or hospital stay.

The best use of Journal comes when you need to draw something, do maths or write something quickly in a foreign language. It's difficult if not impossible to draw something in Word, for instance, and equally difficult to try to type out a calculation.

Beyond creating handwritten notes there are menus, just as you'd find in other programs. Here's Journal and the pen options.

There are lots of menu options, and I won't go over them all here. However, to help you get started, here are some you'll probably use often:

- File menu, New Note: open a new note page, where you can handwrite notes and save them.

- File menu, New Note From Template: Offers a place to open note templates, like To Do List and Month Calendar.

Windows Journal (cont.)

- File, and then Import: to bring in just about any data type, including pictures.

- File, Send To Mail Recipient: send notes in an email.

- Edit, Selection Tool: select text you've handwritten and convert it to typed text from the actions menu.

- Edit, Delete: remove selected text or data.

- Insert, Picture: to add a picture into any Notes page

- Actions, Convert Select to E-Mail: converts selected handwriting to typed text, and places the text in an email.

- Action, Convert Handwriting to Text: converts handwriting to text.

- Tools, Pen: to change the pen type. Similar menu options include Tools, Highlighter and Tools, Eraser.

Programs
Windows Journal ——————————— **3**

Search Everywhere
Search the Internet

Journal ——————————— **2**

1

Windows Journal (cont.)

Creating a new note with the journal

1 Click on Start.

2 In the Start Search window, type 'Journal'.

3 Click on Windows Journal under Programs.

4 Using your stylus (or mouse) write a note or memo.

5 Click on Edit.

6 Click on Select All.

13

5

Note5 - Windows Journal

File **Edit** View Insert Actions Tools Help

		Page Width ▾

Undo Ink Stroke	Ctrl+Z
Can't Redo	Ctrl+Y
Cut	Ctrl+X
Copy as Text...	
Copy	Ctrl+C
Paste	Ctrl+V
Selection Tool	
Select All	Ctrl+A
Select Page	
Cancel Selection	Esc
Delete	Del
Find...	Ctrl+F
Go to Page...	Ctrl+G
Format...	

E 5

nch With Bill

6

4

Windows Journal (cont.)

7 Click on Actions.

8 Click on Convert Handwriting to Text.

9 Use the stylus to correct any errors in the dialogue box.

10 Click on OK.

11 Click on 'Insert in the same Journal note'.

12 Click on Finish.

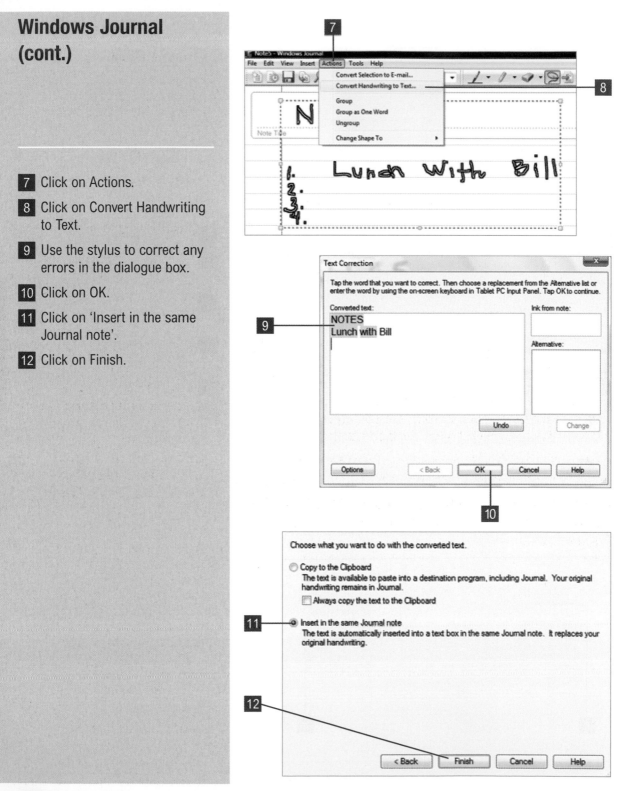

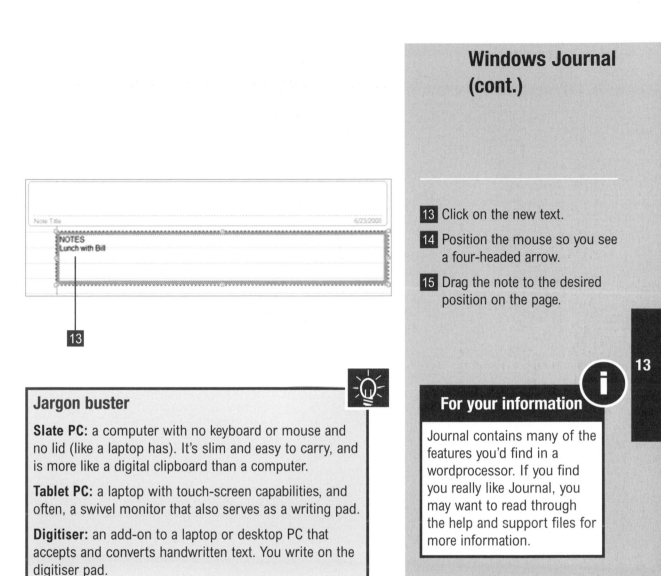

13 Click on the new text.

14 Position the mouse so you see a four-headed arrow.

15 Drag the note to the desired position on the page.

13

Jargon buster

Slate PC: a computer with no keyboard or mouse and no lid (like a laptop has). It's slim and easy to carry, and is more like a digital clipboard than a computer.

Tablet PC: a laptop with touch-screen capabilities, and often, a swivel monitor that also serves as a writing pad.

Digitiser: an add-on to a laptop or desktop PC that accepts and converts handwritten text. You write on the digitiser pad.

For your information

Journal contains many of the features you'd find in a wordprocessor. If you find you really like Journal, you may want to read through the help and support files for more information.

Holidays with a laptop

Introduction

The main reason you have a laptop may very well be the fact that it's a portable. You want to take it with you when you travel for both work and pleasure. You may want to send photos from your travels to others via e-mail, have a tool for keeping a journal or notes, and the option of doing work on the run. You may want to take a slideshow of your own pictures to your relatives' homes, or have the option of talking on a webcam with the family while you're away. You may even have an always-on satellite Internet connection where you can access maps, hotel websites and campsite information. Being mobile brings its own set of problems though, including getting through airport security, having to leave the laptop in a car or hotel room, and going through customs, to name a few. In this chapter you'll learn how to avoid common problems, keep your laptop secure and use your laptop safely.

What you'll do

Clean up your laptop before leaving on a trip

Move sensitive data off the laptop (USB key or external drive)

Encrypt sensitive data on the laptop

Back up your encryption key

Prepare for airline travel

Change the time, language or region

Print a list of contacts

Back up your laptop before you leave

▶

If your laptop is your only computer, you probably have everything of any importance on it. Some of this data may be precious to you, such as family photos, and some may be sensitive – tax information or personal or company documents. When travelling with a laptop then, you have to ask yourself two things:

■ Am I prepared to replace this data if my laptop is stolen, lost or broken? Do I have a valid, tested and working back-up?

■ What will happen if the personal data I have stored on my laptop gets into someone else's hands? Will the thief be able to steal my identity, access my personal bank accounts or otherwise use my personal information to his or her advantage?

If you keep these questions fresh in your mind while preparing for a trip, I can almost guarantee you'll make copies of your data and remove sensitive (and unnecessary) data from the laptop. (It's highly unlikely you'll need last year's tax information while on holiday, for instance, so you should remove it from your laptop, just in case it's stolen.)

Now, with the idea that you need to prepare your laptop in the case of it being lost or stolen (or broken), here are the tasks you need to complete:

■ Copy of all your important files. Keep the back-up at home in a safe place. Here are a few of the folders you should back up and remove personal information from:

  – Desktop: this folder contains links to data you created on your desktop.

  – Documents: this holds documents you've saved, subfolders you created, and folders created by Vista including Fax, My Received Files, Remote Assistance Logs and Scanned Documents.

  – Pictures: images you save to the PC.

  – Videos: videos you save to the PC.

■ After the back-up is complete, remove sensitive information from your laptop. Delete everything that won't be needed on your trip. Examples include tax spreadsheets, confidential company files, personal files, medical information, letters to lawyers, documents that list passwords or sign-in information for websites, and similar data. I suggest you create a second copy of this information on a USB key, CD or DVD.

- Remove and store unnecessary peripherals such as webcams, printers, external drives, Ethernet cables and mice.

- If possible, encrypt personal files that must remain on your laptop. Encrypted files can only be accessed with a password.

- If you must have access to sensitive information while away from home, consider using a secure online data storage service, such as Google Docs & Spreadsheets, Ibackup or Evault.com.

Back up your laptop before you leave (cont.)

Clean up your laptop before leaving on a trip

1 Delete data that is not longer needed. One way to do this is to drag it to the Recycle Bin, but you can also right-click and choose Delete. Once you've finished, right-click on the bin and choose Empty Recycle Bin, otherwise the items can be restored.

2 Back up important data. See Chapter 8.

3 Detach any hardware not needed.

14

Back up your laptop before you leave (cont.)

Move sensitive data off the laptop (USB drive or external drive)

1. If you have a USB drive (sometimes call a pen drive or USB key), insert it into one of the laptop's USB ports. If you do not, connect the laptop to an external or network drive.

2. Right-click any data you want to move. As usual, hold down the Shift key to select files grouped together, or hold down the Ctrl key while clicking on files spread around the screen.

3. Click on Cut.

4. Browse to the location to move the file.

5. Right-click and choose Paste.

Backups and Passwords	6/19/2008 4:49 PM	File Folder
Personal - Wills Resumes	6/19/2008 4:49 PM	File Folder
Taxes		lder
About the Authors2		oft Office ...
Joli Ballew Resume 2008		oft Office ...
Joli's Calendar		dar File

Explore
Open
SnagIt ▶
Send To ▶
Cut
Copy
Create Shortcut

View ▶
Sort By ▶
Group By ▶
Stack By ▶
Refresh

Customize This Folder...

Paste
Paste Shortcut
Undo Move   Ctrl+Z

New ▶

Properties

For your information

If you are flying and need access to a power outlet on the plane, contact the airline and see if you can get a seat close to a power outlet.

Encryption

Encryption lets you protect sensitive data that you must take with you on a laptop. When data is encrypted, only the person with the required 'encryption key' can open the files. The key is created when you choose to encrypt. After encryption, you should back up your key in case anything happens to it. Companies hold encryption keys on smart cards and similar media. Once you've set up encryption, opening, working with and saving encrypted files is seamless for you, but it's a problem for thieves and hackers. When a folder is encrypted, it simply can't be opened without the proper key.

Knowing how encryption works isn't important. However, knowing how to apply encryption to files and folders is. If you have sensitive data you want to protect while on the road, enabling encryption is the way to do it.

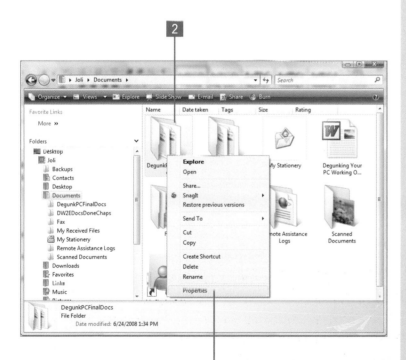

Encrypt sensitive data left on the laptop

1 Note that you can only encrypt data on Vista Business, Ultimate or Enterprise. To encrypt files, go to the windows showing your documents.

2 Right-click on the folder to encrypt.

3 Click on Properties.

14

Back up your laptop before you leave (cont.)

4 From the Properties dialogue box, click on the General tab.

5 Click on Advanced.

6 Click on 'Encrypt contents to secure data'.

7 Click on OK, and click on OK again.

4

General	Sharing	Security	Previous Versions	Customize

DegunkPCFinalDocs

Type:	File Folder
Location:	C:\Users\Joli\Documents
Size:	1.80 MB (1,892,864 bytes)
Size on disk:	1.83 MB (1,921,024 bytes)
Contains:	18 Files, 0 Folders
Created:	Today, June 24, 2008, 19 minutes ago
Attributes:	☐ Read-only (Only applies to files in folder)
	☐ Hidden Advanced...

5

Advanced Attributes ✕

Choose the settings you want for this folder.

When you click OK or Apply on the Properties dialog, you will be asked if you want the changes to affect all subfolders and files as well.

Archive and Index attributes

☐ Folder is ready for archiving

☑ Index this folder for faster searching

Compress or Encrypt attributes

☐ Compress contents to save disk space

6 ☑ Encrypt contents to secure data Details

OK Cancel

7

352

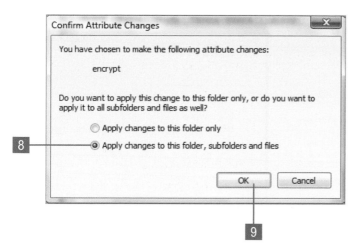

8

9

After you encrypt data, you need to copy your key file so that you can open the encrypted files if something happens to the encryption key on the laptop. If your encryption key file is lost or corrupted, without a back-up there's no way you will be able to access the data. It's that secure. You will also lose data if you store your encryption key on a smart card and that card is lost, stolen or damaged. To make sure you can always access your encrypted data, you should back up your encryption certificate and key.

8 If prompted, select Apply changes to this folder, subfolders, and files.

9 Click on OK.

10 Notice the folder, which is now encrypted, appears in green.

14

Back up your laptop before you leave (cont.)

Back up your encryption key

1. Click onStart.

2. Type certmgr.msc.

3. Under Programs, select certmgr.

4. Click on the arrow next to the Personal folder. It will expand.

5. Click on Certificates.

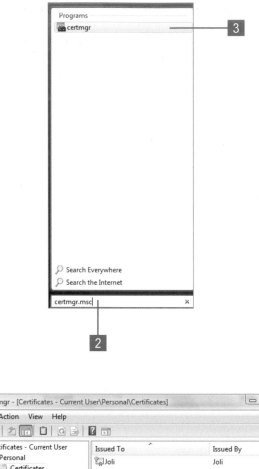

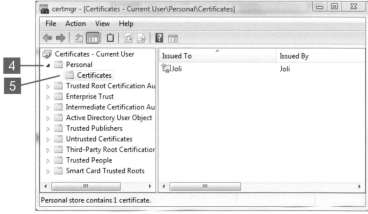

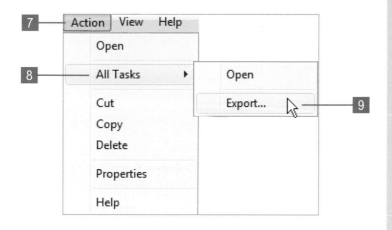

6 Select the certificate. If there is more than one, use the Shift key while selecting the first and last. This will select all of them.

7 Click on Action.

8 Click on All Tasks.

9 Click on Export.

10 Click on Next to start the wizard.

Certificate Export Wizard

Welcome to the Certificate Export Wizard

This wizard helps you copy certificates, certificate trust lists and certificate revocation lists from a certificate store to your disk.

A certificate, which is issued by a certification authority, is a confirmation of your identity and contains information used to protect data or to establish secure network connections. A certificate store is the system area where certificates are kept.

To continue, click Next.

< Back   Next >   Cancel

14

Back up your laptop before you leave (cont.)

11 Click on 'Yes, export the private key'.

12 Click on Next.

13 Click on Personal Information Exchange.

14 Click on Next.

Certificate Export Wizard

Export Private Key
You can choose to export the private key with the certificate.

Private keys are password protected. If you want to export the private key with the certificate, you must type a password on a later page.

Do you want to export the private key with the certificate?

⦿ Yes, export the private key

○ No, do not export the private key ————————— 11

Learn more about exporting private keys

[< Back] [Next >] [Cancel]

12

Certificate Export Wizard

Export File Format
Certificates can be exported in a variety of file formats.

Select the format you want to use:

○ DER encoded binary X.509 (.CER)

○ Base-64 encoded X.509 (.CER)

○ Cryptographic Message Syntax Standard - PKCS #7 Certificates (.P7B)

☐ Include all certificates in the certification path if possible

13 —— ⦿ Personal Information Exchange - PKCS #12 (.PFX)

☐ Include all certificates in the certification path if possible

☐ Delete the private key if the export is successful

☐ Export all extended properties

○ Microsoft Serialized Certificate Store (.SST)

Learn more about certificate file formats

[< Back] [Next >] [Cancel]

14

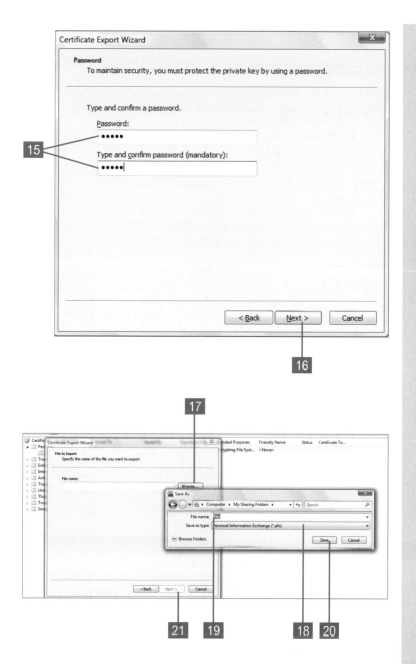

15 Type in a password and confirm it.

16 Click on Next.

17 Click on Browse.

18 Locate a place to save the file. Use a USB pen drive or network drive.

19 Name the file.

20 Click on Save.

21 Click on Next.

22 Click on Finish.

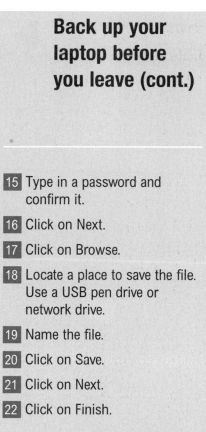

14

Be sure you need your laptop ▶

Have you ever packed a laptop for a trip, lugged it to the airport, got it through security and then never turned it on? It happens all the time. So before you start packing, ask yourself if you will really have time to use your laptop. Here are some questions to help you decide if you'll have time or need to use your laptop:

- Are you staying with relatives? If so, you may be able to use their computer to go online and check email, if that's all you need to do.

- Are you staying in a place with lots of noise? You probably won't get much work done if so.

- Is your trip so busy that you won't have time to use the laptop?

- If you will have a computer available, can you simply take the files you need on a USB pen drive or CD?

- Do you need Internet access to work? If so, will you have a connection available? Are there cafés with free wireless access?

- Are you going to be too busy camping, swimming, hiking and biking to use your laptop? You can always upload the pictures you take once you get home.

- How far are you going to have to carry your laptop bag? Do you have a long walk from where you'll park to the airport terminal, or from the terminal to your hotel? Are you going to be happy carrying your laptop around?

- Can you use your mobile phone or PDA instead of a laptop?

- Will you have enough time to get through security with your laptop? Do you know of any problems taking a laptop through customs in your part of the world?

- Do you have the necessary power adapters if going overseas? If not, can you buy the required adapters?

If you've decided you need to bring a laptop and that you'll have time to use it, you'll want to make sure you pack all of the required accessories, and that you pack correctly. No matter whether you travel by boat, car, airplane or motorcycle, you really do need a padded carrying bag (or case) that will hold everything you need for your laptop. It's time-consuming, disorganised and unsafe to carry just the laptop in one bag, while packing all of its bits in another. Your laptop won't do you much good if the airline loses your luggage, which also contains the power cable. Make sure that the bag for your laptop also contains power cables, an extra battery, Ethernet cable and/or wireless network card.

Make sure the bag you choose has padding. It should also have compartments to keep the components from damaging each other. When I travel, I use an expandable backpack that has wheels and an extendable handle for pulling. Expandable backpacks have lots of compartments, almost always fit in an airplane's overhead locker, are often padded, and can be stowed easily in a car or under a bed in a hotel. A backpack on wheels also helps disguise what you're carrying. It doesn't look like a laptop carrying case; it looks like a backpack. This discourages theft.

Here are some things you should carry in your laptop bag:

- Power cable.
- Wireless network card.
- Ethernet cable (in case WiFi is not available).
- A USB pen drive for back-up.
- An extra battery (for long excursions without power).
- Power adapters.
- A plastic rubbish sack or something similar to wrap your laptop bag in if you have to walk in the rain with it.
- A laptop lock.

Packing your laptop

For your information

Getting through airport security with a laptop requires you to take it out of the bag, so you'll want to make removing the laptop a quick and easy process. I keep my laptop in a compartment all to itself, so there is no problem removing it.

14

Packing your laptop (cont.)

And here are a few things you can pack in the luggage you check in, or in a separate bag for a car or boat trip:

- The operating system disk. You may need to recover the laptop if there is a software failure.

- Warranty information. You really only need this if you're going on a long trip.

- Wireless network detector (if you're running Windows XP). Windows Vista should pick up all local networks.

- If you prefer, a real mouse, external keyboard, headset, webcam and/or a surge protector.

Finally, here are a few things you probably don't need:

- External speakers.

- Travel printers. Many hotels offer free print services, you can probably find an Internet café that offers one, and you can save anything you want to print to a USB pen drive and print it when a computer with a printer becomes available.

Airports across the globe have tightened security in recent years. You have to take off your shoes, belts and jewellery, and place your mobile phone and laptop (and other electronic devices) in a special bin to be X-rayed. Some countries may require security steps you have not yet been exposed to. For instance, you may be asked to turn on your laptop to prove it is a working device. (The same can be true of cameras.) For that reason, you'll want to make sure you have enough power to boot your laptop without having to drag out a power cable and find a plug.

As you would expect, there are plenty of ways to prepare for a trip to the airport with a laptop. Here are a few things to remember:

- Always put your laptop and peripherals in a bag you will carry on the airplane with you. Never check in a laptop.

- Keep your laptop bag with you at all times. If possible, keep the bag underneath the seat in front of you once you're on the plane: that way, you are in control of it.

- It's OK to send your laptop under an X-ray machine; that won't hurt it. What you must do is make sure you're through security before your laptop is through the X-ray machine. People have been known to steal laptops from a security queue.

- Make sure you have some kind of proof the laptop belongs to you. You may want to carry a copy of the sales receipt, have your full name as an option for a user account when logging in, and add stickers on the outside of the laptop with your name and address.

- Regarding the receipt, if you have to go through customs, bring it. You will want to be able to prove, if asked, that the laptop was purchased in your home country, not the country you just visited. You don't want to be forced to pay duties or taxes on it.

- If at any time during your stay at the airport or on the airplane someone seems a little too curious about your laptop, keep in mind they could be looking for a laptop to steal.

- If possible, once through airport security, lock your laptop bag.

Taking your laptop on an airplane

14

Taking your laptop on an airplane (cont.)

Once you've arrived at your destination and are in airport (or hotel), change the clock, language and Region settings on your laptop. There are several options including changing the date and time, changing the time zone, showing additional clocks, adding a clock gadget to the Windows sidebar, and even changing the country or region so that information you obtain online matches your current location. You can also change how numbers, currency, time and date are displayed on your laptop, if you desire.

Preparing for airline travel

1. Purchase a heavily padded carrying case, preferably one with wheels that you can pull behind you. Make sure all required peripherals will fit in it.

2. Pack the case carefully, placing the laptop in a compartment by itself for easy removal. Make sure other components are secure and cannot touch other peripherals and damage them.

3. If you have to work on an airplane but can't get access to a power outlet, carry an extra battery with you.

4. Remove disks from disk drives.

5. If you are unsure what type of power adapter to bring, call the hotel, airline or campsite. Buy the proper adapter and pack it before leaving.

6. Call your host to find out how you can get online while there. You may need to bring a phone cord for dial-up, an Ethernet cable for wired connections, or a wireless network card for satellite service.

Taking your laptop on an airplane (cont.)

7 Call you insurance company and ask if your laptop will be covered on your trip. If not, consider travel insurance. You can contact a travel agent for advice.

8 Charge your laptop battery fully before leaving for the airport.

9 Avoid having your laptop stolen by monitoring it closely. Be especially aware of where the laptop is as it travels through the X-ray machine. If you're worried, in many airports you can ask for manual inspection.

10 If possible, keep your laptop at your feet during the flight.

14

Taking your laptop on an airplane (cont.)

Changing the time, language or region

1 Click on Start.

2 Click on Control Panel.

3 Click on Clock, Language, and Region.

4 To change the time zone, click on 'Change the time zone'.

5 Click on 'Change time zone'. (You must be logged on as an administrator to perform this task.)

6 Select the time zone from the drop down list.

7 Click on OK.

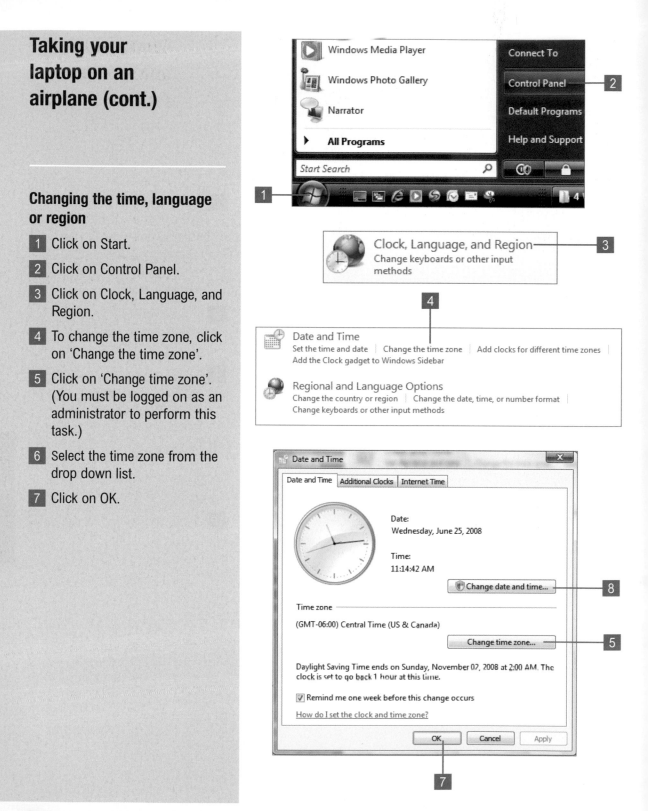

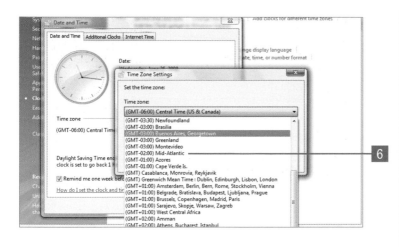

8 With the date and time window still open, click on 'Change date and time'.

9 Click inside the date and/or time options to change them.

10 Click on OK.

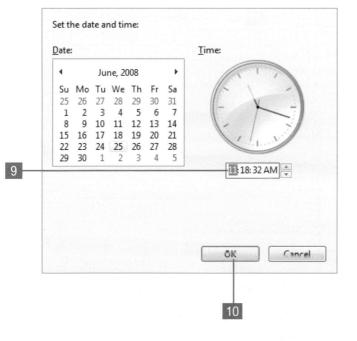

Taking your laptop on an airplane (cont.)

11 To add additional clocks, click on the Additional Clocks tab.

12 Select 'Show this clock'.

13 Select a time zone to add.

14 Click on OK.

15 Click on Start.

16 Click on Control Panel.

17 Click on Clock, Language and Region.

18 Click on Regional and Language Options.

19 From the Formats tab, click on 'Customize this format' if you want to access the tasks to change the number, currency, time or date settings.

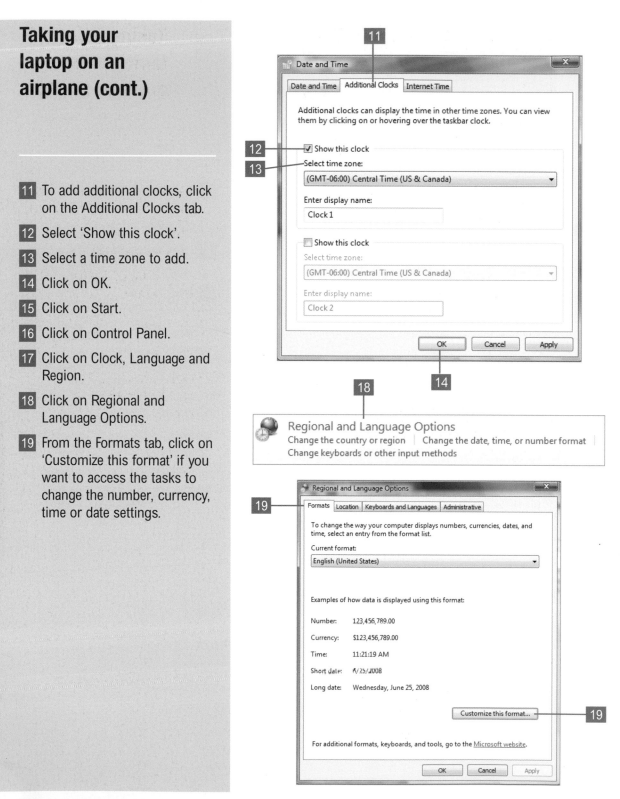

11

Date and Time

Date and Time | Additional Clocks | Internet Time

Additional clocks can display the time in other time zones. You can view them by clicking on or hovering over the taskbar clock.

12 ☑ Show this clock

13 Select time zone:

(GMT-06:00) Central Time (US & Canada) ▾

Enter display name:

Clock 1

☐ Show this clock

Select time zone:

(GMT-06:00) Central Time (US & Canada) ▾

Enter display name:

Clock 2

[OK] [Cancel] [Apply]

14

18

Regional and Language Options
Change the country or region | Change the date, time, or number format
Change keyboards or other input methods

Regional and Language Options

19 Formats | Location | Keyboards and Languages | Administrative

To change the way your computer displays numbers, currencies, dates, and time, select an entry from the format list.

Current format:

English (United States) ▾

Examples of how data is displayed using this format:

Number: 123,456,789.00

Currency: $123,456,789.00

Time: 11:21:19 AM

Short date: 6/25/2008

Long date: Wednesday, June 25, 2008

[Customize this format...] 19

For additional formats, keyboards, and tools, go to the Microsoft website.

[OK] [Cancel] [Apply]

Customize Regional Options

Numbers | Currency | Time | Date

Example

Positive: 123,456,789.00   Negative: -123,456,789.00

Decimal symbol:	.
No. of digits after decimal:	2
Digit grouping symbol:	,
Digit grouping:	123,456,789
Negative sign symbol:	-
Negative number format:	-1.1
Display leading zeros:	0.7
List separator:	,
Measurement system:	U.S.
Standard digits:	0123456789
Use native digits:	Never

Click Reset to restore the system default settings for numbers, currency, time, and date.   Reset

OK   Cancel   Apply

20

21   24

Regional and Language Options

Formats | Location | Keyboards and Languages | Administrative

Some software and services provide you with local information such as news and weather.

Current location:

22   Turkey

OK   Cancel   Apply

23

20 There are many options. Make your changes and click on OK.

21 Click on the Location tab to select a new location.

22 From the dropdown list, select your present location.

23 Continue configuration as warranted. Click on OK when finished.

24 Close the Control Panel by clicking the X in the top right corner.

14

Getting online access

Travelling with a laptop is not always easy, but the benefit of having Internet access often makes up for the trouble of lugging it around. Having such access means you can contract friends and family, send photos, keep a blog of your travels, get local information and even manage bank accounts and pay bills. Beyond that, you can back up the data you create to online servers, or even send it to yourself so you'll have it when you get home.

Getting online isn't the same in all countries around the world, though. A modem from one region may not recognise the dial tone in another region. Even if it does, you may be charged long-distance fees for connecting. So, if you use a dial-up connection, make sure to call your ISP before you leave, tell them where you're going, and ask if you'll have Internet access while there, and if so, how you'll log on and what it will cost. Additionally, you won't always have access to an Ethernet jack that offers Internet access, and if you do find one, you'll probably have to have a user name and password. In most places though, you can get online via satellite. Therefore, before taking off on a long journey with your laptop, consider buying a satellite card and subscription.

Staying safe on the Internet

On your travels, you need to take as many precautions as possible when online, especially if you're in a public place such as an Internet café. There is no way for you to know if the connection you have to the Internet is safe, or if others can access your laptop while you're online.

First, when connecting to a public network, make sure you select 'Public' when prompted by Vista. When you connect to a network you know, like a network in your home, you select Home (or Work) as shown opposite. However, when you're in a public place, when prompted, always select 'Public location'.

Second, make sure your laptop's security applications and software updates are current, and that includes anti-virus software, your firewall and anti-spyware.

Beyond these two very important precautions are several more.
When connecting to the Internet in a foreign place:

- Limit the amount of confidential information you send over
  the Internet. If possible, do not make credit card purchases,
  travel reservations or input your social security number.

- Set up a remote web mail account to enable email access
  from any browser, such as Gmail, Yahoo! Mail or MSN
  Hotmail. Web mail servers have built-in security that you can
  benefit from while travelling.

- Always sign out of any secure website you enter, so that the
  next person can't use your information to make purchases or
  withdraw funds.

- If possible, delete your browsing history. In Internet Explorer,
  you'll find this option under Tools.

14

Getting online access (cont.)

Travelling without a laptop and getting online

In Europe, Canada and the US, most places that offer web access, whether free or for lease, offer drinks, snacks, coffee or beer, and their main business is to sell these items to you while you are online. There are other places too, including launderettes, print shops and convenience stores. In larger cities, you can use your own laptop to get online, but more and more often, you can use a PC made available by the establishment.

If you do plan to travel (with or) without a laptop you can probably find a list of Internet cafés in a local travel or guidebook, but you can also locate such places online before you leave. As you research, you may find that some are equipped with microphones and headsets, cater to a specific age group, allow or do not allow the burning of CDs, access USB ports, or upload or download data. Most of the time, you'll simply have Internet access, and nothing else. Beyond such places, there are options that are almost always free. These include public libraries and hotel lobbies.

For your information

The most secure places to get online using a rented computer are those where the computer is reset to its default settings each time a person quits a session. Before committing, ask the proprietor if this is the case.

Carrying online data

There are several important things to bring with you on your trip if you plan to communicate online. You'll need your contact's email addresses for one. This information will be on your laptop, but if you're not bringing a laptop make sure to print out your contact list. You'll probably also want to list the websites you visit often. You'll have to do this by hand, most likely. And while you may also need your user names and passwords, it's best to commit those to memory (rather than writing them down on paper or saving them to your laptop).

Here are some additional options for enabling access to sensitive data such as user names and passwords:

- Store them in an encrypted folder on your laptop.
- Send them to yourself and access the email when you need to retrieve the data.
- Save the information to a USB pen drive you keep on a keychain that's with you at all times. You may also want to change some information just in case the pen gets stolen. Whereas your actually password may be Wx6658#, save the password as Wx6658#np.

For your information

In the next section, you'll learn how to export your Windows Mail contact list to a file and then print your contact information. You can follow similar steps in other programs to achieve the same thing.

14

Getting online access (cont.)

Printing a list of contacts in Windows Mail

1. Click on Start.
2. Click on your user name.
3. Double-click on the Contacts folder to open it.
4. Click on Export.
5. Select CSV (Comma Separated Values).
6. Click on Export.

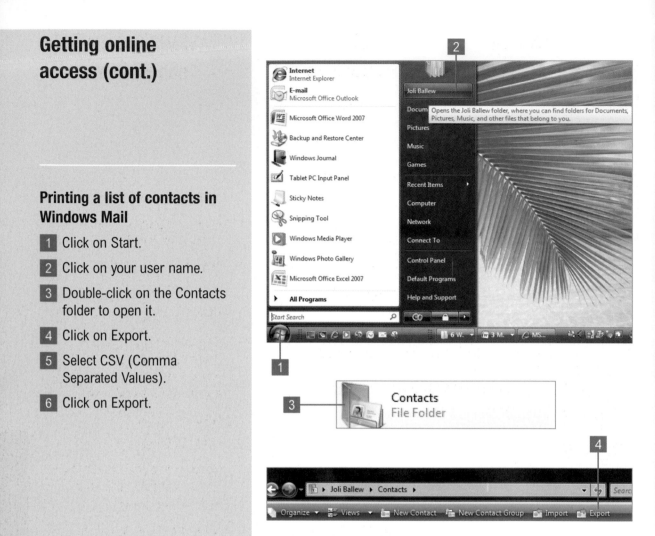

7 Click on Browse.

8 Note the location where the file will be saved, Documents.

9 Type in a name for the file.

10 Click on Save.

11 Click on Next.

12 Select the fields to export. Make sure you select First Name, Last Name, Name, and E-mail Address (at least).

13 Click on Finish.

14 Click on Close.

15 Locate the saved contacts file. It will probably be in your Documents folder.

16 Double-click on the file to open it.

Getting online access (cont.)

17 In the program window, locate the Print command. It may be on a menu bar or under the File menu.

18 Select the printer.

19 Configure any print options.

20 Click on OK.

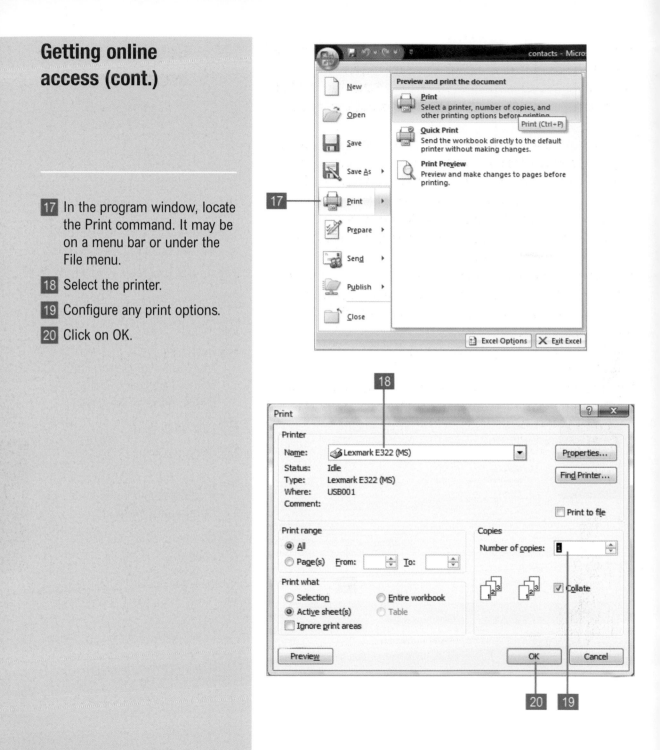

While away you'll want to make sure your laptop is secure. The easiest way to do that is to keep the laptop in your sight. If it must be left in a hotel room or car, hide it. Better yet, in a hotel room use a laptop lock or the safe, and in a car, use the boot.

It's also important to know that while it's common for people in the West to carry a laptop or work on a laptop in public places, in less developed countries this can be seen as a sign of wealth. This may make your laptop – or you – a target for thieves. As noted earlier, carrying the laptop in a bag such as a generic backpack makes you (and it) far less attractive to the bad guys.

Hard drives can also be damaged if you drop them, or if they are exposed to heavy vibration. So, if you're on a safari in a 4x4, leave the laptop at camp. Laptops are also affected by heat and humidity, and the best way to keep a laptop safe is to avoid these types of weather conditions.

Finally, because the power grid is unreliable in many developing countries, always use a surge protector. You may also need to buy an adapter for the electrical plug at your destination.

Physically secure your laptop

14

Maintaining and upgrading your laptop

15

Introduction

There are a few things you have to do to keep your laptop in tip-top shape. One is to clean the laptop, but it's important to note you can't just scrub it with soap and water! You have to know what to do and how to do it, so that you don't harm any of the components. It's also important to take precautions, such as using a surge protector and configuring the laptop's keyboard power button to apply hibernation and sleep options when you press it.

Beyond the physical, it's important to keep the virtual side in good order too. That means using Disk Cleanup and Disk Defragmenter regularly. Doing so will keep unwanted files off your hard drive, and keep files you want optimally stored.

Finally, you may want to add a printer or digital camera, and/or add external or internal RAM. You'll learn how to do all of these things in this chapter.

What you'll do

Clean the outside of the laptop

Clean the keyboard and monitor

Clean the inside of the laptop

Apply surge protection

Apply sleep and hibernate settings

Use Disk Cleanup

Use Disk Defragmenter

Install a printer (or scanner)

Install a digital camera

Use ReadyBoost

Maintain your laptop

Maintaining your laptop, physically at least, doesn't take much effort. You need to keep it clean, make sure it's protected from power surges or lightning strikes, and try to avoid continually turning it on and off. Let's start by cleaning the laptop.

Clean your laptop

On the surface, you may see a few fingerprints, maybe a couple of sticky spots and think all is well. That may not be the case. If you look at the ports on the laptop such as the USB and FireWire ports, you just may find dust, cat hairs or even nicotine build up. If you look closely at the monitor and keyboard, you're likely to find dirt there too. Fingerprints, food particles, pet hair and more accumulate over time. To keep your monitor and keyboard performing optimally, you'll want to remove the grime. Since it's important to keep these areas dirt free, you should clean them two or three times a year, or as needed.

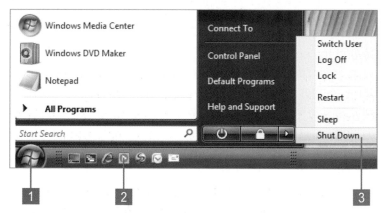

When you clean the inside of a laptop you have to deal with two things: the monitor and keyboard. When cleaning the screen, make sure to first read any instructions that came with it. If you don't have any instructions, try looking up the information on the web. This is important because monitors can be flimsy, and you don't want to damage yours.

Cleaning the outside of the laptop

1 Click on Start.

2 Click on the arrow shown at the bottom of the Start menu.

3 Click on Shut Down.

4 Unplug the laptop from the wall socket.

5 Disconnect all external hardware, including webcam, flash drive and printer.

6 Use a vacuum cleaner with a small attachment to pull dust from the external ports. If there is an air intake, clean that as well.

7 Use compressed air to blow out remaining dust and dirt.

8 Clean any additional crevices with a dry cotton bud.

9 Clean the plastic outside of the case with a cotton rag sprayed with a mild, non-abrasive cleaner. Do not get any electrical part or port wet.

10 Reconnect peripherals.

That said, when cleaning the monitor:

- Use a soft, dry, non-abrasive cloth. Don't use a paper towel. If you can find one and can afford it, buy an LCD cleaning kit.

- Never use ammonia or strong cleaners or spray anything on the screen.

- For tough spots, add a touch of vinegar to the cleaning cloth.

- Clean from top to bottom.

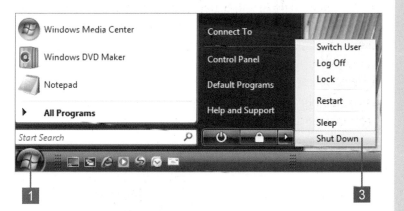

The inside of a laptop can also acquire dust and dirt. This build-up can cause your laptop to run 'hot'. Problems related to heat may cause the computer to shut down unexpectedly, or worse, cause permanent damage to the laptop's internal parts. Thus, the inside needs to be cleaned on occasion as well.

I clean the inside of my laptop once a year. However, this involves opening the laptop's case, which voids the warranty. That said, you have three choices regarding this task. You can:

- Never clean the inside of the laptop, but keep the air vents and other openings free of dust with canned air.

- Take the laptop to a qualified technician every 18 months or so.

- Take your chances and clean the inside of the laptop yourself.

If you choose the last option, the next section shows you how to perform the internal cleaning of a laptop.

Cleaning the keyboard

1 Click on Start.

2 Click on the arrow at the bottom of the Start menu.

3 Click on Shut Down.

4 Unplug the laptop from the wall outlet.

5 Disconnect all external hardware, including external webcam, flash drive and printer.

6 To clean the keyboard, hold the entire laptop upside down with the lid open and shake gently.

7 After shaking gently, and still holding upside down, use compressed air to remove additional dust and grime. (You may need someone to help you with this.)

8 Turn the laptop right side up, and use a toothpick to loosen dirt stuck between the keys.

9 Wipe the monitor clean following the earlier instructions. Remember, never spray anything directly on the screen.

15

Maintain your laptop (cont.)

Cleaning the inside of the laptop

1. Unplug the computer from the wall and disconnect any connected hardware.

2. Find out how to open your laptop case and obtain the required tools. Most open with a flat head screwdriver these days.

3. Open the battery compartment and remove the battery. There will be instructions on how to do this either in the battery compartment itself or in the computer's documentation.

4. Open the laptop case.

5. Ground yourself and expel any stored static electricity by touching a metal desk (or something similar) before touching anything inside the laptop.

Use surge protection

Lightning strikes, electrical power surges and power failures can wreak havoc on your laptop's power supply and internal parts. One good lightning strike can destroy a laptop. To be safe, when your laptop is plugged in, it should be connected to a surge protector.

Make sure when you buy your surge protector you don't end up with a simple extension lead with extra sockets. These don't offer protection – just more electrical sockets. A surge protector often offers additional sockets and protection from power surges for any or all of the following:

- Electrical cables to the laptop.
- Cable, ADSL or other modems.
- Coaxial cable inputs.

Important

Even the most expensive surge protectors may not protect your laptop if lightning hits your home. Since that is the case, it's best to unplug your laptop when a lightning storm approaches.

Using hibernation and sleep

It's not good for a laptop to be turned 'all the way' off and then 'all the way' on often. At least that's what many people believe, including me. Although a point of contention among experts, the facts seem to show that minimising the number of times you boot the laptop will lengthen the life of the CPU, the CPU fan and the hard drive, as well as other components. However, when you leave a computer on all the time, it uses electricity and may create excess heat. This in turn may raise your electricity bill and/or cause heat-related problems for the laptop. To find a happy medium then, I suggest you learn how to use hibernation and sleep settings.

You can put the computer to sleep using the Start button, but with a laptop it's much more convenient to put the computer to sleep (or into hibernation) by closing the lid. You can configure what happens when you close the lid, when you press the power button, or even when you press an available Sleep button on your laptop, from System Settings. You can also configure preferences for each of these based on whether or not your laptop is currently plugged in to an electrical outlet.

Define power buttons and turn on password protection

Choose the power settings that you want for your computer. The changes you make to the settings on this page apply to all of your power plans.

Change settings that are currently unavailable

Power and sleep buttons and lid settings

		On battery	Plugged in
When I press the power button:		Shut down	Shut down
When I press the sleep button:		Sleep	Sleep
When I close the lid:		Sleep	Sleep

First, you must understand the difference between sleeping and hibernating.

In the hibernate mode, the laptop will save any data that has not been saved to RAM, and turn itself off. It will not draw any electricity when it's off. When you awake the laptop from hibernation, you continue where you left off, including having immediate access to open programs and files. Recovering from hibernation takes more time than recovering from the sleep mode. I suggest using Hibernate when you aren't sure when you'll use your laptop again and Sleep when you will use it very soon.

In the sleep mode the computer seems to have turned off, but power is still provided to keep the computer's memory powered. Sleep is a good choice when you leave your PC over lunch and want to save energy. Usually, moving the mouse or pressing a key on the keyboard will bring the computer quickly out of sleep. Recovering from Sleep takes a lot less time than recovering from Hibernate. I suggest you use Sleep when you

6 Remove dust using a dry cotton bud, a small vacuum attachment or canned air. Be extremely careful not to loosen any parts.

7 Do not detach the monitor or keyboard, or force any part of the laptop open. If you can't reach it easily, dust probably can't either.

8 Replace the battery and cover.

15

Maintain your laptop (cont.)

Apply sleep and hibernate settings

1 Click on Start.

2 Click on Control Panel.

3 Click on Mobile PC.

know you'll be accessing your PC in the next 1–24 hours. (Note, since Sleep uses some power, if you do not have access to an electrical outlet, use Hibernate.)

In the next section, you'll configure what happens when you press the power button, press the sleep button and/or close the laptop's lid. You can configure different settings for when the laptop is plugged in to a power outlet and when it's running on batteries. For each, you can choose from Do Nothing, Sleep, Hibernate and Shut Down.

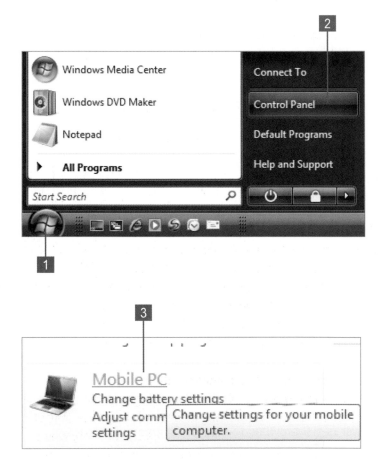

Power Options
Change battery settings | Require a password when the computer wakes
Change when the computer sleeps | Change what the power buttons do
Change what closing the lid does

4

5

« Hardware and Sound ▸ Power Options ▸ System Settings | Search

File Edit View Tools Help

Define power buttons and turn on password protection

Choose the power settings that you want for your computer. The changes you make to the settings on this page apply to all of your power plans.

Change settings that are currently unavailable

Power and sleep buttons and lid settings

	On battery	Plugged in
When I press the power button:	Shut down	Shut down
When I press the sleep button:	Sleep	Sleep
When I close the lid:	Hibernate	Sleep

Password protection on wakeup

⦿ Require a password (recommended)
When your computer wakes from sleep, no one can access your data without entering the correct password to unlock the computer. Create or change your user account password

○ Don't require a password
When your computer wakes from sleep, anyone can access your data because the computer isn't locked.

Save changes   Cancel

4 Click on 'Change what the power buttons do'.

5 Configure the settings as desired. My laptop settings are shown here.

Disk cleanup

Disk Cleanup is a safe and effective way to reduce unnecessary data on your laptop. With such files deleted, your PC will run faster and have more disk space for saving files and installing programs. With Disk Cleanup you can remove temporary files, empty the Recycle Bin, remove set-up log files and downloaded program files (among other things), in a single process.

Disk Cleanup has only changed a little from the version included with Windows XP. The only thing that will stand out initially is that you can choose to clean up only your files or all users' files. Additionally, there is a More Options tab, where you can free up disk space by deleting programs you don't need, and you can now remove all but the most recent System Restore points and shadow copies if desired. Disk Cleanup lets you clean all of your drive's partitions too, to enable you to optimise the entire PC.

15

Maintain your laptop (cont.)

!

Important

You can delete all of the files listed opposite without causing any harm. However, read the description of each and choose wisely. If you recently deleted a lot of files for instance, you may not want to empty the Recycle Bin right away; you may decide you need to restore something from there later. For the most part though, accepting the defaults during the Disk Cleanup process works fine.

Disk Cleanup for (C:)

| Disk Cleanup | More Options |

You can use Disk Cleanup to free up to 474 MB of disk space on (C:).

Files to delete:

☑ Downloaded Program Files	0 bytes
☑ Temporary Internet Files	14.0 MB
☐ Offline Webpages	80.3 KB
☑ Recycle Bin	443 MB
☑ Setup Log Files	3.10 KB

Total amount of disk space you gain: 474 MB

Description

Downloaded Program Files are ActiveX controls and Java applets downloaded automatically from the Internet when you view certain pages. They are temporarily stored in the Downloaded Program Files folder on your hard disk.

View Files

How does Disk Cleanup work?

OK   Cancel

?

Did you know?

If you run Disk Cleanup to clean your files only, you won't see the More Options tab.

Disk Cleanup lets you safely remove the following (you can pick and choose which):

- Downloaded program files: these download automatically when you view certain web pages. They are stored temporarily and accessed when and if needed.

- Temporary Internet files: these contain copies of web pages you've visited so that you can see the pages more quickly when visiting the page again.

- Offline web pages: these are pages that you've chosen to store so you can see them without being connected to the Internet. Upon connection, the data is synchronised.

- Recycle bin: contains files you've deleted. Files are not permanently deleted until you empty the bin.

- Set-up log files: created by Windows during set-up processes.

- Temporary files: created and stored by programs for their own use. Most of these are deleted when you quit the program, but not all.

- Thumbnails: small icons of your pictures, videos and documents. Thumbnails will be recreated as needed, even if you delete them here.

- Per user archived Windows error reporting: files used for error reporting and solution checking.

- System archived Windows error reporting: files used for error reporting and solution checking.

As noted, you can also access the More Options tab, where you can remove programs that you do not use. Clicking on Clean up here opens the Control Panel's Programs and Features window, where you can view installed programs and remove them if desired. Also from the More Options tab, System Restore and Shadow Copies lets you move all but the most recent restore point (which I don't suggest), and old back-up images.

15

Maintain your laptop (cont.)

Using Disk Cleanup

1 Click on Start.

2 In the search dialogue box, type 'Disk Cleanup'.

3 In the results, under Programs, click on Disk Cleanup. (As always, click on Continue or input administrator's credentials when prompted.)

4 Choose 'My files only' to clean your files and nothing else. Choose 'Files from all users on this computer' if you wish to clean additional user's files or if you want access to the More Options tab, where you can delete unwanted programs and unnecessary back-ups and system restore points.

5 If prompted, choose the drive or partition to clean up. If only one drive exists, you won't see the prompt shown here. Choose the letter of the drive that contains the operating system, which is usually C. Click on OK.

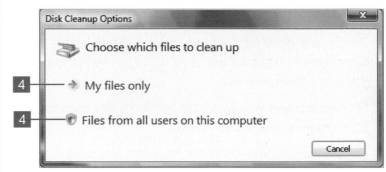

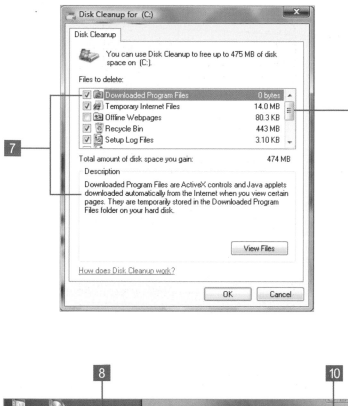

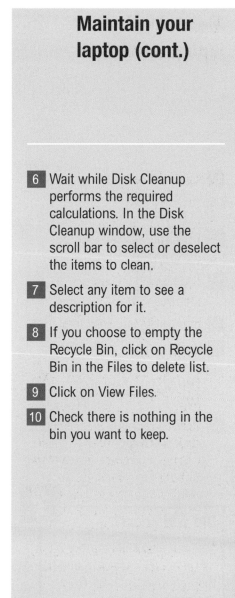

Maintain your laptop (cont.)

6 Wait while Disk Cleanup performs the required calculations. In the Disk Cleanup window, use the scroll bar to select or deselect the items to clean.

7 Select any item to see a description for it.

8 If you choose to empty the Recycle Bin, click on Recycle Bin in the Files to delete list.

9 Click on View Files.

10 Check there is nothing in the bin you want to keep.

15

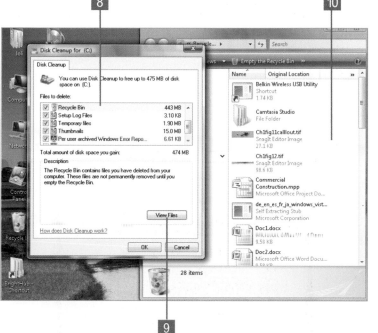

Maintain your
laptop (cont.)

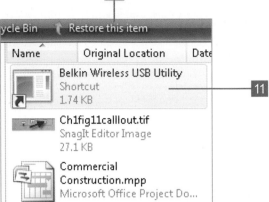

11 If you see something you want to keep, click it one time to select it.

12 From the Toolbar, click on 'Restore this item'.

13 Click on OK to start the cleaning process.

14 Click on Delete Files to start.

15 If you opted to clean the files of all users on the computer in step 4, you'll have access to the More Options tab. Click on it.

16 Under Programs and Features, click on Clean up.

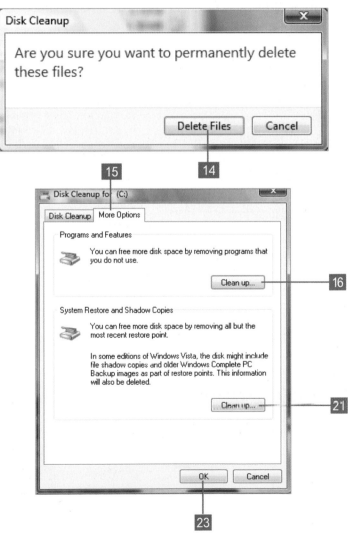

? Did you know?

You can also click a program name once to select it, and then choose Uninstall from the available tabs.

17

Tasks

View installed updates

Get new programs online at
Windows Marketplace

View purchased software
(digital locker)

Turn Windows features on or
off

Uninstall or change a program

To uninstall a program, select it from the list and then

Organize ∨ Views ∨ Uninstall Cha

Name   Publish

Adobe Flash Player ActiveX   Adobe

Belkin 54g USB Network Adapter

Camtasia Studio 4   TechSm

Microsoft Office Professional Plus 2007   Microso

Microsoft Office Project Professional 2007   Microso

Microsoft Silverlight   Microso

Nero 6 Ultra Edition

Nokia Connectivity Adapter Cable DKU-5

NVIDIA Drivers

Realtek AC'97 Audio

Snagit 8   TechSm

Programs and Features

⚠ Are you sure you want to uninstall Microsoft Silverlight?

☐ In the future, do not show me this dialog box   Yes   No

18

Disk Cleanup   X

Are you sure you want to delete all but the
most recent restore point?

If you have several saved restore points, you might not need
the older ones. You can save disk space by deleting them.

Delete   Cancel

22

17 Look through the programs
listed. If you see a program
you know you don't use and
will never need, double-click
on it.

18 Click Yes to uninstall the
program or No to cancel.

19 Work through the program's
uninstall process; each
process is different.

20 If necessary, click the X at the
top of the window to close it.

21 Back at the Disk Cleanup
dialogue box, under System
Restore and Shadow Copies,
click on Clean up.

22 Click on Delete.

23 If the Disk Cleanup dialogue
box does not close
automatically, click on OK to
apply changes or Cancel to
close Disk Cleanup.

15

Maintain your laptop (cont.)

Disk Defragmenter

A hard drive stores the files and data on your laptop. When you want to access a file, the hard drive spins and data is accessed from the drive. When the data required for the file you need is all in one place, the data is accessed more quickly than if it is scattered across the hard drive in different areas. When data is scattered, it's fragmented.

Disk Defragmenter analyses the data on your hard drive and consolidates files that are not stored together. This enhances performance by making data easier to access. Disk Defragmenter runs automatically once a week, in the middle of the night.

You won't ever need to *use* Disk Defragmenter, provided a schedule is set. You'll want to verify Disk Defragmenter is set to run on a schedule though, and if not, create one. Additionally, you can change when Disk Defragmenter runs, if you do most of your computing in the middle of the night – you don't want Disk Defragmenter slowing down your PC while you're trying to work.

Maintain your laptop (cont.)

Using Disk Defragmenter

1 Click on Start.

2 In the search box, type Defrag.

3 Under Programs, select Disk Defragmenter.

4 Verify that Disk Defragmenter is configured to run on a schedule. There should be a tick in the box, as shown here. If there is not a tick, click inside the box to create one.

15

Maintain your laptop (cont.)

5 If you want to change when Disk Defragmenter runs, click on Modify schedule.

6 Select a choice for How often, What day, and What time, using the dropdown lists.

7 Click on OK to close the scheduling box.

8 If you want to run Disk Defragmenter now, click Defragment now. There's generally no need to do this.

9 Click on OK.

For your information

By default all volumes (or hard drive partitions) are selected, so there's no need to click Select volumes to make changes.

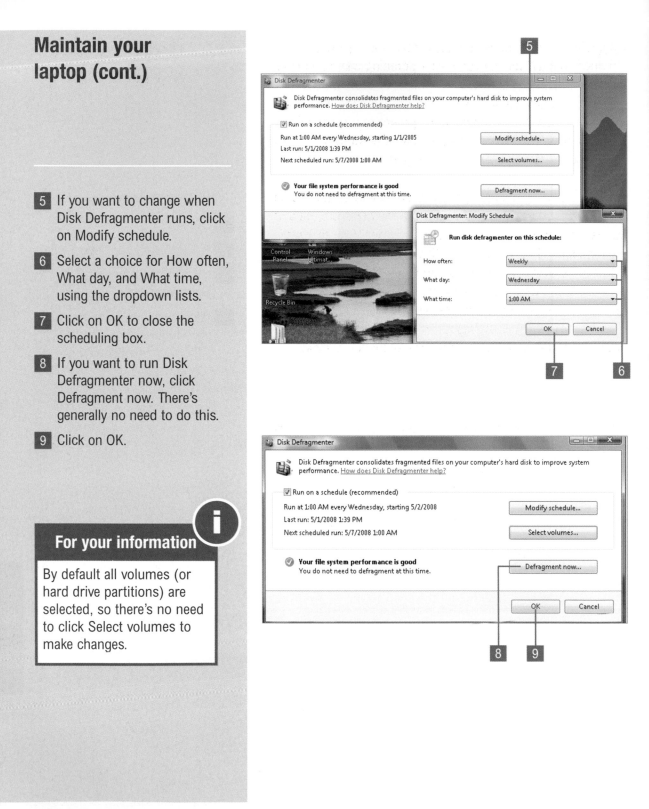

Upgrading a laptop doesn't always mean adding RAM, although that will be covered here. Upgrading can also mean purchasing and installing a travel printer or scanner, or a webcam or digital camera. While I'd never use the term 'upgrade' when describing adding a printer to a home PC, having a small printer you can use in a hotel room or on a long car trip will certainly seem like an upgrade!

Most of the time, adding a printer or camera is a simple affair. You insert a driver CD if one came with the hardware, plug in the new hardware and turn it on, and wait for Vista to install the required driver. It Vista can't find the driver it needs on the CD or in its own driver database on the hard drive, it will connect to the web and look for the driver in Microsoft's online driver database. Most of the time, Vista is successful using one of these methods. For the most part, speakers, headphones, printers, scanners and digital cameras all install this way.

Upgrading your laptop

Important !

On occasion, manufacturers will require you to load software first; then plug in the device; and then turn on the hardware. So read the instructions to know what order to do what, just as a precaution. Often though, this is just a ruse to get you to load unnecessary software, so be aware of what you're installing. For more information read the sections below.

15

Upgrading your laptop (cont.)

Installing a printer (or scanner)

1 Connect the printer or scanner to a wall socket.

2 Connect the printer or scanner to the PC using either a USB cable or a parallel port cable. (USB is a faster connection, if you have a choice.)

3 Insert the CD for the device, if you have it.

4 If a pop-up message appears as shown here, click the X to close the window. Leave the CD in the drive. If Vista wants information on the CD, it will acquire it from there.

5 Turn on the device.

6 Wait while the driver is installed.

Install from a CD or let Vista install hardware?

As noted earlier, I think it's best to connect new hardware, turn it on and let Vista install it. That's because printers, scanners, music players and cameras often come with extra software, and loading a driver from the CD also installs that software by default. This means if you blindly install what's on a CD, you may end up with a hard drive full of unnecessary applications. Why add printer software when you can print from any open application? Why add a scanning application when you can use the Windows feature to scan photos?

Here's an example of a camera program that wants to load QuickTime. If installed, this program will boot when Windows does, run in the background and use system resources, even when it isn't needed.

● Digital Video Software Installation

● QuickTime 5.0 Installation

Need more examples? Consider a digital video camera. It may come with an application for uploading and editing the video you take. However, Vista comes with Movie Maker, which will do all of that. In this case, it isn't necessary to load the software – it would only fill up your hard drive and use unnecessary resources. Printers often come with photo management software too, but Vista's Photo Gallery is all you need. If you need more than what Vista offers, consider Photoshop Elements; the software that comes with printers is usually either not any better than what Vista offers or harder to use. Finally, while portable music players may come with software to help you buy and manage music, Vista has Windows Media Player, and of course, you can download iTunes (which you may prefer over any other choice). I'm trying to pound the point home; don't load the programs on the hardware's CD unless you are sure you have to. You'll know

15

Upgrading your laptop (cont.)

Installing a digital camera

1. Read the directions that come with the camera. If there are specific instructions for installing the driver, follow them. If not, continue here.

2. Connect the camera to a wall socket or insert fresh batteries.

3. Connect the camera to the PC using either a USB cable or a FireWire cable. USB is generally used with digital cameras, and FireWire with video cameras. Your camera may have both. Connect using the method outlined in the instructions, or use USB if no information is available.

4. Insert the CD for the device, if you have it.

5. If a pop-up message appears, click the X to close the window. Leave the CD in the drive. If Vista wants information from the CD, it will acquire it from there.

6. Turn on the camera. Place it in Playback mode if that exists. Often, simply turning on the camera is enough.

7. Wait while the driver is installed.

if you need the software by reading the information that comes with the hardware. Anyway, you can install it later if need be.

Here's one more example from a digital camera's CD. Clicking Software installation offers the following: PhotoStitch, a program for merging overlapping images into a panorama, useful if you want to do that; and ZoomBrowser, an application that lets you organise and print images. This may not be necessary, as Vista's Photo Gallery has everything you probably need. Why double-up on programs or load ones you won't use? In this case, I think it's best to only install the driver.

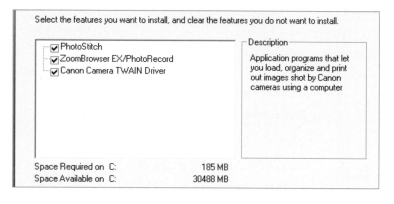

For your information

If you try to load a driver from the CD, and opt out of installing other programs, you may see an error message. If so, just click on 'This program installed correctly', otherwise you'll be hounded indefinitely.

ReadyBoost

ReadyBoost is a technology that lets you add more RAM (random access memory) to a PC easily, without opening the case. Adding RAM often greatly improves performance. ReadyBoost lets you use a USB flash drive or a secure digital memory card (like the one in your digital camera), as RAM, if it meets certain requirements. Just plug the device into an open slot on your PC and, if it is compatible, choose to use the device as RAM.

Using ReadyBoost

1 Insert a USB pen drive, portable music player or memory card into an available slot on your laptop. USB pen drives must be at least USB 2.0 and have at last 64 MB of free space: but don't worry about that, you'll be told if the hardware you're using will work or not in a moment.

2 Wait while Vista checks to see if the device can perform as memory.

3 If prompted to use the flash drive or memory card to improve system performance, click on 'Speed up my system'. If the device isn't fast enough to use with ReadyBoost, opt to never test this device again if desired.

15

Upgrading your laptop (cont.)

4 Click on Start.

5 Click on Computer.

6 Right-click on the new icon for the hardware selected to serve as ReadyBoost.

7 Choose Properties.

8 Click on the ReadyBoost tab.

9 Define how much of the device's memory to use for performance, and how much to use for file storage. Move the slider all the way to the right if you do not need to use the device for storage.

10 Leave the device plugged in.

11 Click on OK.

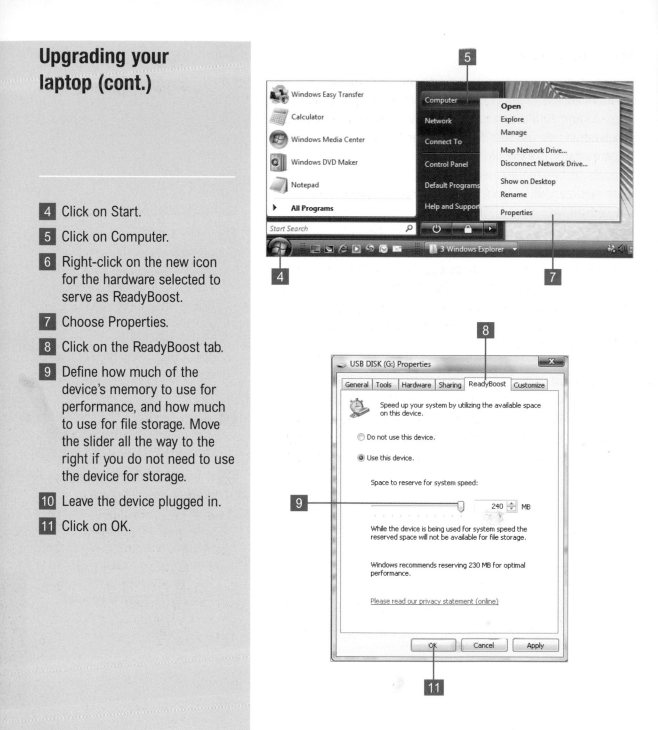

Adding internal RAM

Adding internal memory to a laptop is not difficult or expensive. In fact, I think adding RAM to a laptop is easier than adding it to a desktop. That's because, generally, RAM is accessible via the back of the laptop, and you only need open the proper slot to install it.

Before you can add RAM though, you have to know a few things. First, you need to find out what kind of memory chips your laptop uses, how much is already installed, and whether or not your laptop has an empty 'slot' to take more. There are several ways to find these things out. The first is to refer to the information that came with your PC. The easiest is to visit the manufacturer's website. There, you can often input your laptop's serial number (and/or model number), and get the information you need.

If you can't find out what you need to know via these two options, visit **www.crucial.com**. Crucial offers a memory adviser, and you can use it to scan your laptop. The scan will tell you what kind of RAM you need, and if you have an empty memory slot (which defines whether you can upgrade or not).

A report from Crucial will tell you:

- How many, if any, empty slots are available.
- How much RAM you can add.
- Options for buying the RAM.

Because there are so many kinds of memory, including but not limited to DDR3, DDR2, DDR, SDRAM and EDO, it's extremely important you follow these guidelines.

Upgrading your laptop (cont.)

For your information

If your laptop has less than 1 GB of RAM, consider upgrading to 2 GB or more. You'll see a big difference. This is especially important if you play games, use demanding programs or do a lot of switching between programs.

15

Upgrading your laptop (cont.)

To find out how much RAM you have

1 Click on Start.

2 Right-click on Computer.

3 Click Properties.

4 Under System, refer to Memory (RAM).

Windows Easy Transfer	Recent Items
Calculator	Computer
Windows Media Center	Network
Windows DVD Maker	Connect To
Notepad	Control Panel
All Programs	Default Programs
	Help and Support

Open
Explore
Manage

Map Network Drive...
Disconnect Network Drive...

Show on Desktop
Rename

Properties

Start Search

System

Manufacturer:	Hewlett-Packard Company
Model:	a1720n
Rating:	**3.2** Windows Experience Index
Processor:	Intel(R) Core(TM)2 CPU 6300 @ 1.86GHz 1.87 GHz
Memory (RAM):	1.00 GB
System type:	32-bit Operating System

After buying the RAM, you'll need to slot it in. The chips will come with instructions, but for laptops, you pretty much only have to turn off, unplug the laptop, open the proper slot on the underside and insert the RAM in the same way as the chips already there.

Jargon buster

RAM: random access memory. This is where Vista stores its data, whether it be for printing a document, performing a calculation, or fixing a photo.

Surges: unexpected increases in the voltage of an electrical current. Surges have the potential to damage sensitive electrical equipment. (Sags are the opposite of surges, equally dangerous, and are a drop in electrical current.)

Appendix: Avoiding laptop disasters

Because of the nature of a laptop and how you may use it, it's easy to cause damage to it. While you would have to be negligent to drop a desktop PC into a swimming pool, it's much more likely you'd drop a laptop there, provided you tripped at the proper moment and were standing, well, by a swimming pool. Because of the obvious and not so obvious ways you can cause a laptop disaster, this appendix is devoted to avoiding them.

Commonsense precautions

After reading the first paragraph, we hope you won't go near any swimming pools with your laptop. It is certainly possible for a cruise ship to rock just enough to send the computer sliding off your lap while you're checking email, or to drop it in the water after tripping over a float while walking to your beach chair. That said, there are lots of practices to be aware of while working on your laptop (or walking around with it):

- Always place your laptop on a stable surface. You do not want it falling off. This is especially true in a car or a cruise ship.

- Try to keep the laptop away from vibrating surfaces. This could loosen internal parts.

- When you do find a place for your laptop, keep drinks and food away from it. If anything spills on your keyboard, the entire laptop could be ruined. (If you do spill something on your laptop, turn it upside down, with the lid open, and very, very gently, position it so the liquid can drain out for a few hours.)

- Always allow enough room around the laptop so it can 'breath'. There are ventilation vents and holes that need space around them. If you feel the computer getting hot, make sure its vents are getting adequate air and put the computer in Sleep mode for an hour.

- Keep cables and power cords away from any area where people could walk on them or trip on them. This could cause the laptop to fall or cause injury to others.

- When in a car, keep the laptop in its case and preferably in the boot. This will keep the laptop from hitting you in the event of an accident.

Health precautions

There are some precautions you need to take to protect your health too. This includes not using a plugged-in laptop near water. You could get electrocuted! Here are some others:

- Men who use a laptop on their laps for long periods may decrease their sperm count. It's the heat sperm doesn't like. Consider a laptop desk.

- A laptop uses wireless signals to access the web and look for open networks (even when you aren't connected to one). Wireless signals are also used in hearing aids, heart pace makers and other medical devices. Keep your pacemaker at least 15 cm away from the laptop.

- Don't overload an extension lead. Doing so could cause a fire. Be especially careful in hotel rooms and older homes, as the electrical system may not be up to necessary standards.

- Don't compute and drive at the same time. You could cause an accident (not to mention getting car sick).

- If you start feeling any eyestrain or headaches, take a break from the computer. In fact, it's best to look away from the computer every 15 minutes or so and focus on something far away to relax your eyes.

- If you start feeling pain in your fingers or hands, you may be using the computer too much, especially if this is a new feeling.

Laptops and physical precautions

Yes, you know you shouldn't force cables into holes they don't belong in, and you should not expose the computer to water, rain or excess humidity. But did you know you should also keep your laptop away from magnetic fields and direct sunlight? Both could damage your laptop. It's true, and there's more:

- Don't place your computer on a radiator or the boot of a car. You want to keep it away from heat.

- If you're on holiday in the desert, shield the laptop from flying dust or dirt particles.

- Close the lid when moving from room to room. Turn the laptop off if you will be moving it by car or bus.

- When possible, keep the laptop with you or inside a house, a cool car or hotel room. This will minimise temperature changes.

- Avoid using the laptop on a bed, couch or blanket as material may bunch up and clog ventilation holes.

- When this laptop's lid is closed, avoid placing objects on it.

Jargon buster

Activation – The process you must complete to verify you have a valid copy of Windows Vista including a proper Product ID. You usually activate Vista online, the first time you turn on the PC. This is mandatory.

Adware – Internet advertisements (which are also applications) that often include additional code that can be used to track a user's personal information and pass it on to third parties, without the user's authorisation or knowledge.

Aero – Aero changes how the Windows Vista interface looks.

Aero Glass – Visual reflections and soft animations that are applied when Aero is selected as the display setting.

Applications – Software installed on your PC other than the operating system. Some applications come preinstalled, like Windows Calendar, Windows Mail and Internet Explorer. Third-party applications are software you buy separately and load yourself, such as Microsoft Office or Photoshop.

AV-in – Accepts input from various audio/video devices.

Backup and Restore Center – This feature lets you perform back-ups, and in the case of a laptop failure, put them back. However, there are other back-up options too, including copying files to a CD or DVD, copying pictures and media to an external hard drive, USB drive or memory card, or storing them on an Internet server.

Bandwidth – A guide to how much data you can send and receive on a paid connection, like a smart phone or Internet connection.

Battery bay – This holds the laptop's battery. Sometimes you have to use a screwdriver to get inside the bay, other times you simply need to slide out the compartment door.

Battery lock – Locks the battery in position.

Battery release latch – This latch holds the battery in place, even after the bay door has been opened. You'll need to release this latch to get to the battery.

Bluetooth – A technology used to create 'personal' networks for the purpose of connecting devices that are in close range (like a mobile phone and an earpiece). A laptop may come with built-in Bluetooth capabilities (although this is not common), or you can add them by buying a USB Bluetooth dongle.

Bluetooth dongle – A small device, about the size of a USB pen drive, that connects directly to a USB port on the outside of the laptop.

Boot up – When a laptop is powered on, it goes through a sequence of tasks before you see the desktop. This process is called the boot-up process. Laptops can be rated by many factors, and one of those factors is how long the 'boot-up process' takes.

Browse – Looking for a file, folder or program is the process of drilling down into Vista's folder structure to locate the desired item.

Burn – The process of copying music from a laptop to a CD or DVD. Generally music is burned to a CD, since CDs can be played in cars and generic CD players; videos are burned to DVDs since they require much more space and can be played on DVD players.

Contacts Folder – This holds your contacts' information, which includes email addresses, pictures, phone numbers, home and businesses addresses.

Control Panel – A place where you can change laptop settings related to system and maintenance, user accounts, security, appearance, networks and the Internet, the time, language and region, hardware and sounds, visual displays and accessibility options, and programs.

Cookies – Small text files that include data that identifies your preferences when you visit particular websites. Cookies are what allows you to visit, a website and be greeted with your name and suggestions based on your past visits.

Copy command – Copies data to Vista's clipboard (a temporary, holding area). The data will not be deleted from its original location even when you 'paste' it somewhere else. Pasting copy data will copy the data, not move it.

CPU – Central Processing Unit. This is the main 'computer chip' inside your laptop.

Cut – To remove a selected text, picture or object.

Cut command – Copies the data to Vista's clipboard (a virtual, temporary, holding area). The data will be deleted from its original location as soon as you 'paste' it somewhere else. Pasting cut data moves the data.

Desktop Folder – This folder contains links to items for data you created on your desktop. Computer, Network and Recycle Bin aren't listed, but shortcuts to folders you create and data you store on the Desktop are.

Digitiser – An add-on to a laptop or desktop PC that accepts and converts handwritten text. You write on the digitiser pad.

Documents Folder – This folder contains documents you've saved, subfolders you created and folders created by Vista including Fax, My Received Files, Remote Assistance Logs and Scanned Documents.

Downloaded Program Files – Files that are download automatically when you view certain web pages. They are stored temporarily in a folder on your hard disk, and accessed when and if needed.

Downloads Folder – Empty by default. It offers a place to save items you download from the Internet, like drivers and third-party programs.

Dialogue box – A place to make changes to default settings in an application. Clicking File and then Print, for instance, opens the Print dialogue box where you can configure the type of paper you're using or select a printer.

Disk Cleanup – A tool included with Vista that offers a way to reduce unnecessary data on your PC. With Disk Cleanup you can remove temporary files, empty the Recycle Bin, remove set-up log files and downloaded program files (among other things), in a single process.

Disk Defragmenter – A tool included with Vista that analyses the data stored on your hard drive and consolidates files that are not stored as one. This enhances performance by making data easier to access. Disk Defragmenter runs automatically once a week, in the middle of the night.

DPI – Dots per inch. The number of dots (or pixels) per inch on a computer screen.

Driver – Software (or code) that allows a device to communicate with Vista and vice versa.

DV – Digital video, generally used by DV cameras.

DVD drive – A physical piece of equipment that can play and often record DVDs.

DVI port – Used to connect the laptop to a television set or other DVI device.

Email address – A virtual address you use for sending and receiving email. It often takes this form: yourname@yourispname.com.

Emoticon – a graphic used to show emotion such as a smiley face, a face with a frown, etc. Most emoticons are faces.

Enhancements – Features in Windows Media Player that you can use to improve your music, including a graphic equaliser.

Ergonomics – The science of working without causing injury to yourself. Injury can include back strain, eye strain and carpal tunnel syndrome.

Ethernet – A technology that uses cables to transmit data and network laptops.

Ethernet cable – Wire used to connect PCs to routers and cable modems.

ExpressCard slot – Used to insert an ExpressCard where you can expand your laptop's capabilities by offering additional ways to connect devices. ExpressCards are often used to offer wireless capabilities.

Extended Warranty – An insurance policy that you buy along with the manufacturer's warranty. This is supposed to cover everything, including drops and spills. Often though, extended warranties fail to pay up in such an event (which is spelled out in the fine print).

Favorites Folder – This folder contains the items in Internet Explorer's favourites list. It may also include folders created by the computer manufacturer or Microsoft.

Filter Keys – A setting you can configure so that Windows ignores keystrokes that occur in rapid succession, such as when you accidentally leave your finger on a key for too long.

FireWire – Also called IEEE 1394, a way of connecting digital video cameras, professional audio hardware and external hard drives to a PC. FireWire connections are much faster than USB, so are better for large amounts of data, like digital video.

Flip and Flip 3-D – A way to move through open windows graphically instead of clicking the item in the Taskbar.

Form data – In Internet Explorer, this is information that's been saved using the Internet Explorer's autocomplete form data functionality.

If you don't want forms to be filled out automatically by you or someone else who has access to your PC and user account, delete this.

Gadget – In Vista, an icon on the sidebar such as the Weather or Clock gadget.

GHz – Short for gigahertz, this term describes how fast a processor can work. One GHz equals one billion cycles per second, so a 2.4 GHz computer chip will execute calculations at 240 billion cycles per second. Again, it's only important to know that the faster the chip, the faster the PC.

GPU – Graphics processing unit. A processor used for drawing graphics. Having a processor just for graphics frees up the main CPU, allowing it to work faster on other tasks.

Hard drive – A physical piece of equipment where your data is stored. Hard drives are inside a laptop, but you can buy additional, external hard drives to back up data. Digital music, photos and video take up a surprisingly large amount of hard drive space.

History – In a web browser, this is the list of sites you've visited and any web addresses you've typed. Anyone who has access to your PC and user account can look at your list to see where you've been.

Hotspot – A WiFi hotspot lets you connect to the Internet without using a cable. Sometimes this service is free, provided you have the required wireless hardware.

Icon – A symbol on the screen representing a file, program or device.

Instant Messaging – Text and instant messaging require you to type your message and click a Send button. It's similar to email, but it's instantaneous; the recipient gets the message right after you send it. Instant messaging is the term generally reserved for text communications between two or more computers; text messaging is a term generally reserved for communicating between mobile phones.

Interface – What you see on the screen when working in a window.

Internet – Groups of computers that communicate via land lines, satellite and cable for the purpose of sharing information and data. The World Wide Web is a software system that uses this network.

Internet server – A computer connected to the web that stores data. Hotmail offers Internet servers to hold email and data, so you do not have to store it on your PC. Internet servers allow you to access information from any computer that can access the Internet.

ISP – Internet service provider. A company that provides Internet access, usually for a fee.

Kensington lock slot – a way to connect the laptop to a lock to prevent it from being stolen.

Line-in jack – An input on a laptop that accepts audio from external devices, such as CD players.

Link – A shortcut to a web page. Links are often offered in an email, document or web page to allow you to access a site without having to actually type in its name. In almost all instances, links are underlined and in a different colour than the page they appear on.

Links Folder – This folder contains shortcuts to documents, files and other folders.

Load – A web page must 'load' before you can access it. Some pages load instantly while others take a few seconds.

Magnifier – A tool in the Ease of Access suite of applications. You use Magnifier to increase the size of the information shown on the screen.

Mail – Windows Mail comes with Vista. It can send and receive email, manage your contacts, manage sent, saved, and incoming email, and read newsgroups.

Mail Servers – A computer that your ISP configures to allow you to send and receive email. It often includes a POP3 incoming mail server and an SMTP outgoing mail server. Often the server names look something like pop.yourispnamehere.com and smtp.yourispnamehere.com.

Malware – Stands for malicious software. Viruses, worms, spyware, etc.

Menu – A title on a menu bar (such as File, Edit, View). Clicking this menu button opens a dropdown list with additional choices (open, save, print).

Menu bar – A bar that runs across the top of an application that offers menus. Often, these menus include file, edit, view, insert, format and help.

Modem port – A connector on the outside of a laptop that lets you plug your laptop into a phone jack using a standard telephone cord. Once connected, you can access the Internet using a dial-up connection.

Mouse keys – Instead of using your mouse, you can use the arrow keys on your keyboard or the numeric keypad to move the mouse pointer on the desktop or inside programs or documents.

Music Folder – Contains sample music and music you save to the PC.

Narrator – A basic screen reader included with Vista. This application will read text that appears on the screen to you, while you navigate using the keyboard and mouse.

Network – A group of computers, printers and other devices that communicate wirelessly or through wired connections.

Network (from the Start menu) – The Network window offers links to computers on your network and the Network and Sharing Center. You can also add printers and wireless devices here.

Network adapter – Hardware that lets your computer connect to a network, such as the Internet or a local network.

Network and Sharing Center – A collection of features where you can easily access network connections, sharing options, networked computers and devices, and diagnose and repair features.

Network Discovery – a state where computers can find other computers on the network. Network Discovery must be on to locate and communicate with network devices.

Network Map – Details each of your network connections graphically, and allows you to distinguish easily among wired, wireless and Internet connections.

Notification area – The area of the taskbar that includes the clock and the volume icons, and also holds icons for applications that are running in the background. You may see icons for your anti-virus software, music players, updates or security alerts.

Operating System – Software that controls your computer, such as Windows Vista. You use Vista to find things you have stored on your laptop, connect to the Internet, send and receive email, and surf the web, among other things.

Page Setup button – Clicking Page Setup opens a dialogue box where you can select a paper size, source, and create headers and footers. You can also change orientation and margins, all of which is dependent on what features your printer supports.

Parental controls – You can apply such controls to limit the hours a user can access the laptop, which games they can play and what programs they can run (among other things).

Paste command – Copies or moves the cut or copied data to a new location. If the data was cut, it will be moved. If the data was copied, it will be copied.

Pen cursors – Visual feedback for actions you perform with your stylus. If you want to see visually when you single-tap or double-tap with the stylus, or when you perform the equivalent of right-clicking, you can enable pen cursors.

Pen flicks – A move you make with the stylus that is similar to flicking your wrist. This is an easy way to move quickly through web pages and documents, and perform editing tasks like cut, copy, paste, undo and delete, using a stylus.

Per user archived windows error reporting – Files used for error reporting and solution checking.

Phishing – A technique used by computer hackers to get you to divulge personal information like bank account numbers. Phishing filters warn you of potential phishing websites and email, and are included in Vista. In other words, an attempt by a unscrupulous website or hacker to obtain personal data including but not limited to back account numbers, social security numbers and email addresses.

Pictures Folder – Contains sample pictures and pictures you save to the PC.

Pixel – The smallest unit of data that can be displayed by a computer. Resolution is defined by how many pixels you choose to display.

Playlist – Songs that you can save and then listen to as a group or burn to a CD, or copy to a portable music player.

POP3 Server Name – The name of the computer that you will use to get your email from your ISP. Your ISP will give you this information when you subscribe.

Power cable – Connect the laptop to the wall socket (power outlet). You can connect and disconnect the power cable at any time, even when the laptop is running.

Power plan – Settings that you can configure to tell Vista when and if to turn off the computer monitor or display, and when or if to put the laptop to sleep.

Print button – Clicking on this opens a box where you can configure the page range, select a printer, change page orientation, change print order and choose a paper type. Additional options include print quality and output bins. Of course, the choices offered depend on your printer. If your printer can only print at 300 x 300 dots per inch, you can't configure it to print at a higher quality.

Print preview button – Clicking on this opens a window where you can see what a printout will actually look like. You can switch between portrait and landscape views, change the Page Setup dialogue box and so on.

Processor – Short for microprocessor. The silicon chip that contains the central processing unit (CPU) inside a computer. Generally, the terms CPU and processor are used interchangeably. CPUs do almost all of the computer's calculations and are the most important piece of hardware in a computer.

Programs – See Applications.

Public Folder – Folders where you can share data. Anyone with an account on the laptop can access the data inside these folders. You can also configure the Public folder to share files with people using other computers on your local network.

Publish – In Windows Calendar, a way to distribute a calendar electronically so that it is seen with others. The calendar can be seen via an online source like a web page or on the user's own network. In Windows Movie Maker, finishing a film.

RAM – Random access memory. The hardware inside your laptop that temporarily stores data that is being used by the operating system or programs. The more RAM you have, the faster your laptop will (theoretically) run and perform.

ReadyBoost – A way to add more memory to a PC using a USB pen drive or a secure digital memory card (like the one in your digital camera), as RAM, if it meets certain requirements. Just plug the device into an open slot on your PC and, if it is compatible, choose to use the device as RAM.

Recycle Bin – A folder where deleted files are stored until you decide to empty it. This serves as a safeguard, allowing you recover items accidentally deleted or items you thought you no longer wanted but later decide you need. Note that once you empty the bin, the items are gone forever.

Registration – A non-mandatory task that you generally perform during the Vista activation process. By registering you can get email about Vista and new products. Registration is not mandatory.

Remote Desktop Connection – A Vista program you can use to access your laptop over a phone line from somewhere else, like an office or hotel room.

Resolution – The number of pixels shown on a computer screen. Choosing 800 by 600 pixels means that the desktop is shown to you with 800 pixels across and 600 pixels down. When you increase the resolution, you increase the number of pixels on the screen.

RF-in – A jack socket that accepts input signal from digital TV tuners.

Rip – The process of copying files from a physical CD to your hard drive, and thus your music library.

Router – Equipment used to send data from laptop to computer on a network. A router 'routes' the data to the correct PC and also rejects data that is harmful or from unknown sources.

Scratch-out gestures – A gesture you make with the stylus in Vista that allows you to delete your own handwriting by using the following: strikethrough, and vertical, circular and angled scratch out.

Screen Saver – A picture or animation that covers your screen and appears after your laptop has been idle for a specific amount of time that you set. You can configure your screen saver to require a password on waking up for extra security.

SD card slots or card readers – Slots on the outside of the laptop used to accept digital memory cards found in digital cameras and similar technologies.

Searches folder – Contains preconfigured search folders including Recent Documents, Recent E-Mail, Recent Music, Recent Pictures and Videos, Recently Changed, and Shared By Me. If you need to find something recently accessed or changed and don't know where to look, you can probably locate it here. These folders get updated each time you open them.

Setup log files – Files created by Windows during set-up processes.

Sidebar – A desktop component that lies on top of the Desktop. It's transparent and offers by default, a calendar, the weather and a clock. You can delete and add sidebar items, called gadgets, to show the information you want to see. You can also hide the sidebar.

Slate PC – A PC with no keyboard or mouse, and no lid (like a laptop has). It's slim and easy to carry, and is more like a digital clipboard than a computer.

SMTP server name – The name of the computer that you will use to send email using your ISP. Your ISP will give you this information when you subscribe.

Snipping Tool – A feature in Vista that allows you to drag your cursor around any area on the screen to copy and capture it. Once captured, you can save it, edit it and/or send it to an e-mail recipient.

Sound Recorder – A tool in Vista with only three options: Start Recording, Stop Recording, and Resume Recording. You can save recorded clips as notes to yourself or insert them into films or slide shows.

Spam – Unwanted email. Compare spam to junk faxes or junk post.

Speech recognition – Software that allows you to control your laptop with your voice.

Standard toolbar – A toolbar that is often underneath a menu bar (in an application window) that contains icons, or pictures, of common commands. Common commands include New, Open, Save, Print, Print Preview, Find, Cut, Copy, Paste, Undo and Date/Time.

Sticky Keys – This setting allows you to configure the keyboard so that you never have to press three keys at once (such as when you must press the Ctrl, Alt, and Del keys together to shut down or restart Windows). With Sticky Keys, you can use one key to perform these tasks. You configure the key to use for three-key tasks.

Sticky Notes – A tool that enables you to create short handwritten or voice notes. Just like real sticky notes, you can jot down ideas, reminders or create lists using the pen or stylus, or create a voice clip by speaking into the microphone.

Surge protector – A device to protect a computer from power surges.

Surges – Unexpected increases in the voltage of an electrical current. Surges have the potential to damage sensitive electrical equipment. (Sags are the opposite of surges, equally dangerous, and are a drop in electrical current.)

S-Video – A port or technology used to connect the laptop to a television or other compatible display.

Sync – Synchronisation. The process of comparing data in one location to the data in another, and performing tasks to match it up. If data has been added or deleted from one device, for instance, it can also be added or deleted from the other.

Sync Center – An application in Vista that helps you keep your files, music, contacts, pictures and other data in sync between your laptop and mobile devices, network files and folders, and compatible programs such as Outlook.

System archived Windows error reporting – Files used for error reporting and solution checking.

System Restore – If enabled, Vista stores 'restore points' on your PC's hard drive. If something goes wrong you can run System Restore, choose one of these points, and revert to a pre-problem date. Since System Restore only deals with 'system data', none of your personal data will be affected.

System restore point – A snapshot of the laptop that Vista keeps in case something happens and you need to revert to it, because of a bad installation or hardware driver.

Tablet PC – A PC that contains a stylus you can use to handwrite notes on a touch screen. Some Tablet PC screens swivel.

Tablet PC input panel – Stores the tablet PC tools. Here you can write notes in your own handwriting and then enter the converted text anywhere text is accepted. If you have a tablet PC with a touch screen, you can write directly In the Panel using the stylus. If you have a laptop, you can write by moving your mouse.

Tags – Data about a particular file, such as a photo, song or album. Tags can be used to group pictures or music in various ways. Some tags are applied automatically when you import pictures from a digital camera, including the date they were uploaded, along with any name you applied to the imported group. You can create your own tags.

Tap – Hitting the stylus on a touch tablet's PC screen for the purpose of inputting data, selecting options or opening web links.

Taskbar – The bar that runs horizontally across the bottom of the Vista interface, and contains the start button, quick launch area and notification area. It also offers a place to view and access open files, folder and applications.

Temporary Files – Files created and stored by programs for use by the program. Most of these temporary files are deleted when you quit a program, but some remain.

Temporary Internet files – Files that contain copies of web pages you've visited on your hard drive, so that you can view the pages more quickly when visiting them again.

Text messaging – Text and instant messaging require you to type your message and click a send button. It's similar to email, but it's instantaneous; the recipient gets the message right after you send it. Instant messaging is the term generally reserved for text communications between two or more laptops; text messaging is a term generally reserved for communicating between two cell phones.

Thumbnails – Small icons of your pictures, videos and documents. Thumbnails will be recreated as needed should you choose to delete them using Disk Cleanup.

Touch Input – Many newer tablet PCs have screens you can touch with your finger. With this technology you can perform tasks with your finger instead of a stylus, mouse or keyboard.

Touchpad – A pointing device that is usually located in the centre of the laptop keyboard or at the bottom of it. Place your finger on the touchpad or trackball and move it around to move the mouse.

Transition – In Movie Maker, a switch from one clip to another, such as fading in or out.

USB – Universal Serial Bus. A port you use to connect devices. USB devices include mice, external keyboards, mobile phones, digital cameras and USB pen drives.

VGA port – An external monitor port. With this port you can connect your laptop to a secondary monitor or network projector where you can mirror what you see on the laptop's screen or extend the screen to the second monitor. A VGA port is a 15-pin port.

Video format – The video file type, such as AVI or WMA.

Video messaging – A form of instant messaging where one or both users also offer live video of themselves during the conversation.

Videos folder – Contains sample videos and videos you save to the PC.

Virus – A self-replicating program that infects laptops with intent to do harm. Viruses often come in the form of an attachment in an email.

Visualisations – Produced by Vista and Windows Media Player, these are graphical representations of the music you play.

Web browser – An application you can use to surf the Internet such as Internet Explorer or Firefox.

Webcam – A camera that can send live images over the Internet.

Website – A group of web pages that contain related information. Microsoft's site contains information about Microsoft products, for instance.

Window – When you open a program from the Start menu, a document, folder or a picture, it opens in a 'window'. Window, as used in this context, is synonymous with an open program, file or folder and has nothing to do with the word Windows, used with Windows Vista.

Windows Calendar – A calendar included in Vista.

Windows Defender – A Vista tool that offers protection against Internet threats. It's enabled by default and it runs in the background. However, if you ever think your laptop has been attacked by an Internet threat (virus, worm, malware) you can run a manual scan here.

Windows Firewall – The firewall will help prevent hackers (people whose job it is to get into your laptop and do harm to it) from accessing your PC and data. The firewall blocks most programs from communicating outside the network (or outside your PC). If you want to allow a program to communicate outside your safety zone you can 'allow' a program by adding it to an 'exceptions' list.

Windows Media Center – Available in Vista Home Premium and Ultimate editions, an application that allows you to watch, pause and record live television, locate, download, and/or listen to music and radio, view, edit and share photos and videos, and play DVDs.

Windows Mobility Center – An application that lets you adjust your mobile PC, tablet PC or laptop settings quickly, including things like volume, wireless and brightness.

Windows Update – If enabled, when you are online, Vista will check for security updates automatically and install them. You don't have to do anything, and your PC is always updated with the latest security patches.

Worm – A self-replicating program that infects laptops with intent to do harm. However, unlike a virus, it does not need to attach itself to a running program.

Troubleshooting guide

Choosing and buying a laptop

What should I consider when buying
a laptop?   12

What is ergonomics?   13

What types of connections should
I insist on?   14

What questions should I ask the
salesperson?   15

What is a 'processor' and 'RAM' and
how much should my new laptop have?   15

What is a hard drive, and how big a hard
drive should my laptop have?   15

What type of laptop should I buy if I just
want to use email?   16

What type of laptop should I buy if I
want to create my own home films
on DVDs?   16

What should I look for on the
manufacture's website?   17

I plan to take my laptop on a safari
and on a mountain climbing trip.
Should I get a 'rugged laptop'?   17

Should I invest in an extended warranty?   18

The outside of the laptop

How can I find out what all of this stuff
is on the outside of my laptop?   20

What is a USB port and how do I use it?   22

What is FireWire and how do I use it?   22

What is Ethernet and how do I use it?   23

What is Bluetooth and how do I use it?   24

How do I add another monitor?   25

How do I add external speakers?   26

What port do I use to configure a dial-up
connection to the Internet?   26

How do I insert or remove the battery?   27

What additional ports do I have (S-Video,
DVI, SD, ExpressCard, etc.)?   28

The inside of the laptop

Where's the power button?   30

Where's the volume?   30

Where's the microphone?   31

Where's the webcam?   32

What do all of these weird keyboard
keys do?   33/36

How can I use the arrow keys? 36

What are 'function' keys? 37

What is a touchpad and how do I use it? 38

Getting started with Windows Vista

How do I activate Vista? 41

What is the Welcome Center? 42

I can't find the Welcome Center. 43

What are the Vista editions? 47

What are these icons on the Desktop?
What do they do? 52

What applications are included with Vista? 54

How do I open a Vista application? 59

What accessories come with Vista? 60

How do I access the accessories? 65

What is the taskbar? 67

How do I personalise the taskbar? 69

What is the sidebar? 70

How do I enable the sidebar 71

How do I add gadgets to and
personalise the sidebar? 72

How do I use Instant Search to find
something on my PC? 78

How I do I shut down my laptop safely? 79

What's the difference among sleep, shut
down, log off and other options? 80

Personalising Windows Vista

How do I enable Aero (or disable it)? 85

How do I change the desktop
background? 89

How do I change or apply a screensaver? 92

How do I change what icons appear
on my desktop? 96

How do I create a shortcut on my
desktop for a program I use often? 99

How do I delete a shortcut from the
desktop? 104

How do I change the screen resolution? 107

How do I change my mouse pointer? 108

How do I make Vista have the
'classic' look? 110

How do I change the font size? 113

Vista's accessibility options

What options are available to me as a
disabled person? 122

How do I make the computer read to me? 118

How can I magnify what's on the screen? 121

How can I input data without touching
the keyboard? 122

How can I make the keyboard easier
to use? 126

What are the most common keyboard
shortcuts? 128

How do I train the computer to recognise my voice?   138

Security

What are Vista's security features?   142

Should I create user accounts for others who access my laptop?   144

How do I create a user account?   145

I'm using an administrator account. Is that safe?   147

How do I protect my laptop using passwords?   153

How do I enable System Restore?   154

How do I get required updates for my laptop?   157

How can I get the most from Windows Firewall?   158/160

How can I get the most from Windows Defender?   159/161

What do I do if Security Center produces warnings?   164

What can I do with parental controls?   165

How to I enable parental controls?   166

What is the easiest way to back up my data?   170

What can I do to stay safe while surfing the Internet?   171

How can I get help when I need it?   174

Getting online

How do I choose an internet service provider?   184

What information should I obtain from my ISP?   184

How do I create a connection to the Internet once I've obtained the proper information from my ISP?   187

How do I create a wireless connection to the web?   190

Where can I view and manage my Internet connection?   192

What is a hot spot?   194

How do I connect to a hotspot?   196

Working with media

How do I copy a CD I own to my laptop?   200

How do I play music on Media Player?   202

How do I copy music from my laptop to a CD I can listen to in my car?   205

How do I get pictures off my digital camera and on my laptop?   208

What photo-editing options are available on my laptop?   210

How do I edit photos?   210

How can I add information to my saved pictures?   213

How many ways can I share pictures with others?   217

How do I email a picture? 219

How do I watch a DVD in Media Player? 222

How do I create a data DVD? 227

What is Movie Maker? 229

How can I share films I create with
Movie Maker? 232

How do I get footage from my DV
camera into Movie Maker? 234

How do I edit data in Movie Maker? 238

How do I watch live TV? 248

How do I record TV? 251

Messaging

What's the best program for instant and
video messaging? 257

How do I download and install a
messaging program? 258

How do I get a messenger ID? 261

How do I send an instant message to
another computer? 267

How do I set up my mic and web cam for
video messaging? 273

How do I make PC-to-PC phone calls? 276

How do I have a video conversation? 277

Mobility Center

What is Windows Mobility Center? 279

How can I extend battery life? 283

What is the battery meter? 284

How do I turn off my wireless card
while I'm on an airplane? 286

How do I enable settings for
presentations? 288

Can I synchronise my portable music
player with Windows Vista? 289

How do I perform a sync? 292

How do I connect an external display
like a projector or TV? 295

Tablet PC tools

What is the tablet PC input panel? 298

How do I enter handwritten text? 298

How do I change handwriting input
settings? 304

How do I use the Snipping tool to
capture something on my screen? 318

How do I use Sticky Notes to create a
reminder for myself? 322

How do I train in handwriting
recognition? 326

How do I add web components,
numbers, and symbols? 330

How do I add words to the handwriting
dictionary? 331

How do I change input panel
preferences? 332

What are gestures and how do I
use them? 335

What are Windows Flicks and how do I
use them? 337

How do I start a journal with Windows Journal? 341

On holiday with a laptop

Should I delete any data before leaving on a trip? 348

How do I move sensitive data off the laptop? 350

How can I safeguard data I want to take on my laptop (in case it's stolen)? 351

How can I know if I really need to bring my laptop with me? 358

What's the best way to pack a laptop? 359

How can I prepare my laptop for airline travel? 361

How do I change the time, language or region once I arrive at my destination? 364

What options do I have for getting online while I'm away? 368

How can I stay safe when I'm online? 368

If I don't bring my laptop with me, can I still check my email somehow? 370

How do I print a list of contacts in Windows Mail? 372

Maintain your laptop

How do I clean the outside of the laptop? 378

How do I clean the keyboard and monitor? 379

How do I clean the inside of the laptop? 380

Do I need a surge protector? 380

What do Sleep and Hibernate offer? 380

What is Disk Cleanup and how can I use it to keep my computer in top condition? 386

What is Disk Defragmenter and do I need to use it? 390

How do I install a printer (or scanner)? 394

How do I install a digital camera? 396

How can I add RAM to my laptop without opening the case? 397